4.1.08

The Early Modern Corpse
and Shakespeare's Theatre

The Early Modern Corpse and Shakespeare's Theatre

Susan Zimmerman

Edinburgh University Press

© Susan Zimmerman, 2005, 2007

Edinburgh University Press Ltd
22 George Square, Edinburgh

First published in hardback by
Edinburgh University Press in 2005

Typeset in Sabon and Futura by
Norman Tilley Graphics, Northampton and
printed and bound in Great Britain by
Antony Rowe Ltd, Chippenham, Wilts

A CIP record for this book is available from the British Library

ISBN 978 0 7486 3363 0 (paperback)

The right of Susan Zimmerman
to be identified as author of this work
has been asserted in accordance with
the Copyright, Designs and Patents Act 1988.

Contents

Recognitions

During the gestation of this book, I complained a lot to my friends about its hardships, but while doing so I was also aware, at least intermittently, that the circle of friends and fellow-scholars contributing to my venture was growing ever wider. As most authors know, this new life-support system is the surprise benefit of writing a book, one that comes clearly into focus only in looking back. I have many debts, and I rejoice in all of them.

Leeds Barroll, Catherine Belsey, and Peter Stallybrass have been indefatigable mentors for many years – challenging, generous, and always hugely stimulating. They have made possible my best ideas.

Many other remarkable friends, old and new, made inestimable gifts of their own. Some read parts (or all) of the book, several wrote letters in support of the project, and everyone was happy to brainstorm. I am especially grateful to Harry Berger, Jr., Dympna Callaghan, Lynn Enterline, Kenneth Gross, Heather A. Hirschfeld, Jean E. Howard, Nora Johnson, Rayna Kalas, Julia Reinhard Lupton, Cynthia Marshall, Jeffrey Masten, Linda E. Merians, Lena Cowen Orlin, Kristen Poole, James R. Siemon, Bruce R. Smith, Gabrielle M. Spiegel, Barbara M. Stafford, Garrett A. Sullivan, Valerie Traub, and Valerie Wayne.

My readers for Edinburgh University Press, Peter Stallybrass and John Drakakis, were, as is their wont, astute and incisive in their comments. John Drakakis has generously supported my scholarship with his customary grace and good will on several other occasions as well.

The award of a Research Fellowship from the National Endowment for the Humanities in 2000 made possible a substantial period of research at the Folger Shakespeare Library that proved crucial to the development of my project. In 2002, the Folger itself awarded me a short-term Fellowship, for which I owe particular thanks to Gail Kern Paster, Director of the Library, and Barbara A. Mowat, Director of Academic Programs. In both instances, Queens College, CUNY, was fully supportive in arranging for leave from my teaching responsibilities. In addition, the College provided a Scholar Incentive Award during the year of my NEH grant.

I am very fortunate in my colleagues in the English Department at

Queens College. Our Chair, Nancy C. Comley, has always been personally and professionally generous. The ironic, irreverent style of my good friend Maureen Waters has made critical conversation a joy. Charles H. Molesworth debated literary theory with me on many occasions, and Steven F. Kruger advised on the medieval portions of the manuscript.

In 1996–97, and again in 1997–98, I had the privilege of chairing the Folger Institute Evening Colloquium which featured monthly group discussions of ongoing research projects. I am deeply grateful to Lena Cowen Orlin, former Executive Director of the Folger Institute, for inviting me to chair these sessions, and also to several participants who have maintained an interest in my own work, including Cynthia B. Herrup, Kathleen Lynch, Michael Neill, Tanya Pollard, Georgianna Ziegler, and again Jean E. Howard, Nora Johnson, Jeffrey Masten, and Bruce R. Smith. I owe a special debt to the late Susan Snyder, who took an active role in both colloquia.

As everyone knows who has had the pleasure of working at the Folger Shakespeare Library, the Reading Room staff is in a class by itself – informed, attentive, eager to resolve problems, and inspired in no small part by its energetic leader, Richard Kuhta, Eric Weinmann Librarian. I have benefited for many years from friendships with Laetitia Yeandle, Curator of Manuscripts (retired); Georgianna Ziegler, Head of Reference; Betsy Walsh, Head of Reader Services; and Harold Batie, Circulation Assistant. In more recent days, I have cheerfully exploited the ready services of Rosalind Larry, LuEllen DeHaven, and Camille Seeratan.

At the Edinburgh University Press, it was my good fortune to work with Jackie Jones, Head of Publishing and Deputy Chief Executive, who approaches every challenge with a refreshing mixture of professionalism and friendliness; and James Dale, Managing Desk Editor, who guided the text through the press with care and efficiency. It was always a pleasure to work with the staff at EUP.

In the end, of course, the affection and understanding of family and friends are the *sine qua non* of any authorial undertaking. My heartfelt debt to my sister, Judy Becker, extends well beyond this book; and I am especially grateful as well to L. David Levi, Colleen Murphy, and Sara Withers.

The book is dedicated to my husband, Leeds Barroll, the great gift of my life.

Copyright Permissions

I am grateful for permission to reprint earlier versions of several essays in this book: 'Killing the Dead: The Ghost of Hamlet's Desire,' in *Shakespeare Jahrbuch* 140 (Spring 2004): 81–96; 'Animating Matter: The Corpse as Idol in *The Second Maiden's Tragedy*,' *Renaissance Drama*, n.s.31 (2002): 215–43; 'Duncan's Corpse,' in *A Feminist Companion to Shakespeare*, ed. Dympna Callaghan (Oxford: Basil Blackwell, 2000), 215–43. Portions of an earlier essay – 'Marginal Man: The Representation of Horror in Jacobean Tragedy,' in *Discontinuities in Contemporary Renaissance Criticism*, eds. Viviana Comensoli and Paul Stevens (Toronto: University of Toronto Press, 1998: 223–51) – were used intermittently throughout the text.

Chapter 1

Dead Bodies

This book is a study of death and representation – specifically, the representation of dead bodies on the English Renaissance stage. Even at first glance this statement may seem to elide a contradiction. How exactly does one 'perform' a dead body? Or, to consider the statement's more disquieting implications, what is it about the body itself that marks it as dead? What does a mimesis of the corpse presume to represent, and how and why does it fail?

Because this study would connect performance conventions of the theatre in England to early modern concepts of the corpse, I focus on two major discourses from the period that attempt to redefine the meaning of 'dead': the religious discourse on idolatry and the scientific discourse on anatomical dissection. Albeit for wholly different, if equally controversial, reasons, it was in the interests of both Protestant reformers and medical anatomists to identify the concept of 'dead' with the materiality of the body, as exemplified pre-eminently by the corpse. My fundamental interest is in the cultural dynamics of these attempts at ideological imprinting as they connect to the theatre. How might the newly defined materiality of early modern religion and science have reconfigured theatrical conditions for the actor's 'impersonation' of the corpse?

I did not, however, begin this study with that question in mind. Instead, I was prompted by a curiosity about the corpse as a transhistorical signifier, in ritual and in language, for the inexplicable and the inexpressible. And because this signifying function of the corpse cannot be separated from that of the body, the most compelling theoretical question for my purposes turned out to be interestingly circular: what are the ritual and psychic processes by which the subject constructs the body itself as a prototype of the unknowable and the unspeakable?

That the body serves as a hermeneutic matrix for the human being is most readily discerned in those categorical if slippery distinctions that seem to originate in bodily phenomena: outer and inner, visible and invisible, tangible and intangible, substantial and insubstantial, continuous and discontinuous. Put simply, these and other such categories structure the body in terms of problematic relationships between what seems apparent and what remains obscured or hidden. But they also keep the concept of the body as a totality in place. Occluded or interior body parts and functions, however impenetrable and mysterious, none the less do not ordinarily undermine the subject's perception of the integrity of the body-as-a-whole,[1] except, of course, in sickness and in death.

The irremediable mortality of human life points to the tenuousness of the body's conceptual construction and establishes the *dead* body as the entity that must somehow be accommodated by the collapsed categories of its predecessor. From an anthropological perspective, the fearsomeness of the corpse resides in its putrefaction, or *un*becoming; that is, in the dissolution of those boundaries that mark the body's former union of parts. The phenomenon of putrefaction thus situates the corpse as a crux – probably *the* crux – in any effort to interpret the interdependence of life and death in human experience. Pre-eminent emblem of the organic process ('nature'), which simultaneously generates and obliterates life, the putrefying corpse literally embodies the unitary principle of life and death.

This chapter, which serves as an introduction, is in fact a retrospective description of this study's foundations. It attempts to explain the theoretical premises that I have come to understand more fully through the process of writing and to set out the issues (explored in later chapters) that situate the corpse in an early modern historical framework. Throughout the book, my historicist emphasis is frequently inflected with psychoanalytical theory. In considering, for example, what the transvestite acting convention contributed to the staging of the early modern corpse,[2] I have focused on the shifting signals generated by the practice, its tendency to confuse or re-configure gender categories. My psychoanalytical assumption here is that to sabotage the symbolic order is to prise open a chink to the unconscious, where gender identity, however synchronically constructed, fails to protect against intimations of self-dissolution. Thus I view transvestite representations of the early modern corpse as a historically distinctive theatrical phenomenon, which on one level subverts socially constructed gender categories, and on another disturbs fundamental psychic defence mechanisms.

In Chapter 1, then, I set out an articulation of the intellectual framework of this work. The chapter is divided into two sections, each of which is subdivided in order to conjoin theoretical and historical analyses. In the first section I examine anthropological and psychoanalytical theories of the corpse before considering early modern concepts of its signification; and in the second I position early modern theatrical conventions in the context of

Walter Benjamin's theory of the *Trauerspiel*. My aim in adopting this structure is to situate the corpse at a critical nexus that connects local and universal signifiers in a reciprocal, productive tension.

1. The corpse as signifier: a diachronic view

Among recent anthropologists, Georges Bataille provides the most fully formulated theory of the simultaneous horror and attraction that the putrefying corpse inspires in the subject.[3] Bataille's theory depends, first, on establishing the interdependence of violence and taboo. According to Bataille, the taboo signifies the human subject's refusal to participate in nature's unimaginable 'orgy of annihilation' (61); it seeks to deny the excessive violence that constitutes the natural process of death and renewal. If left unrestrained, the transformative drive of 'nature' leads to the void – the cancellation of what Bataille calls discontinuous, or individuated, selves. However, the taboo would disrupt or forestall this unconfined, terrifying continuity of reproduction and death, nature's 'virulent activity of corruption' (56). Based on the denial of disequilibrium, the taboo serves as an organising principle for social constructs, in particular those dealing with sexuality/reproduction and death. Bataille argues that by inspiring fear, disgust and horror in the subject, the taboo seeks to regulate primary forms of human violence, and thereby to defy the larger scheme of radical instability that constitutes the subject's world.

Interestingly, however, Bataille's system also identifies the taboo as a symptom of the subject's desire. Because violence can 'never be anything but partially reduced to order' (4), the taboo is always subject to transgression. It cannot, in fact, function *as* taboo unless it is transgressed, since the need for taboo implies the subject's underlying propensity for violence.[4] Thus Bataille proposes that what gives the taboo its deepest significance is the 'counterpoise of desire' (37). Against the subject's insistence on discontinuous (individuated) being is opposed a desire to approach the void: 'desire originates in its opposite, horror' (59). The subject thus perceives the fusion or death of living forms in the proliferation of life, nature's exuberant continuity, as an erotically charged horror: the taboo that would hold the generative power of corruption and decay at bay originates in a kind of fatal attraction.

Further, Bataille claims that the ambivalent power of the putrefying corpse is implicit in the biological structure of the living body. He puts this graphically: 'the sexual channels are also the body's sewers'; there are 'unmistakable links between excreta, decay, and sexuality'. The 'mingled horror and fascination' aroused in the subject by the corpse are akin to common responses to the body's by-products – excrement, menstrual blood (56–8). For Bataille, and for the anthropologist Mary Douglas as well, putrefaction is, finally, the foremost signifier of marginal, indeterminate being. What Douglas calls 'dirt' is in fact all being that escapes the categories of a symbolic system, and in so doing evokes the horror of, and desire for, originary formlessness – Bataille's void.[5]

In her study of human abjection as a 'conglomerate of fear, deprivation and nameless frustration' (15), Julia Kristeva uses similarly explicit terms to evoke the power of marginal being:

> A wound with blood and pus, or the sickly, acrid smell of sweat, of decay, does not *signify* death ... refuse and corpses *show me* what I permanently thrust aside in order to live. These body fluids, this defilement, this shit are what life withstands, hardly and with difficulty, on the part of death. There, I am at the border of my condition as a living being. My body extricates itself, as being alive, from that border ... If dung signifies the other side of the border, the place where I am not and which permits me to be, *the corpse, the most sickening of wastes, is a border that has encroached upon everything* [my italics] ... The corpse ... is the utmost of abjection. It is death infecting life ... It is thus not lack of cleanliness or health that causes abjection but what disturbs identity, system, order. What does not respect borders, positions, rules. The in-between, the ambiguous, the composite. (3–4)[6]

Kristeva's project, grounded in Lacanian psychoanalysis, is to connect the subject's experience of the abject to pre-discursive human experience.[7] For Kristeva, the experience of the abject is strongly linked to the subject's fear of indeterminate being, or being-on-the-borders, because as a 'conglomerate of ... *nameless* [pre-discursive] frustration' (15; my italics), abjection is 'a drive economy' without an object. It involves, instead, 'recognition of the *want* on which any being, meaning, language, or desire is founded', that is, 'the experience of *want* itself as logically preliminary to being and object – to the being of the object' (5). Kristeva's informing idea is that the 'want' of pre-discursive experience originates in the infant's violent separation from its mother, and in the 'pre-objects', and 'semi-objects' that 'stake out the transition from a state of indifferentiation to one of discretion (subject/object)' (32).

> There would be a 'beginning' preceding the word ... In that anteriority to language, the outside is elaborated by means of a projection from within, of which the only experience we have is one of pleasure and pain. The non-distinctiveness of inside and outside would thus be unnamable, a border passable in both directions by pleasure and pain. (61)

The danger of abjection is that it threatens to engulf the totality of the subject's identity as constructed by the symbolic order, drawing one 'toward the place where meaning collapses' (2), where the subject, 'fluctuating between inside and outside, pleasure and pain, would find death, along with nirvana' (62).[8]

By identifying the abject with the mother (variously called 'the archaic mother', 'the maternal authority', the 'maternal entity'), and by locating 'the immemorial violence with which a body becomes separated from another body in order to be [exist]' in 'the archaism of [a] pre-objectal relationship', Kristeva is reconfiguring the significance of the radical split in the subject's psychic development. Kristeva contends that, prior to language, there is 'a primal mapping of the body that I call semiotic' (72), a corporeal imprint that inheres in the fantasy of originary oneness. Abjection makes available the traces, or 'memory', of 'our earliest attempts to release the hold of *maternal* entity' (10–11), traces inflected with the mutual attractions of repugnance and *jouissance*. Separation from the pre-symbolic mother, then, occasions a splintering prior to the radical split that produces a 'primal repression': 'the abject is the violence of mourning for an "object" that has always already been lost' (15), a fear of incompleteness that is at the same time a fear of 'sinking irretrievably' into the maternal archaic.[9]

Kristeva thus argues that abjection points towards 'the boundary between semiotic authority and symbolic law' (73), a boundary shadowed by a powerful maternal presence that disturbs the subject's identity in the symbolic order. If all boundaries mark the discomfiting ambiguous and in-between, then certainly the archaic mother, original 'non-object' of desire, existing in the subject only as a trace and by means of a 'primal repression' of pre-symbolic experience, represents the prototypical ambiguity.[10] Nevertheless, for Kristeva, the archaic experience as such does not fully explain the subject's association of filth (Douglas's 'dirt') with bodily borders, especially the borders and body products of the female:

> Why does *corporeal waste*, menstrual blood and excrement, or everything that is assimilated to them, from nail-parings to decay, represent – like a metaphor that would have become incarnate – the objective frailty of symbolic order? (69–70)

In probing this question, Kristeva's speculations intersect most closely with those of Bataille and Douglas.

Kristeva contends that both excremental and menstrual defilements 'stem from the *maternal* and/or the feminine, of which the maternal is the real support' (71) because they are associated with the ambiguities of generation. If, to cite Bataille once again, 'nature' constitutes an 'orgy of annihilation' that is paradoxically life-generating, a fusion or union of living forms in the transformative activity of corruption, then death and reproduction are inextricable in the natural order. Fear of the archaic mother thus 'turns out to be essentially fear of her generative power'

(Kristeva, 77), a creative potency that seems to connect, in Douglas's phrase, with 'the powers inhering in the cosmos' (161), and that ultimately cannot be fully harnessed by taboo.

This creative potency is deeply imbricated in female sexuality. For Bataille, eroticism (for both genders) 'opens the way to death' (24) because it leads to the exultant union of discontinuous beings (orgasm as *le petit mort*). But because sexual experience re-enacts (or pre-enacts) the life-and-death dynamic of reproduction, it is the prospective mother who carries the burden of death-dealer, at least in patriarchal societies. Female sexuality thus represents the means by which the female body is empowered to exercise its life- and death-dealing potencies, that is, its power as breaker of existing entities in sexual self-dissolution, and as generator of new entities in the gestation and birthing of infants. Unsurprisingly, this same body has served, as Douglas claims, as the traditional locus of taboo, and its eroticism and fertility govern most rituals of defilement or purification. Such rituals are aimed, on the one hand, at exorcising impurities from the human body so as to render it sexually pure, an 'unchanging lapidary form' that functions as the enemy of 'ambiguity and compromise'; and, on the other hand, at protecting the social order against the death implicit in the 'dirt', or indeterminacy, of this body's by-products, particularly menstrual blood (viewed as a human being *manqué*) (Douglas, 162, 96; see also 140–58, *passim*).

Taken collectively, then, the psychoanalytical analysis of Kristeva and the anthropological findings of Bataille and Douglas provide a compelling rationale for the identification of death with marginality, and of both with the female. If the human body 'must be clean and proper in order to be fully symbolic ... must bear no trace of its debt to nature' (Kristeva, 102), then the potential for pollution in the female body is second only to that of the corpse. If the corpse, 'the most sickening of wastes, is a border that has encroached upon everything', it is the wastes generated by the female body that most nearly approach that border. The corpse may be the 'utmost of abjection ... death infecting life' (4), but it is in the subject's 'memory' of the archaic mother that abjection originates. Thus the female body exerts a powerfully ambiguous attraction for the subject in which life-affirming desire is deeply inscribed with the unbecoming of death.

2. Early modern dead bodies

The foregoing theory would establish two diachronic principles: that the body serves as a primary matrix for human perception; and that the corpse encapsulates the subject's ambivalent response to bodily borders and to the absence of categorical distinctions. If the inside/outside of the living body suggests, problematically, a visible, integrated totality enveloping an invisible and partially fluid interior, then putrefaction is the destructive/generative process by which inner/outer, visible/invisible collapse into one another. The corpse signifies – or, as Kristeva would have it, *shows* – the phenomenon of becoming/unbecoming which symbolic categories are designed to exclude. It is a paradoxically sensible mystery – seeable, touchable, smellable – but a mystery none the less. As such the threat of the corpse can be exorcised only by means of a surrogate, such as woman, whose surrogate function derives, according to Kristeva, from her originary role as archaic mother.

These theoretical perspectives on the corpse help to clarify its significance in the Christian belief system and also, for the purposes of this study, in early modern controversies about Christian doctrine. Because Christianity is based on the concept of a God/man, that is, a deity constituted by a hypostatic or inextricable union of divine and human natures, the body itself has been a major focus of theological speculation throughout Christian history. During the sixteenth century, Protestant reformers in England reconfigured the terms of this debate by repudiating Catholicism's persistent foregrounding of the body and its images in ritual practices (including funerary and burial rites). But Protestant resistance to Catholic anthropomorphism, as I shall argue in later chapters, revealed a more fundamental anxiety about the function of materiality itself in matters of the spirit.

Given the basic blueprint of Christian belief, it is hardly surprising that the Protestant agenda was fraught with difficulty. All early modern Christians, Catholic and Protestant alike, agreed that the *sine qua non* of their religion was the sacrificial death of Christ and his subsequent Resurrection. The body of Christ was thereby deeply imbricated in the Christian mysteries, and its transfiguration and ascension into heaven only reinforced the centrality of the hypostatic union to the Christian redemptive scheme. It was, in fact, the transfiguration of Christ's resurrected body that served as model for the fusion of body and soul in the heavenly beatification of the redeemed believer. And it was the body of Christ in the form of the Eucharist that enabled an inversion, as it were, of the Incarnation: the ingestion of the God/man, the divine/corporeal, in the human bodies of the faithful. Fundamentally, then, all the Christian mysteries were about bodily transformations: the generation of life from death, or, as Bataille would put it, the fusion of living forms from material disintegration. At bottom, the generative corpse, most ancient of enigmas, was the unavoidable centre of the Christian theory of transcendence.

From this perspective the Catholic/Protestant divide in England[11] can be viewed as a struggle over the meaning of Christ's humanity, or as elaborated in the controversy over idolatry, over the meaning to be attached to the material body in the Christian system. To the great discomfort of reformers, late medieval Catholicism focused intensely on the implications of the Incarnation, on the profoundly ambiguous and deeply sacred connections between the corporeal and spiritual in the person of Christ.[12] In keeping with this preoccupation, Catholic ritual and iconography appropriated the mysteries of bodily processes themselves as a mode of understanding – an analogue for – the paradoxes of Christianity. Because medieval Christianity conceived of the self, in Caroline Walker Bynum's phrase, as a 'psycho-somatic unity',[13] the intricate relationships among body parts, fluids and functions provided a symbolic map for the relationship between body and soul. And because this same labial body was paradoxically destined for changeless eternal life, medieval theologians were heavily invested in interrogating the signification of the corpse as the raw material, so to speak, of beatification.

To Protestant reformers, however, the Catholic preoccupation with the corporeal dangerously distorted the relationship between body and soul by implying that generative power might be a constituent property of materiality – that the material body (before and after death) could have an independent or autonomous viability, a 'life' without benefit of informing spirit. Their anxiety about the consequences of this distortion prompted an effort to reformulate materiality as definitively *dead*, and the homily on idolatry, 'Against Peril of Idolatry and Superfluous decking of Churches' (first published in English in 1563), launched an attack on material images that implicitly included materiality itself.[14] Interestingly, the homily's polemic ignores the generative potential of the corpse by insisting that the corpse is axiomatically dead; it is, in fact, the only material entity that can fully demonstrate what 'dead' means. In thus postulating the deadness of the corpse as a self-evident premise, the homily succeeds in hardening the distinction between material and spiritual and in neutralising the problem of transfiguration. Fundamentally, the homily would shift the Catholic emphasis on the body as a hermeneutic matrix to the soul as ascendant spiritual principle, from the humanity of Christ to the divinity of God the Father.

But the homily's reliance on strategies of denial and deflection, including excoriating rhetoric, suggests just how difficult it was to decentre the body of the Catholic imagination and to efface the concept of the indeterminate corpse.[15] The evasive tactic of appropriating the corpse as standard for 'dead', for example, suggests a strong if negative recognition of its disruptive power, as does the homily's misogynistic diatribe against the painted woman as a 'dead' material icon and agent of male sexual corruption.[16] By displacing distrust of bodily phenomena onto female sexuality and thereby redirecting the problem of bodily borders, the homily marginalises further the signification of the corpse. This castigation of the female body undoubtedly exploits a long-standing association of harlot and idol in Judeo-Christian tradition. None the less it is interesting to note that the substitution of woman for corpse resonates strikingly with the scapegoat function described by Kristeva and Douglas – the woman as a surrogate for the subject's fear of physical dissolution, the woman as taboo.

'Killing' the corpse was, then, a major desideratum of English religious reformists. But it also figured crucially, if for different reasons, in promoting the new science of anatomical dissection. Anatomists who would legitimate the use of corpses for medical research and instruction were forced to defend themselves against the accusation that dissection desecrated the dead. Popular culture regarded the taboo against such practices as a safeguard or protection against the mysterious power of the corpse – its supposed ability to communicate death, for example, or to rejuvenate the living through its *mummia*, or body fluid. For centuries, recognition of this power had been manifest in English techniques for dressing and 'containing' the dead, in folk customs surrounding the burial process, in funerary rituals prescribed by the Catholic Sarum Manual (which Protestants tried to supersede in successive editions of The Book of Common Prayer), and during the late Middle Ages, in the transi tombs with their grotesque sculptures of vermiculation. Notwithstanding the counter-influences of reformist religious discourse, the idea of the corpse as quasi-sentient and empowered was still strongly inscribed in the communal imagination.[17]

As a consequence there was a popular suspicion that, in publicly exposing the internal secrets of the corpse, the new anatomists presumed literally to strip away the mystery of what cannot – or should not – be made visible: the boundaries between the living and the dead. Significantly, the corpse at the centre of the frontispiece of Andreas Vesalius's *De Humani Corporis Fabrica*, published in England in 1545, is that of a woman; and it is literally her womb, the mystery of reproduction itself, which Vesalius opens for display. In seeking to unravel the body's creative processes, to explicate divinely ordained orders of being, the anatomist seems to play the role of sacrilegious anarchist, unleashing an atavistic, unsignifiable power. Ultimately, the success of the effort by medical science to disempower the corpse as fetish, like that of religion to demystify the material idol, depended on establishing the dead body as detritus, devoid of informing spirit.

What is particularly noteworthy about the religious and scientific struggle to define corporeality in early modern England is that the issues at stake were not yet shaped by the Cartesian mind/body dichotomy.[18] On the contrary, hegemonic discourse found it difficult to co-opt the corpse because of a continuing, if largely conscious, popular fascination with the ambiguities of bodily borders. As we have seen, psychoanalytical theory contends that conscious and/or unconscious recognition (including pre-linguistic recognition) of the permeable boundaries between living and dead, material and immaterial, is a constituent element of human subjectivity. I would argue, accordingly, that English iconoclasm and anatomical science were fundamentally about the interdiction and regulation of this elusive recognition, about the reordering of psycho-social categories of perception in the service of new orthodoxies.

3. Illusory embodiment[19]

In considering the theatrical, or staged, corpse, I am primarily concerned with how the early modern theatre took part in ongoing controversies concerning the dead, in the nexus between theatrical representation and ideological conflict. But early modern performative agency is itself an antecedent issue, especially as it pertains to the distinctive conventions of the public stage.

Theatrical mimesis of any kind, however historically located, is to a significant degree anti-illusionist: an audience agrees to be complicit in a fiction that performance itself foregrounds as artifice.[20] But in considering the mimesis of the early modern theatre, it is helpful to distinguish first between what Harry Berger Jr terms the 'citational' and the 'ritual'. Berger's citational text is one that claims to be validated by an unimpeachable authority and would reinforce the assumed immanence of 'reality' in language: it posits an inherent link between language and a presumably knowable external world. Ritual, on the other hand, subverts those categories of language that shape citational texts by intimating that which they would occlude:

> ritual can reveal the sources of disorder, can make invisible dangers visible, only because the citational texts of a culture have selectively visualized as invisible certain kinds of danger, thereby repressing others ... Those invisible disorders that cannot be signified, cannot be bound by some polar or analogical operation to the range of phenomena classified by language and accessible to perception, remain buried in the margin of surplus meaning. (161)

Although itself enabled by the symbolic order, ritual none the less pushes against the categorical parameters of that order.

The 'margin of surplus meaning' to which Berger refers also figures in Victor Turner's anthropological theory of performance as ritual. According to Turner, 'the dominant genres of performance in societies at all levels of scale and complexity tend to be *liminal phenomena*' (25), that is, phenomena that move beyond the *limen*, or threshold, of the ordinary, to evoke the unfamiliar, the imperfectly understood, that which has been disengaged from categorical moorings:

> [drama] may be likened to loops in a linear progression, when the social flow bends back on itself ... and puts everything so to speak into the subjunctive mood as well as the reflexive voice. Just as the subjunctive mood of a verb is used to express supposition, desire, hypothesis, or possibility ... so do liminality and the phenomena of liminality dissolve all factual and commmonsense systems into their components and 'play' with them in ways never found in nature or in custom, at least at the level of direct perception.[21]

Eschewing, then, the idea of mimesis as the imitation of a knowable reality, Turner emphasises performance as a generative and potentially transformative representational process, a scrambling of that (already unstable) semiotic system which none the less undergirds the subject's fantasy of a fixed natural order.[22]

In this context, I would argue that early modern theatre in England was pronouncedly ritualistic, foregrounding the liminality of performance by its indifference to illusionist machinery and its strong propensity for meta-theatrical reflection ('anti-naturalist before the event', as Francis Barker puts it).[23] These are, I believe, closely connected components of a single stylistic pattern – the generating mechanisms of the English Renaissance stage. For example, the prevalence of language in which actors describe themselves as *playing* a fiction seems connected to the anti-illusionist structures of public theatres, as well as to the circumstances and con-ventions of performance (including the disruptive exigencies of early modern scheduling and repertory). More importantly, perhaps, the unruly mixtures of genres, plots, source materials and tonalities, the well-known 'gallimaufry' of Renaissance dramatic texts, militate against a sustained suspension of disbelief, for both actors and spectators. Thus the hallmark of this theatre is an insistence on its own theatricality, a resolute artificiality; and this quality is conceptually linked to what Turner calls the 'subjunctive mood' of liminal experience. By continually playing with the boundary between actor and spectator, between fiction and the enactment of it, English Renaissance theatre chose to explore the limits and the possibilities of dramatic impersonation.[24]

Moreover, in this self-conscious ambience, the absence of the female body from the stage could only have underscored the fluid permutations of the performance dynamic. 'Transvestism', or the appropriation of female roles by cross-dressed boys, was probably the most far-reaching meta-theatrical convention of Renaissance stagecraft in that it simultaneously

constructed and deconstructed the social paradigms of gender differentiation. As Phillipa Berry eloquently puts it, the missing female body
was 'an immense figurative resource' precisely because it was missing: the
'maximum undecidability' and 'hybridity' of cross-dressed impersonation
'delineates ghostly traces of the "more" that is mysteriously inherent in [all]
absence and loss'.[25] By filling the gap that marked a missing gender with
a hybrid of indeterminate gender and thereby eschewing the security of
gender categories, theatrical transvestism evoked 'the margin of surplus
meaning' not only in hybridity, but also in language and in desire.

As the ultimate hybrid, the utmost in marginality situated at the
furthermost border, the corpse signifies the body/not-body that resists
impersonation altogether, an entity in the grips of a primordial – or, as
Christianity would have it, transfiguring – process. Thus the (impossible)
representation of the corpse on the Renaissance stage was further and
profoundly complicated by the hybridity of transvestism in representations
of female corpses. As Douglas has demonstrated, patriarchal societies
traditionally single out female reproductive potency and eroticism as a
source of defilement, the designated scapegoats for man's fear of, and
attraction to, death. But the early modern theatrical 'woman' was a
confusing representation of this displacement in so far as s/he portrayed not
a gender, but a dispensation from gender categories, as well as from the
behavioural proscriptions associated with them. Thus, on one level, the
cross-dressed actor/woman offered spectators a stimulus for erotic
fantasies, a means of imagining or intimating sexual experience outside
socially prescribed boundaries, notwithstanding the 'ghostly traces' of
death which underlay this eroticism. But the double conundrum of the
cross-dressed corpse, a personification of death in a visual emblem of
collapsed genders, pointed more disturbingly towards the arbitrariness of
all categorical defences by occluding the woman's customary function as a
scapecoat for death.

It would thus seem that the symbolic potential of bi-gendered corpses
could be harnessed in the theatre with enormous effect to disrupt the
psychic programming of spectators, and I believe that some early modern
playwrights (Shakespeare pre-eminent among them) were indeed able to do
this. None the less, within the large corpus of English Renaissance tragedy,
including so-called revenge tragedy,[26] such sophisticated exploitation of
the possibilities of liminality is exceptional. More typically, plays of blood
and/or revenge foregrounded an explicit, even outrageous, sensationalism
that would seem to preclude serious symbolic import. Such taboo subjects
as incest, patricide and necrophilia were treated in a hyperbolic fashion,
exaggerated to such a degree as to seem almost to trivialise the horrific
subject matter. Certainly, cross-dressed corpses figure importantly in many

plots, but the ambience of these plays often gives them a parodic, even comic quality – indeed, corpses are sometimes featured in scenes that strive in part for deliberate comic effects. And therein lies an almost ridiculous paradox: that the corpse as a theatrical travesty should be weighted, at least theoretically, with an impossible signified, that is, the indeterminacy that eludes signification altogether. The sensationalist tragedy of Renaissance England is, then, difficult to reconcile with the dramatic potential of the theatrical corpse, especially as inflected by the transvestite convention.

This incongruity suggests a crux in the relationship of ideology to practice that may be stated as follows: what happens to the symbolic potential of the corpse, synchronically and diachronically, when it is accommodated to theatrical conventions that are aggressively meta-theatrical and sensational? Or, to re-articulate the question by once again reversing the perspective: *why* might the early modern English theatre have elected to represent the corpse according to such conventions? In this connection, and in terms of both questions, Walter Benjamin's theory of the *Trauerspiel* is deeply illuminating.

4. English Renaissance *Trauerspiel*

For Benjamin, the *Trauerspiel* is a drama of sorrow or mourning (*trauer*), considered as both stage performance and game (*spiel*).[27] Its style is dis-tinguished by a conjunction of the allegorical and the baroque which serves to express a deep philosophical scepticism, one rooted in a response to the Christian ethos. Ostensibly, Benjamin would describe the baroque theatre of Counter-Reformation Germany; what he sees as the crisis in Christianity is its ideological failure to supersede the perceived destructiveness of material nature – a failure made all the more apparent by the Reformation's violent discord over the status of materiality in Christian theology. Benjamin's attention to the German baroque is, however, primarily a means of extrapolating those conceptual and stylistic features of the *Trauerspiel* that apply equally to playwrights from other traditions. Thus, for example, he identifies similarities in the dramaturgy of Shakespeare and Calderón which presumably derive from their mutual absorption in the *Trauerspiel gestalt*.

Benjamin defines this *gestalt* in contrast to that of *Tragödie*, or classical drama, which represents the destructiveness of human life through a mythic 'rite of heroic sacrifice' (18) to a transcendental ideal.[28] The sorrow of the *Trauerspiel*, on the other hand, springs from man's desperation about his subjugation to an inchoate physis, or natural world. Giving voice to the torment implicit in the elusive relationship between material and spiritual realms, the *Trauerspiel* is earth-bound, absorbed in the enigma of the physis, marked by an 'obsessive physicality' (17) and always aware of the 'proximity of literal [Christian] hell' (19), the 'abyss of damnation' (16). Whereas in the universe of *Tragödie* the structural continuity and coherence of the play itself signify the immanence of the 'hidden god', a 'harmonious inwardness' (17), the *Trauerspiel* represents 'reality' as discontinuous and grotesque – 'grotesque' in its original meaning (*grotta*) of mysterious, buried, subterranean (171).

For Benjamin, 'allegory' thus signifies a mode of representation that disrupts the fantasy of coherence and continuity. *Tragödie* depends on symbols because it 'insists on the indivisible unity of form and content': 'the unity of the material and the transcendental object, which constitutes the paradox of the theological symbol, is distorted into a relationship between appearance and essence' (160). The allegory of the *Trauerspiel*, on the other hand, suggests the fragmentary, the ambiguous, the polysemic: 'what ruins are in the realm of things' – collapsed fragments of a former totality – 'allegories are in the realms of thought' (178). In both the 'dry rebuses' of the ruin and the emblems of allegory, 'the false appearance of totality is extinguished' (176): human history is represented, not as the process of an eternal life, but as that of an eternal transience, an irresistible decay. The *Trauerspiel* holds 'not the faintest glimmer of any spiritualization of the physical' (187). On the contrary, it 'sees in historical events, in architecture, in the collateral edifice of the human body and of the body politick, properties for a grievous pageant' (18).

Paradoxically, however, the style of this 'grievous pageant' is, in Benjamin's lexicon, 'baroque', that is, hyperbolic and ostentatious. For Benjamin the baroque is the stylistic correlative of drama preoccupied with the ceaseless self-generation of the physis because to pile up fragments 'without any strict idea of a goal' (178), as a ruin does, is to mock, as it were, the sheer gratuity of materiality. Thus the 'extravagant pomp' of the 'play of mourning' calls attention to its 'obviously constructed quality' (177), its disjointed structure: fragmented and grandiose, like the physis, the *Trauerspiel* occludes the 'hidden god' in its own proliferating excesses. Because decaying objects are 'the polar opposite to the idea of transfigured nature', the penchant of the *Trauerspiel* is for 'the artificial light of apotheosis' (179, 180).

Ineluctably, then, the mystery at the core of the *Trauerspiel* is that of the corpse, primary signifier of the life implicit in disintegration: 'the allegorization of the physis can only be carried through in all its vigour in respect of the corpse': the corpse is 'quite simply [its] pre-eminent emblematic property' (217–18). In a statement that resonates powerfully with that of Kristeva, Benjamin describes the subject's attachment to the corpse:

> Seen from the point of view of death, the product of the corpse is life. It is not only in the loss of limbs, not only in the changes of the aging body, but in all the processes of elimination and purification that everything corpse-like falls away from the body piece by piece. It is no accident that precisely nails and hair, which are cut away as dead matter from the living body, continue to grow on the corpse. There is in the physis, in the memory itself, a *memento mori* ... (218)

Because there is no escaping the recognition of death in living matter, and the ultimate surrender of living matter to the transformative process of death, it is the corpse that informs the 'physically obsessed' play of sorrow:

> ... the characters of the *Trauerspiel* die, because it is only thus, as corpses, that they can enter into the homeland of allegory. It is not for the sake of immortality that they meet their end, but for the sake of the corpse. (217–18)

Benjamin would thus demonstrate the interdependence of 'allegory', understood as emblematic fragmentation, and the 'baroque', understood as ostentatious style, as symptomatic of a play's philosophical and affective orientation, its 'mourning' for mortality. For Benjamin, Shakespeare is chief mourner in the English Renaissance, and the qualities found in at least some of his tragedies – the broad canvas and proliferation of plots, the heightened language, the discordant, often melodramatic tonalities and the sense of probing, even tormented scepticism – betray an 'earth-bound' rather than transcendental focus.[29] I would argue further that the meta-theatricality of Renaissance performance practices, the eschewing of sustained dramatic illusion, fragments the English Renaissance *Trauerspiel* further by distinctively foregrounding the self-reflective artificiality of drama itself.[30]

Always attentive to the innovations of Shakespeare, Benjamin also credits him with developing the *intrigant* as an important counterweight to the protagonist of the *Trauerspiel*. (Iago is a prime example.) In Benjamin's system, the *intrigant* represents *Lustspiel*, or comedy, the 'essential inner side of mourning' (125), the obverse of the 'death's head' (166): 'just as earthly mournfulness is of a piece with allegorical interpretation, so is ... frustration in the triumph of matter ... [of a piece with] devilish mirth' (227). Although Benjamin associates this figure with the rogue/fool of fifteenth-century religious drama, the 'devilish mirth' of the *intrigant* is more properly a 'mirthless laughter', a 'bitingly provocative scorn' (126).[31] In the *Trauerspiel*, the *intrigant* has several functions: to mitigate the play's stylistic extravagance by grounding it in a viciously comic counter-play; to represent the calculation and self-regard of hopelessness (as opposed to the hope, however desperate, of the mourner); and to manipulate the actions of others, often sadistically:

> What tempts [the *intrigant*] is the illusion of freedom – in the exploration of what is forbidden; the illusion of independence – in the secession from the community of the pious; the illusion of infinity – in the empty abyss of evil. (230)[32]

Thus the *intrigant* completes the circle of sorrow, as it were, by representing a response to the physis that is at once hopeless and base.[33]

Benjamin's theory of the *Trauerspiel* was not, of course, developed with Shakespeare (or any other playwright, for that matter) primarily in mind, despite its elevation of Shakespeare and Calderón. On the contrary, what Benjamin proposes is something much larger: a philosophical rationale for how a post-classical, materialist aesthetic might take shape in drama. Working within the intellectual tradition of Western Europe, Benjamin identifies 'materialist' with 'Christian', that is, the problem of materiality in relation to a God/man lies in the transcendental weight that the flesh must bear in the Christian tradition.[34] Classical tragedy did not need to confront the conundrum of transcendental materiality; the *Trauerspiel* was enjoined to address it directly, particularly after the crisis of the Reformation. It did so with a tortured uncertainty as to the redemptive potential implicit in the physis, and ultimately, of course, implicit in the corpse.

Notwithstanding the breadth of its framework, Benjamin's theory of the *Trauerspiel* is, I believe, acutely relevant to our understanding of English Renaissance tragedies of blood. The analogy I am making here is of course a loose one. Indeed, Benjamin's paradigm is inappropriate to synchronic historical analysis, and his positioning of Shakespeare as *éminence grise* in the *Trauerspiel* tradition need not be accepted in all its particulars. But Benjamin does provide a provocative argument for bridging the problem of the material body in Christianity with the problem of the material body on the public stage, one that resonates almost uncannily with the relationship of the English theatre to religious and scientific controversies of its own time.

Caught in a double bind during the Reformation's challenge to Catholic hermeneutics because of its own anthropomorphic imaging, the early modern theatre interrogated the properties of the material body, including that of the performer, in the midst of an ideological crisis about that very issue. Throughout this book I will be arguing that the corpse, 'pre-eminent emblematic property' of the *Trauerspiel*, was at the centre of this crisis, and that in the controversy over idolatry the corpse as Christian conundrum was conceptually inextricable from the corpse as fetishistic object in popular culture. Thus, for example, the English response to anatomical dissection may be understood as an instance in which the complexities of corpse-fear found social expression in a single, protracted resistance.

Benjamin's *Trauerspiel* also provides a conceptual framework, as I have indicated, for the stylistic excess, fragmentation of form, and meta-theatrical reflexivity found in English tragedies of blood. But curiously, Benjamin neglects to address (or does so only parenthetically) the function of women in the *Trauerspiel* – a factor of singular importance, ideologically and stylistically, to the plays at issue here. Benjamin's diffidence is puzzling considering the affinity of his view of the *physis* with that of Bataille, Douglas and Kristeva – specifically, his awareness of its runaway reproductive energy, of the corpse as its 'homeland'. None the less, whereas these theorists link the subject's fear of the *physis* directly with the generative power of the female, Benjamin's connections are oblique. For example, in remarking on the 'decisive importance' of the chaste woman in the German martyr-drama, he describes the 'assertion of chastity' as a futile attempt to subdue 'a state of emergency in the soul, the rule of the emotions' (74), thereby intimating, but not clarifying, the use of woman as scapegoat for the uncontrollable.

Viewed from the perspective of the Lacanian process of desire, of course, it can be argued that the existential dilemma delineated by Benjamin is, in the end, gender-neutral. Putrefaction is not, after all, restricted to a single gender, and the fragmentation of the corpse would seem to deny that originary wholeness that is the fantasy of all human subjects: thus at bottom the *Trauerspiel* voices the angst of the human condition. Yet in English tragedies of blood, gender is very much at issue: indeed, protagonist and *intrigant* alike are largely defined in terms of their responses to the perceived threat of the female. Thus it may be both apt and ironic that the transvestite convention represents gender on the English stage by means of an inversion; and that this inversion, while showcasing gender differences, simultaneously evokes the unspeakable margins of being in which all distinctions, including those of gender, collapse.

The following chapters present a detailed examination of the relationship of the public theatre to the culture of the dead in early modern England. Because major shifts in the religious imaging of the body/corpse undoubtedly had an impact on the theatre's approach to its own embodied representations, Chapter 2 considers the reformulation of Catholic hermeneutics and sacramental practices during the English Reformation. It contrasts late medieval modes of conceptualising the material body – as seen, for example, in the doctrine of purgatory, the writings of the mystics and the *Legenda Aurea* – with Reformation attempts to demystify the Catholic *gestalt* of the dead. This chapter concentrates in particular on two Reformation discourses: the homily on idolatry, and Foxe's *Book of Martyrs*.

Chapters 3 to 5 examine representations of the corpse in plays by Middleton, Massinger, Webster and Shakespeare, with attention to early modern contestations over the dead as well as to the challenge that the corpse posed to theatrical representation itself.

Prior to examining the so-called 'Herod' plays – Middleton's *The Second*

Maiden's Tragedy and Massinger's *The Duke of Milan* – Chapter 3 examines the performance conventions of the public stage, especially as they pertain to the 'impersonation' of the female corpse. The chapter argues that in adapting the necrophiliac legend of Herod the Great to a Reformation context, these plays present the dead woman, sensationally, as idol and as erotic object. Chapter 4 focuses on two major tragedies that are steeped in a far more unsettling, if no less sensational, graveyard ambience: Middleton's (?) *The Revenger's Tragedy* and Webster's *The Duchess of Malfi*. Examining first modes by which ambivalent attitudes towards the semi-animate corpse were inscribed in English practices of embalming, postmortem examination and burial, as well as in public resistance to the new practice of anatomy, the chapter considers the quasi-liminal dead that haunt these plays. My analysis of the *Duchess*, in particular, emphasises the sophisticated modes by which Webster inscribes psychological complexities in scenes of extraordinary barbarism, thereby evoking the eroticism implicit in the violation of taboo.

Chapter 5 argues that in *Macbeth* and *Hamlet*, Shakespeare comes brilliantly close to representing the unrepresentable, that is, the indeterminate being that escapes signification, the corpse itself. Both tragedies convey a 'fatal vision' in which 'nothing is but what is not' by exploiting the horrific potential of the palpable unseen: in *Macbeth*, Duncan's indeterminate but pervasive blood; in *Hamlet*, the leprous, disintegrating body occluded by the 'complete steel' of Hamlet Sr's ghost. My argument in this chapter is that these plays tap into early modern cultural anxieties at the same time that they stretch the possibilities of theatrical representation, conjuring powerfully that which cannot be given substantive shape, the dissoluble and transfixing corpse.

Throughout Chapters 2 to 5, theoretical perspectives and historical evidence coexist in what I see as a mutually productive tension. From the beginning of my project, my methodological aim has been to demonstrate the viability of an analytical paradigm that foregrounds the transactions between past and present, history and theory. For this purpose, the conundrum of the staged corpse has proved to be a uniquely suitable subject.

Notes

1. In her groundbreaking study of eighteenth-century modes of perceiving the body, Barbara Maria Stafford is similarly concerned with the conundrum of 'a visible natural whole made up of invisible dissimilar parts'. She states the central issue eloquently: 'The difficulties of imaging the body illuminate that supreme representational problem: how does one seize the liquid inner and

outer of things?' See *Body Criticism: Imaging the Unseen in Enlightenment Art and Medicine* (London and Cambridge, MA: MIT Press, 1991), 12, 45.

2. This uncomfortably loaded contemporary term is none the less widely used in critical discourse with reference to early modern cross-dressing.

3. See George Bataille, *Erotism: Death and Sensuality*, trans. Mary Dalwood (San Francisco: City Lights Books, 1957).

4. In *Powers of Horror*, Julia Kristeva points out the importance of Bataille's emphasis on the weakness of prohibition, on the subject's incomplete submission to taboo. See *Powers of Horror: An Essay on Abjection*, trans. Leon S. Roudiez (New York: Columbia University Press, 1982), 64.

5. See Mary Douglas, *Purity and Danger: An Analysis of the Concepts of Pollution and Taboo* (London: Routledge, 1991). Mikhail Bakhtin, in his theory of the grotesque/carnivalesque, is also concerned with the connections between reproductive and excretory functions, and with the continuum of death, decay and rebirth. Carnival provides a means of transgressing physical and social boundaries through inversion and bodily excess: 'The essence of carnival lies in change, in death–rebirth, in destructive–creative time' (Tzvetan Todorov, *Mikhail Bakhtin: The Dialogical Principle*, trans. Wlad Godzich (Minneapolis: University of Minnesota Press, 1984), 79). For Bakhtin, however, carnivalesque transgression represents a form of communal transcendence, of gaiety; Bakhtin's grotesque is not horrific. See Mikhail Bakhtin, *Rabelais and His World*, trans. Helene Iswolsky (Bloomington: Indiana University Press, 1984), esp. 59–144, 303–67. See also Todorov, *Mikhail Bakhtin*.

6. Kristeva's description of bodily borders owes much to Jacques Lacan. In *Écrits: A Selection*, trans. Alan Sheridan (New York and London: Norton, 1977), Lacan discusses 'the anatomical mark (*trait*) of a margin or border' (314) on the body itself. Lacan's full commentary has been concisely summarised by Susan Stewart as follows:

> the cuts and gaps on the body's surface – the lips, the anus, the tip of the penis, the slit formed by the eyelids … allow the sense of 'edge,' borders, or margins by differentiating the body from the organic functions associated with such apertures. Because these cuts or apertures are described on the very surface of the subject, they have no specular image, no outside that they represent … What is both inside and outside the body (feces, spittle, urine, menstrual blood, etc.) tends to become taboo because of its ambiguous and anomalous status.

See Susan Stewart, *On Longing: Narratives of the Miniature, the Gigantic, the Souvenir, the Collection* (Baltimore and London: Johns Hopkins University Press, 1987), 104. See also Lacan, *Écrits*, 314–16.

7. Lacan's system itself addresses one form of such experience in the imaginary or mirror stage of psychic development (which Kristeva's abject theoretically antedates). Lacan's imaginary takes place prior to the subject's induction into the symbolic order of language and the Law, and the concomitant division between the subject's conscious and unconscious (the radical split). In (mis)-recognising its mirror image as a unit, or coherent entity, the infant enacts an imperfect differentiation of self from other (image) at the same time that it projects a desire for wholeness. After the induction into language, the subject's desire for wholeness represents an effort to exceed language – the very condition of human subjectivity. But the differential structure of language itself (I am not synonymous with my conscious self; I am not you) precludes the

20   *The Early Modern Corpse and Shakespeare's Theatre*

subject from ever becoming identical either with itself, or with an other. See Jacques Lacan, 'The Signification of the Phallus', in *Écrits*, 281–91. For an unusually cogent analysis of this essay, see Catherine Belsey, 'Desire in Theory: Freud, Lacan, Derrida', in *Desire: Love Stories in Western Culture* (Oxford: Blackwell, 1994), 42–71.

8. Kristeva's conjunction of death and nirvana derives from Lacan's concept of the Real, that is, the inaccessible impossibility that escapes symbolisation, but that the subject returns to in death with the obliteration of the signifying network itself. Lacan's *das Ding* represents the primal pleasure in the Real that the subject seeks to recover as the object of both libido and the death drive, which are inextricably intertwined. *Das Ding* is what holds out the promise of Lacanian *jouissance*, an enjoyment in excess of the pleasure available to the speaking subject. The lack in the enjoyment that can actually be experienced prompts the subject to pursue successive objects of desire: for Lacan, this continual process of substitution is itself a symptom of, or substitute for, the death drive, the purest form of the compulsion to repeat. For a brilliant discussion of the imbrication of death in desire, see Lacan's 'Desire and the Interpretation of Desire in *Hamlet*', in Shoshana Felman, ed., *Literature and Psychoanalysis: The Question of Reading: Otherwise* (Baltimore and London: Johns Hopkins University Press, 1982), 11–52. For an account of *das Ding*, see Jacques Lacan, *Seminar 7, The Ethics of Psychoanalysis, 1959–60*, trans. Dennis Porter (New York: Norton, 1992), 70.

9. In her book on the representations of the female corpse in the visual arts, Elizabeth Bronfen offers a concise but eloquent description of this ambivalence. On the one hand, the mother's body represents 'the fantasy of a fusion ... the impossible union in life with the lost primordial'; on the other, as 'midwife of individuation', the mother forces the separation by which unitary identity is lost. See *Over Her Dead Body: Death, Femininity and the Aesthetic* (Manchester: Manchester University Press and New York: Routledge, 1992), 33.

10. In some respects, Kristeva's theory of abjection resonates with Freud's theory of the uncanny; Freud, however, is describing a quasi-conscious 'trace' as opposed to a pre-discursive 'want'. For Freud, the uncanny appears as a 'harbinger of death', a 'double' (235) that connects disturbingly to 'what is known of old and long familiar' (220). As such, the uncanny is manifested as the in-between: both familiar and concealed, it exists in the margins of consciousness. Although an experience of the uncanny can be triggered either by an infantile repression or by the revival of an animistic belief that has been previously surmounted, the fear of castration/death, often symbolised by female genitalia, is common to both situations. The uncanny aspect of female genitalia is the repressed, (un)familiar body of the mother, the intra-uterine existence (symbol of life and death). Thus the 'ghostly harbinger of death' manifests itself through the generative potencies of the female/mother, and leads the subject 'back' to the creative formlessness of life/death. See 'The "Uncanny"', *The Standard Edition of the Complete Psychological Works of Sigmund Freud*, ed. and trans. James Strachey, Vol. 17 (London: Hogarth Press, 1968), 218–56. For a useful analysis of the death drive itself in Freudian theory, see Jonathan Dollimore, *Death, Desire and Loss in Western Culture* (New York: Routledge, 1998), 180–97.

11. By opposing 'Catholic' and 'Protestant' I do not mean to imply homogeneity of belief or practices among sects that might fit under the rubric of either term.

Here and elsewhere, my study concentrates on iconographical and sacramental differences in representing the body. See Chapter 2, note 2, p. 66; and notes 65 and 66, pp. 79–80.

12. For example, the redemptive blood that flowed from the side of the crucified Christ was seen as a material form of spiritual nourishment, as was, of course, the Eucharist. Medieval sacramental symbolism is discussed in detail in Chapter 2.

13. See Carolyn Walker Bynum, *The Resurrection of the Body in Western Christianity, 200–1336* (New York: Columbia University Press, 1995), 11.

14. The homily was published as part of *The seconde tome of homelyes* (STC 13663). Chapter 2 includes an explication of the centrality of the corpse to the homilist's argument.

15. The developmental conjunction of the words 'cors' (from the sixteenth century spelled 'corse'), 'corps', 'corpse' in medieval and early modern England is itself suggestive of the ambiguities implicit in the conceptualisation of the dead. During these periods, the distinction between a body and a dead body was indicated either by an adjective (as in Hamlet's address to the ghost as a 'dead corse', 1.4.52) or by context, since the same word could be used for both. 'Cors' and 'corps' (a perverted spelling of the Old French 'cors', but with no change in pronunciation) were prevalent in England by 1500; pronunciation of the 'p' in 'corps' did not begin in England until the late fifteenth century; 'corpse' as a distinct word (and pronunciation) was a rare variation until the nineteenth century (although 'corpses' occasionally appears as a plural from the sixteenth century). See *The Compact Edition of the Oxford English Dictionary*, Vol. I (Oxford: Oxford Unviersity Press, 1971), 1011. I am grateful to Jeffrey Masten for calling my attention to this issue.

16. After a long and intemperate attack on the Byzantine Empress Irene, who supposedly played a major role in the ninth-century controversy over idols, the homily castigates an array of pagan goddesses and Catholic saints. See Chapter 2, pp. 52–6.

17. Chapter 4 address the significance of the corpse in English popular culture and funerary rituals.

18. In discussing pre-Cartesian subjectivity, Francis Barker makes a similar point: 'the early [modern] body lies athwart that divide between subject and object, discourse and world'. See *The Tremulous Private Body: Essays on Subjection* (London and New York: Methuen, 1984), 24.

19. I have borrowed this phrase from Stephen Greenblatt's essay 'Shakespeare Bewitched', in Susan Zimmerman, ed., *Shakespeare's Tragedies* (Basingstoke and London: Macmillan, 1998), 109–39.

20. I do not mean to imply here that, in contradistinction to the theatre, other forms of mimetic art provide access to 'reality', understood as knowable being that exists prior to representation. From a poststructuralist perspective, the interpretable always replaces the knowable in the operation of language. As Harry Berger Jr succinctly puts it:

> The distinction between the knowable and the interpretable is that between given and taken, reflected and constructed, prior and consequent meaning ... The knowable is [supposedly] already 'there' in the world as prior meaning; the interpretable is what awaits the acts that produces consequent meaning. ('Bodies and Texts', *Representations* 17 [Winter 1987], 151)

21. Victor Turner, *The Anthropology of Performance* (New York: PAJ Publications, 1988), 25.

22. Turner's theory elaborates that of the ethnologist Arnold van Gennep, who used the terms 'marginality' and 'liminality' 'to denote the central of three phases' (i.e. limbo) in what he called 'rites of passage'. 'Rituals *separated* specified members of a group from everyday life, *placed them in a limbo* that was not any place they were in before and not yet any place they would be in, then *returned* them, changed in some way, to mundane life' (see Turner, *The Anthropology of Performance*, 25, *passim*; see also his *From Ritual to Theater* (New York: PAJ Publications, 1982)).

23. Barker, *The Tremulous Private Body*, 18.

24. For a fuller discussion of early modern theatricality, see Chapter 3.

25. See Philippa Berry, *Shakespeare's Feminine Endings: Disfiguring Death in the Tragedies* (London and New York: Routledge, 1999), 10.

26. 'Revenge tragedy', a modern critical term, has been loosely applied to sensationalist plays of the Elizabethan and Jacobean periods that focus on protagonists' strategies of revenge. I prefer the term 'tragedies of blood', which suggests a theatrical excess germane to the mode of representation.

27. Benjamin makes an important distinction between 'plays which cause mourning' and 'plays through which mournfulness finds satisfaction: plays for the mournful.' See Walter Benjamin, *The Origin of German Tragic Drama*, trans. John Osborne (London and New York: Verso, 1998), 119.

28. George Steiner, from the Introduction to Benjamin's book.

29. Without invoking Benjamin, Berry argues in similar terms that a 'disturbing figurative excess' in Shakespeare unsettles ordinary sensory response and provides access to 'a polymorphous and heterodox version of material vitality [that is] concealed behind the cultural facades of death' (*Shakespeare's Feminine Endings*, 8, 9).

30. In a passage about the German martyr-drama (a type of *Trauerspiel*), Benjamin discusses the 'minimal ... illusionistic intention' (75) of the medieval passion play, whose episodic structure he associates elsewhere with the works of both Shakespeare and Calderon.

31. Steiner cites Cain as the first *intrigant* 'because fratricide had made him homeless. All "intriguers" after him have been the rootless creatures of their own devices' (18). Certainly, the Cain of the medieval cycle plays is a prototypical *intrigant*, as is Herod, who figures significantly in Benjamin's commentary. For more on Herod's contribution to the *Trauerspiel*, see Chapter 3, p. 95, and *passim*.

32. At one point Benjamin describes the *intrigant* himself as a puppet ('The comic figure is a *raisonneur*; in reflection he appears to himself as a marionette', 127), suggesting that the *intrigant*'s plots against others replicate his own sense of helplessness in an arbitrary and controlling physis. This description might be applied with equal aptness to Cain and Iago.

33. Some malcontents in English tragedies of blood might also be considered *intrigants*, for example, Bosola in Webster's *The Duchess of Malfi*, and Vindice in Middleton's (?) *The Revenger's Tragedy* (although Vindice also serves as the protagonist of the play). These plays are discussed in Chapter 4.

34. It is worth noting that although Benjamin considers Shakespeare's works as critical to the development of the *Trauerspiel*, he believes that *Hamlet*

ultimately transcends the form: 'It is only in [Shakespeare's] prince that melancholy [*sic*] self-absorption attains to Christianity.' There are, then, at least some instances (although none in the tradition of the German baroque) in which the pervasive pessimism or despair of the *Trauerspiel* leads to 'new life' (158).

Chapter 2

Body Imaging and Religious Reform: The Corpse as Idol

Among the objectives of the Protestant reformists was the transformation of Catholic hermeneutics, specifically – at least in the context of this analysis – the Catholic reliance on body imaging for the interpretation of Christian mysteries. Fundamentally, the Reformation's attack on the anthropomorphism of idolatry was symptomatic of its preoccupation with the dangers implicit in materiality and its properties: the materiality of the image or idol, the materiality of the body, and – at the most profound and originary level – the materiality of the corpse.

Because representations of the corpse on the English stage resonate unavoidably with the Reformation controversy over idolatry, this chapter examines the intellectual framework for this controversy by contrasting late medieval concepts of the Christian body (alive and dead) with those of the Reformation. Section 1, 'The material body and Christian sacramentalism', offers a summary of the key issues in contestation from a reformist perspective. Section 2, 'The incorruptible body and the material corpse in the late Middle Ages', considers late medieval approaches to the paradox of the corpse, first in theology, then in iconographic and literary modes by which versions of this paradox became known to the faithful. Section 3, 'Reconfiguring the dead in Reformation England', analyses reformist attempts to demystify Catholic attitudes and practices concerning the material corpse. In Sections 2 and 3, I examine major shifts in the conceptualisation of idols primarily in terms of contrasting, parallel texts such as the late medieval martyrology the *Legenda Aurea* and Foxe's *Book of Martyrs*. In short, this chapter focuses on what might be called the cultural transformation of metaphor on the assumption that any spectator viewing a corpse on the English public stage would have the acrimonious debate over the religious signification of the body consciously or unconsciously in mind.

1. The material body and Christian sacramentalism

The linchpin and unfathomable mystery of Christianity is that of an incorporated deity, a man/God. In Christian theology, an omnipotent God gratuitously assumed human form so that he might be brutally sacrificed, thereby earning for ordinary mortals the right to transcend mortality itself, to live everlastingly. The central doctrines of Christianity – the Incarnation, the Crucifixion and the Resurrection – all proceed from the concept of a God whose redemptive function is imbricated in a human body. Analogously, it is the mortal body of the Christian believer that is paradoxically immortalised, or trans*figured*. Further, a crucial redemptive experience functioned as a kind of mystification of bodily forms in that the concept of the Eucharistic sacrament as promulgated by Catholicism made possible the ingestion or incorporation by the faithful of Christ's body (itself incorporated in the Host). Thus it is to be expected that, beginning with the patristic tradition, Christian theology has been continually engaged in clarifying problematic relationships between divine/human, material/spiritual, living/dead, invisible/visible: any discourse concerning Christ as God is at bottom a discourse about the body.[1]

My particular interest here is the opposition of Protestant reformers in early modern England to what they viewed as the idolatrous practices of Catholicism, practices presumably inscribed in a distortion of the proper Christian theology of the body.[2] The zealous offensive launched by the reformers in England and elsewhere was relentless, even obsessive, but their agenda for eradicating images, relics, shrines and pilgrimages could not be justified solely on the basis of long-standing abuses or even gross commercialism.[3] Rather, Catholic corruption functioned symptomologically for a problem that was less easy to target. In the view of the new Protestant intelligentsia, the Catholic system of worship hypostatised the body, thereby privileging the material principle over that of the spiritual in the Christian system of belief. Put simply, the Reformation's virtually intractable dilemma was to reformulate the prevailing concept of the body/soul relationship so as to counteract the materiality of Catholicism, but without repudiating the paradoxes at the heart of Christian doctrine.

As many Protestant reformers saw it, what was at stake in the controversy over idolatry was the fate of Christianity itself: the culturally inscribed worship of idols was tantamount to the repudiation of the Christian redemptive process. For a Christian to confuse a statue with the saint that the statue supposedly emblematised, for example, was not simply an error in judgement. Rather, it suggested a serious contamination in the believer's faculty of judgement, a flaw so fundamental as to threaten a precipitous slide down the slippery slope to damnation. Idolatry was a seminal sin that invariably generated others, a proliferating disease of the spirit.

On what might be called the first level of ideological contestation, the reformers argued that the moral deterioration implicit in idolatry was rooted in narcissistic self-absorption. Because all material images were dead, the worship (or idolising) of dead images in lieu of the living God served as the foremost symptom of the fall, of man's self-aggrandising procilivity to demystify the deity by worshipping lifeless, anthropomorphic images of himself. To assume that an incomprehensible God (or for that matter any heavenly creature) could be represented at all was insultingly presumptuous; to model representations of the deity after the human body (notwithstanding the Incarnation of Christ) was to obliterate the immeasurable distance between God and his creations; and to confuse the dead material image and the living spirit was further to collapse hierarchies of being by which God remained mysterious and antecedent. Thus as a symptom of man's overvaluation of himself, idolatry was synonymous with the sin of presumption or pride – the root of all evil.

Further, it was not only the hubris implicit in confusing the categories of divine and human that constituted idolatrous behaviour. Homage to idols was thought to have a strongly erotic dimension as well, and Protestant reformers were quick to exploit the exegetical tradition that connected the worship of false gods to lustful appetite. If the desire to substitute a dead, tangible image for the living, invisible God was a sin deriving from man's distorted notion of his own importance, this desire simultaneously signified man's overestimation of bodily forms themselves and was virtually certain to involve the sin of concupiscence. In Judeo-Christian exegesis it was, of course, chiefly the woman (especially the 'false' or cosmeticised woman) who was demonised as a lust-driven idolater, but in a rhetorical double-take, the cosmeticised woman herself functioned as an erotic idol. As 'sins of the flesh', then, idolatry (the human construction and institution of false gods) and concupiscence (excessive investment in the sensual pleasures of the body) were inseparable: concupiscence was at the heart of idolatry.

Moreover, concupiscence was itself symptomatic of a more dangerous, if more subtle, moral corrosion in the idolater – that is, her denial of her spiritual integrity, or the proper union of body and soul, and her corollary affirmation of the principle of fragmentation over that of coherence or identity. Fundamentally, the transfigured self of the Christian subject in heaven represented a state of plenitude or fulfilment. That is, the ideal (if mysterious) conjoining of body and soul in the eternal, beatified state of the redeemed Christian rendered seemingly opposite categories of being profoundly interdependent. It was, therefore, in the earth-bound, *un*redeemed and post-lapsarian subject, contaminated by original sin, that the relationship between material and spiritual principles was necessarily unstable; and this disequilibrium between the subject's constituent elements signified alienation from self as well as from God. Predictably, the problematic status of the post-lapsarian body rendered it vulnerable to further destabilising corruption, so that the pleasures of bodily experience became especially suspect as occasions of sin.

The difficulty of reconciling ideal (transfigured) and debased (un-redeemed) notions of the human body within a single redemptive scheme was, of course, a perennial concern of Christian theology prior to the Reformation. But to the Protestant reformers, Catholic insistence on bodily images in their rituals of worship perversely glorified post-lapsarian corruption by tacitly affirming the ascendancy of the material over the spiritual. It was, in fact, the conceptual connections between Catholic hypostatisation of the body and the dissolution of Christian identity that made sense of Protestant opposition to such seemingly disparate phenomena as cosmeticised women, relics and painted statues.[4] The false face of the cosmeticised woman, for example, served as a symptom of spiritual confusion by creating, as it were, a second self, one divorced from the natural body but pretending to identity with it. In presenting an artificial self, the cosmeticised woman was, in effect, creating an idol of her own bodily beauty and thereby blurring the ontological status of her natural body with that of the idol. Protestants believed that similar ontological confusions, although in different registers, inevitably accompanied the Catholic practices of revering relics and statues, both of which also functioned as idols. In worshipping these artifacts, the faithful not only confused material signifiers with immaterial entities, they also embraced the concept of falsely autonomous, or wholly debased, material bodies.

But it was the ontological status of the corpse – in a sense, the ultimate relic – that foregrounded most dramatically the complexity of the re-lationship between redeemed and debased bodies in the Christian system. Paradigmatically, the corpse occupied a problematically liminal space. The horror of its putrefaction, a punishment for original sin, underscored the corrupt and compromised status of the post-lapsarian body; but the destination of the reconstituted corpse in the eternally changeless subject simultaneously rendered putrefaction as a transformative process, integral to redemption. Indeed, the function of putrefaction *as* transformation – that is, the generation of change *through* fragmentation – seemed to collapse distinctions of any kind between states of being, an issue of serious concern to Catholic theologians for centuries. To reformists, however, Catholic preoccupation with the liminal properties of the corpse during the late Middle Ages dangerously distorted the doctrinal status of the dead. None the less, as we shall see, reformist efforts to revise this attitude met considerable resistance on both the theological and social level, so that the corpse may be said to encapsulate symbolically the challenge implicit in the Protestant project.

At bottom, then, the physical destruction of idols, even when profoundly disruptive of social and religious institutions, was not in itself a solution to the problem of idolatry in the early modern period. As many Protestant reformers seemed to recognise, the chief obstacle to the elimination of idolatrous practices was a culturally entrenched habit of (mis)perception that Catholicism had inculcated for centuries. What the Protestants set out to accomplish was no less than the transformation of cultural paradigms, the dismantling of customary modes of imaging the body in both learned and popular cultures that were thought to subvert the principles of Christian belief.

2. The incorruptible body and the material corpse in the late Middle Ages

On a fundamental level, the 'habits of thought', to borrow Debora Kuller Shuger's apt phrase, of medieval and early modern England are closely allied in that both shared 'the sacramental/analogical character' (11) of pre-modern, or pre-Cartesian thought. That is to say, the Cartesian disposition to categorise by means of binary oppositions (mind/body), generally considered to be symptomatic of the advent of modernism, was unlike the disposition of prior English culture – medieval and early modern alike – to conceptualize by means of ambiguities and interconnections. Moreover, the Christian system of belief as developed by the Church Fathers, who established the historical and intellectual credentials of Christianity, served as a profoundly formative link between medieval and early modern England. But in attacking the materiality of Catholic practices, Protestant iconoclasts were simultaneously enjoined to reformulate the hermeneutic categories by which Christianity had been understood in preceding centuries. And because the reformers needed to draw sharper distinctions between the material and the spiritual, their theology functioned so as to modify the pre-modern proclivity for non-categorical thinking.

In attempting to track aspects of this conceptual shift, I would like to focus, first, on medieval modes of interpreting Christian doctrine through body imagery, concentrating principally on the high Middle Ages (the fourteenth and fifteenth centuries). This period is not only contiguous with the English Reformation, it also saw the emergence of several religious phenomena, in England and elsewhere, that intensified the Catholic disposition to use the body as hermeneutic matrix. These included the visionary transports of the mystics, which foregrounded the body; the preoccupation with purgatory, a site for the bodily suffering of the dead; and the culmination of the cult of the saints in body-oriented popular devotions (shrines, relics, pilgrimages and miracles). Collectively, these developments convinced sixteenth-century reformers that Christianity was gravely endangered, that their own age was witnessing the apex of Catholic capitulation to a false concept of materiality that inevitably generated a rampant materialism.

According to Caroline Walker Bynum, the late medieval emphasis on body imaging in interpretations of the Christian mysteries was more precisely an emphasis on bodily process. Rather than focus on Christ's relationship to God the Father, and on the teleological significance of the Incarnation in the divine design for human redemption, as many influential reformers did, Catholicism chose to explore the implications of Christ's humanity. The body of Christ thereby figured as the central emblem for the redemptive process, but even more importantly, the transformative functions of the body itself were seen as deeply imbricated in Christ's redemptive act. Thus it seemed wholly appropriate in both literary and iconographic traditions of the Western Church to represent the Christian mysteries according to an interlocking system of body metaphors, metaphors that not only tended to collapse distinctions between the material and the spiritual, but between gender categories as well. Bynum encapsulates this orientation in arguing that medieval Christianity, and its representations, were profoundly anti-dualistic.[5]

Bynum demonstrates, for example, how the concept of Christ as bi-gendered served to foreground images of nurture and of mutilation which linked Christ's sacrificial birth to his sacrificial death. In this framework, Christ's Nativity and Crucifixion signified interdependently. Thus in medieval iconography, the crucified body of Christ gave birth, through the bloody wound in his side (occasioned by the piercing of his body with a lance), to the Church (Adam and Eve were frequently depicted beneath the Cross, receiving the stream of redemptive fluid).[6] This 'delivery' was prefigured by Christ's own birth, and later in the cutting and bleeding of his foreskin at the circumcision,[7] so that the bloody wound in Christ's side signified both male and female reproductive agency. Further, medieval depictions of Christ with bleeding breasts linked blood as nurture (mother's milk) with blood as power (potency implicit in the cut phallus): Jesus as Mother and Jesus as Man of Sorrows fed the Christian subject – like Adam and Eve at the foot of the Cross – with the milk/blood of life.[8]

The bi-gendered Christ was also foregrounded by medieval pre-occupation with the bodily process by which Christ took on human shape in the womb of his mother, the Blessed Virgin Mary. Because Christ had no human father, he was enfleshed solely by a woman and nourished by her before and after birth; conversely, as tabernacle or vessel for the deity, the flesh of Mary was in some sense assimilated to the divinity of Christ. Thus the prevalence in medieval devotions of *vierges ouvrantes,* objects in which a statue of Mary nursing Christ opened to show God inside, and of medieval portraits conflating the nurturing function of the Virgin/Mother with the sacramental function of the Eucharistic feast. In certain of these portraits, the Virgin was shown offering to the viewer both the infant Christ (whose own breasts were frequently engorged with milk) and her maternal breast, suggesting that the flesh and milk of the Virgin, analogous to the bread and wine of the Eucharist, might themselves be understood as divine food, or Host. As Rubin puts it: 'a strong bond was created between the eucharistic body reborn at the mass and the original body born from a virgin womb ... Eucharistic poetry and mysticism reveled in this myth, of a virgin mother and her divine son unceasingly born and unceasingly mourned' (142–3).[9]

It was, of course, the function of Christ as food that raised the paradox of natural process to the level of the sacerdotal and invested it with redemptive power. In the 'symbolic cannibalism' (Bynum, *F&R*, 185) of the Eucharistic feast, made possible by the mystery of transubstantiation (the phenomenon by which Christ was materially present in the substances of bread and wine) the faithful consumed and ingested the body and blood of Christ. This participatory act served as analogue to Christ's Incarnation – his partaking of a nature other than his own through the body of the Virgin: the ordinary Christian incorporated (or fused with) the man/God and was thereby empowered to transcend her own mortality, that is, to be redeemed. Thus the Mass, by re-enacting the Crucifixion, and by offering the sacrificed flesh and blood of the Saviour to the faithful as nutrient, paradoxically enabled a spiritual transformation in which death, the inevitable end of bodily process itself, might be obviated.[10]

But if the Eucharist enabled a spiritual transformation, it was the actual consumption of Christ's flesh as a means to this end that occupied the medieval imagination. The host did not symbolise Christ's body; on the contrary, 'pious folk ... experienced miracles in which the bread turned into bloody flesh on the paten or in the mouth of the recipient';[11] and disbelievers in Christ's physical presence were likely to be terrified by the sight of bleeding morsels of flesh at the moment of consecration during the Mass, or at the communion service.[12] Duffy emphasises the common fear that power could 'leak' from the Host: its 'blood affected even the dead metal of the chalice ... no layman or woman might even touch the sacred vessels with their bare hands' (110). The imaginative construction of a bloody host – the body of Christ crucified – was, in fact, crucial to the mystery of transubstantiation as both substance and symbol:

> The juxtaposition of simplest [*sic*] natural act, of eating, with the holiest and most taboo-ridden of nourishments, the human body ... in any other contexts would be abhorrent and unutterable ... [But in] the routine workings of sacramental power – an image of the fullness of life-giving ... dwells in the image of utmost transgression. (Rubin, 359–60)

The pain/pleasure dichotomy in the sacramental cannibalism of the Eucharist, rendered through topoi of eating and bleeding, was especially apparent in the spiritual biographies of the mystics. Although in the late Middle Ages there were mystics of both sexes (Rubin, 316–19), women outnumbered men; in addition, 'the vast majority of stigmatics were women' (*F&R*, 173), and it was women who were the chief promoters of Eucharistic devotion.[13]

Certainly the physicality of sacramental experience served as an analogue for the mystics' visionary transports, so that the ingestion of Christ was frequently described as an ecstatic sexual union.[14] This pervasive paradigm was not, however, invariably heterosexual since ecstatic experience was common to male mystics as well, such as Bernard of Clairvaux and Meister Eckhart; and, perhaps more importantly, since the gender of Christ himself was unstable in the writings of the mystics. As the complex iconographic inversions of the circumcised Christ as mother/bride make clear, 'applications of male/female contrasts' may have functioned 'to organize life symbolically', but 'medieval thinkers used gender imagery fluidly, not literally' (*F&R*, 218).[15]

The imagery of orgasmic transport characteristic of mystic experience is eloquently expressed in the thirteenth-century accounts of Mary of Origines (by the hagiographer James of Vitry) and of the poet Hadewijch, respectively:

> The holy bread strengthened her heart; the holy wine inebriated her, rejoicing her mind; the holy body fattened her; the vitalizing blood purified her by washing ... For it was the same to her to live as to eat the body of Christ ... Indeed she felt all delectation and all savor of sweetness in receiving it, not just within her soul but even in her mouth ... Sometimes she happily accepted her Lord ... in the pure and gorgeously embellished marriage bed of the heart.

> Then he gave himself to me in the shape of the sacrament, in its outward form, as the custom is; and then he gave me to drink from the chalice ... After that he came himself to me, took me entirely in his arms, and pressed me to him; and all my members felt his in full felicity ... so I was inwardly satisfied and fully transported ... (Bynum, *F&R*, 119–20)[16]

At other times, female mystics imagined themselves nursing from the breasts of the crucified Jesus, whose sustenance was inextricable from his suffering, as in the writings of the fourteenth-century theologian/mystic Catherine of Siena, among others:

> We must do as a little child does who wants milk. It takes the breast of its mother, applies its mouth, and by means of the flesh it draws milk. We must do the same if we would be nourished. We must attach ourselves to that breast of Christ crucified, which is the source of charity, and by means of that flesh we draw milk. The means is Christ's humanity which suffered pain, and we cannot without pain get that milk that comes from charity. (96)

A more tortuous depiction of Jesus as mother, in this instance giving birth on the Cross, is provided by Marguerite of Oingt:

> My sweet Lord ... are you not my mother and more than my mother? ... For when the hour of your delivery came you were placed on the hard bed of the cross ... and your nerves and all your veins were broken. And truly it is no surprise that your veins burst when in one day you gave birth to the whole world. (97)[17]

These metaphors suggest that the mystics imagined the dual function of the body as agent of ecstatic fulfilment and as agent of suffering to be indistinguishable, but in their ascetic practices there also seemed to be a deliberate effort to deny the body altogether, to negate it through abnegation. Such practices commonly included 'thrusting nettles into one's breasts, wearing hair shirts, binding one's flesh tightly with twisted ropes, enduring extreme sleep and food deprivation, performing thousands of genuflections and praying barefoot in winter ... jumping into ovens or icy ponds ... [and] whipping or hanging themselves in elaborate pantomimes of Christ's Crucifixion' (Bynum, *F&R*, 132, 184). For women, self-starvation, an extreme but celebrated practice, sometimes led to the inability to menstruate or even to excrete (*RoftheB*, 224). Although it is easy enough to dismiss such behaviour from a contemporary perspective as a medieval form of masochism, to do so is to overlook the way in which these excesses followed a certain theological logic – at least within the already extravagant context of mysticism itself. That is to say, the penitential regimen of the mystics can be said to offer an illustration *in extremis* of a paradox common to all Christians – the need to deny the body and its processes, while simultaneously acknowledging the fact that Christian redemption, and ecstatic experience, could be experienced only in terms of these processes.

The conundrum here lay in the Christian idea of ultimate redemption as a state of stasis. The transfigured, incorruptible body of the resurrected Christian, the Christian in heaven, transcended or transfixed the very birth-and-death cycle which enabled the redemption itself. Because corruptibility was inimical to perfection, which obviates the need for change, the perfection of the transfigured body exempted it forever from bodily process. In a sense, then, the body as a channel for perfection seemed incongruent with its final state of beatitude.

Once again, if in a different register, the bodies of Christ and his mother served as prototypes for the Christian ideal – here, the ideal of stasis. Christian theology argued that these bodies were axiomatically incorruptible because (for different reasons, of course) they had never been spiritually contaminated by original sin, for which death and dissolution were the consequences.[18] Nor were they marred by sexual sin, a requirement that figured prominently, certainly by the Middle Ages, in the Christian ethos. The requirement that Christ's mother be a virgin, for example, derived in part from the Judaic identification of sexuality with contamination (at least in the prohibitions of Leviticus) and partly from the development of a distinctively Christian ethos in which virginity was hypostatised.[19] Because it was wholly sinless, Mary's body was invulnerable to putrefaction prior to her Assumption by Christ into heaven,[20] as was, of course, Christ's body in the tomb prior to his Resurrection. By extension, then, the miraculous preservation of a saint's body from physical corruption was thought to be incontrovertible proof of holiness.

When seen in terms of these theological principles, the mystics' extreme denial of bodily pleasure through self-starvation and flagellation appears to be a deliberate effort to waste the body itself as a symbolic prelude to transfiguration and the end of bodily process.[21] Moreover, the seeming contradiction in their mixed metaphors of eroticism and renunciation suggests the difficulty of accommodating a theory of redemption in which bodily process ends in bodily stasis, and in which the physicality of spiritual union is affirmed (as in the Eucharistic rituals of consumption and consummation) at the same time that the physicality of carnal union is denied, or even demonised. Further, by focusing on extreme expiatory practices that might result, at death, in the immunity of their bodies to ordinary corruption, the mystics ignored or obscured the transitional state between death and beatitude which posed such a vexing problem for ordinary Catholics, and certainly for Catholic theologians.

The relationship between the dead and the transfigured body was figured, finally, by the corpse, an encapsulating emblem for the polar contrasts encompassed by Christianity. The corpse, as a dead body, was paradoxically generative, not static, and in two seemingly opposite directions. On the one hand, putrefaction bore witness to the mortal punishment imposed by God for original sin: in a horrific analogue to Holy Communion, body rot became food for worms, re-incorporated as a debased life-form.[22] For man to be reborn, cleansed of the original taint, he must first undergo death and decomposition. But the principle of bodily transfiguration – or re-formation ending in stasis – was implicit in the process of decomposition, because the corpse, whether enfleshed or consumed, did not represent the final destination of the dead body. At the

Last Judgement, the body/corpse would be glorified – that is, rendered eternally changeless or *in*corruptible – in a brilliant heavenly fusion with the soul. Since there could be no immortality in heaven for souls without bodies (and in Christianity, this was the crucial point), the Christian believer was enjoined to conceive of the putrefying corpse not only as food for worms, but also as the raw material, as it were, of the beatified self. To put this another way, Christian doctrine predicated a continuity, or relationship between two states of bodily being, that seemed dramatically incongruent.

Not surprisingly, during the late Middle Ages the manner of this relationship was the subject of elaborate, even tortuous, theological speculation. Although mainstream philosophers adhered to the general principle that (to cite the Fourth Lateran Council of 1215) 'all rise again with their own individual bodies, that is, the bodies which they now wear',[23] interpretations of exactly how this change was transacted varied considerably. In this contestation, Thomas Aquinas's principles concerning the relationship between mortal and immortal bodies, as formulated in his *Summa Theologica*, dominated theological discourse about corporeality for centuries.

Adapting his hylomorphic theory from Aristotle, Aquinas argued that matter (potency or, in its secondary form, body) and form (soul) together constituted the substance of man: to separate matter and form in the individual was, in effect, to destroy the integrity of the self. But since the promise of Christianity, as confirmed by Christ's Resurrection, was that the believer lived after death, this integrity – that is, the union of matter and form – could not be destroyed. Thus Aquinas's argument for unicity of form between mortal and immortal bodies suggested a temporary suspension of self, that is, that 'the soul as a substantial form survives the death of the body, but the full person does not exist until body (matter) is restored to its form at the end of time' (Bynum, *F&R*, 228).[24] Scholastic philosophy, as adumbrated by Aquinas and others well into the fourteenth century, thereby affirmed that ontological completeness required the union of body and soul, here and in the hereafter, although Aquinas deemed the soul capable of the vision of God prior to its reunification with the body.[25]

Other philosophers, however, elaborating the Augustinian concept of desire, which affirmed the longing of the soul itself for completion in the body, emphasised a sensual striving in the relationship between form and matter which served as an impetus for their reunification after death. In this framework, broadly defined, material and/or structural continuity between mortal and immortal bodies – that is, continuity of specific particles, or matter, and continuity of specific members, or shapes – was of paramount importance. Bonaventure, for example, a contemporary of Aquinas, affirmed that desire is, in Bynum's words, 'at the heart of the person; it is the metaphysical cement binding body to soul', so that the beatified body constitutes 'the emotional, experiencing self' in a fully particularised, if glorified, form (*RoftheB*, 253–4). In his *Sentence*, Bonaventure puts it as follows:

> Thus the soul is united with love [*affectus*] to the substance of the flesh which first it vivified, because it is not completely satisfied unless it is joined to her wherever she may have been hiding.[26]

This shift of emphasis provided the body, as that which the soul desired, with a powerful dynamism lacking in the Thomistic model of unicity, a charismatic quality informing all of the body's constituent parts.[27]

Disputation concerning the resurrected body inevitably led to a plethora of narrowly formulated issues with which medieval philosophy was famously preoccupied for centuries (often to the derision of later generations, including, of course, the Protestant reformers). But eschatological questions such as the following inspired serious debate at universities and elsewhere: Will glorified bodies taste, see and smell? Will the same matter that originally constituted a body part (for example, a finger) return to the same location? Will the transfigured body retain its age, height and gender? Will bodily organs be visible in the glorified body? How is a hermaphrodite transfigured? What happens to individuals who are mutilated or eaten? What happens to the embryo of a pregnant women who is eaten? And so on.[28]

On one level, the insistent literalness of these questions, and their unrelenting focus on the details of physical transformation, seem absurdly reductive. But when viewed as symptoms of a cultural disposition, these instances tell a different story. As Bynum suggests, in the Middle Ages it was almost 'impossible to speak of immortal souls without clothing them in their quite particular flesh', without insisting 'that persons *are* in some sense their bodies, not merely souls temporarily inhabiting matter' (*F&R*, 235, 224). At bottom, theological preoccupation – scholastic and non-scholastic – with the particularities of resurrection represented a resistance to dualism, a refusal to eliminate the body as a co-constituent of the self. It was also symptomatic of a willingness to confront – at times, apparently, with profound discomfort – the difficulty of reconciling human revulsion at the putrefying corpse with the centrality of putrefaction itself as a stage in the process of Christian transformation. Notwithstanding the complexity of the theological landscape, 'the idea of a person bequeathed by the Middle Ages to the modern world' derived, fundamentally, from a materialist eschatology that affirmed 'a sense of self as psychosomatic unity' (*RoftheB*, 11).[29]

For the laity, Catholic eschatology was represented in the visual and literary traditions of medieval popular culture, which, according to Jacques Le Goff, 'tell us more than theology does about the relation between belief and society, about mental structures, and about the historical role of the imaginations'.[30] Although it is a mistake, as Patrick J. Geary has argued, to assume 'a dichotomous view of [medieval] society that would distinguish "popular" and "elite" religions as part of largely separate cultural systems',[31] one may none the less note the reciprocal transaction between eschatological theory and the multidisciplinary interpretations of that theory for (and by) the Catholic populace. During the fourteenth and fifteenth centuries, this tension between symbolic systems was especially apparent in the emergence of the concept of purgatory, which came to have a life of its own in the popular imagination.[32]

Theological discourse about purgatory, like that about resurrection and transfiguration, focused on the status of the redeemed after death, but the possibility of a punishment other than damnation – an intermediate cleansing by fire prior to admittance to heaven – newly foregrounded the period between death and the Last Judgement. At bottom, the relationship of putrefaction to the resurrected body was still the troubling issue in Christian eschatology, but purgatory provided, as it were, a new twist: if Christians ordinarily awaited the Last Judgement for the beatification of their bodies, what entity was it that suffered in purgatory, and *how* did it suffer? Further, were the inhabitants of purgatory released *en masse* at the end of the world, or did their access to the Beatific Vision depend on other factors, such as the severity of their sins and the intensity and duration of their punishment? And how could purgatory as a redemptive process be reconciled with a range of sufferings virtually identical to those of the damned?

For Le Goff, the establishment of purgatory as a Christian doctrine by the Second Council of Lyons in 1274[33] represents far more than a shift in theological focus: it signals 'a substantial modification in the spatial and temporal framework of the Christian imagination' (1).[34] As a function of eschatological time, the interval between death and redemption is theoretically not amenable to temporal or spatial measurement, but purgatory seemed to invite consideration of precisely such practical and logistical questions. As a consequence, theologians faced the daunting task of finding a way to describe, or even to conceptualise, purgatory in terms that did not diminish its eschatological status: to think of it as 'intermediate' or 'in-between' was itself to assume a historical or linear concept of time; to assume an assembly of sufferers was to suggest that they could be located spatially. Certainly, medieval theologians such as Aquinas, elaborating on the earlier speculations of Augustine and Gregory the Great,[35] among others, took pains to describe purgatory as a state (that is, a metaphysical

mode of being inherently other than that of the pre-deceased) from purgatory as a place situated in time. But theological discourse was itself replete
with references to terrestrial concepts of duration, such as years or hours,
and to terrestrial dimensions for space.

Further, continual reference in theological discourse to the '*souls* in
purgatory' complicated the already problematic status of the dead body
prior to resurrection. Orthodox medieval theology, as we have seen,
assumed a suspension of body/soul integrity in the interval between the
putrefaction of the body and its transfiguration, while insisting on this
integrity in the resurrected self. But when this soul-in-transition was
positioned in purgatory, it seemed to function as a body did – that is, it
was subject to varieties of pain ordinarily transmitted through the senses.
Theologians could, of course, find ways to accommodate this new
phenomenon: most opinion, according to Le Goff, assumed that 'once
separated from the body, the soul was endowed with a materiality *sui
generis*, and punishment could then be inflicted upon it in purgatory *as
though it were corporeal*' (6–7; my italics).[36] But fine distinctions such as
these were likely to be far less important to the ordinary Christian, who had
strong reason to identify subjectively with the new doctrine.[37]

As a concept, purgatory seemed to narrow the gap between the saved and
the damned: it was, after all, like hell in that it affected the lives of ordinary
Christians with a fearful urgency and was difficult to imagine outside the
context of bodily pain. If the faithful could now hope to enjoy the Beatific
Vision prior to the Last Judgement (a privilege formerly associated
primarily with the saints, who presumably went directly to heaven after
death),[38] they were none the less confronted with the more immediate
prospect of undergoing terrible suffering for an unspecified period of time.
Moreover, they were enjoined to imagine the pre-deceased – their family
and loved ones – as already *in extremis*, caught helplessly in the agony of
the purgatorial fire. Small wonder, then, that the venial sinner was preoccupied with the varieties and degrees of what appeared to be bodily
torment in purgatory, and with death as a potentially violent transition to a
terrifying hereafter.[39]

Further, although the purgatorial landscape – *pace* theological emphases
– was domesticated in popular imagery (*bodies* burned in some *place* in
some *temporal* dimension),[40] it was also imagined as 'a topography of
nightmare, not of solid reality', as Greenblatt has recently argued. At least
in literary representations of purgatory, 'time and space are warped, the
laws of physics are suspended, and the boundaries between the living and
the dead blurred' (91).[41] In these visionary dreamscapes, the grounding of
purgatory in the familiar actually heightens the dreamer's sense of displacement: like time and space, even intimacy is warped by estrangement, and

the comfort of reaching out to the dead is weighted with fear. For the faithful, purgatory seemed to inspire an irreconcilable alloy of hope and dread.

Aware of the unsettling ambiguities of its doctrine, the Church seemed determined to exploit them. Ironically, the clergy had reason to be concerned that the existence of purgatory might lessen the fear of damnation among Christians and foster a complacency about sin: after all, even an eleventh-hour repentance could suffice to save a sinner from irreversible punishment. Thus it was important to represent purgatory not only as an 'ante-room of heaven' but also as 'an outpost of hell' (Duffy, 343), to ensure that hope was balanced, if not eclipsed, by anxiety. At the same time, however, the Church did provide a recourse – the so-called suffrages – by which the faithful might exert a measure of control over the suffering of their loved ones in the afterlife, and by extension over their own fear of punishment to come.[42]

By making available an elaborate variety of suffrages – masses, prayers and religious activities, such as pilgrimages – that could be set against a purgatorial sentence and thereby shorten it, the Church simultaneously allayed the anxiety of the laity and extended its influence over their everyday lives. All suffrages were, of course, regulated by the Church in kind and degree through the dispensing of indulgences, or remissions from purgatorial suffering for specified periods of time, usually in exchange for a 'donation'. As is well known, the Church exploited this system during the late Middle Ages to its great financial advantage, with insufficient attention to the manifold abuses later condemned by Protestant reformers. But suffrages were of momentous importance to future generations of Christians for another reason as well: they created a new intimacy, or communality, between the living and the dead, which also functioned to extend social networks on earth.[43] In effect, Aquinas's fears about the domestication of purgatory were fully realised. The concept of the dead as distanced, and of the hereafter as Other, proved impossible to maintain against the powerful identification of the faithful with what seemed to be their suffering counterparts in the afterlife.[44]

But if the emergence of purgatory represented, at least in retrospect, a watershed in the development and administration of Christian doctrine, it was also profoundly congruent with well-established medieval Christian beliefs, especially as mythologised in popular culture. The suffering body in the person of the crucified Christ was, after all, the central emblem in Christianity; it was this suffering that the mystics sought to emulate. Moreover, the paradigms established by Christ for redemptive suffering foregrounded, as we have seen, the paradoxical relationship between partition/process and unity/stasis: in delivering his Eucharistic body to be ingested by the faithful, Christ redeemed and sacramentalised, as it were, the disintegrative process to which all bodies are subject. Redemption meant that the violence of earthly suffering and of putrefaction would end in transfiguration, the binding together of the fragmented self; damnation guaranteed the violence of eternal suffering, precluding any possibility of reintegration. Thus the damned were the inverse of the saved, a worst-case scenario extending endlessly; and the purgatorial soul, ambiguously situated in an antechamber of heaven that was also an outpost of hell, newly dramatised the conceptual linkages between these states of being.

In this sense, purgatory did not disrupt the hierarchical ordering of the Christian redemptive scheme. On the contrary, the suffering of the souls in purgatory could be represented by means of the topoi that already connected the suffering of Christ with that of the saved, and the suffering of the saved with that of the damned. Christian iconography thus provided, as it were, variations on a single paradoxical theme, juxtaposing images of bodily partition with those of bodily incorruption. But because the final state of wholeness – whether that of the resurrected Christ, his saints or the ordinary Christian – was meaningless without prior mutilation and/or fragmentation, and because the damned were doomed to an eternity of such horror, ecclesiastical iconography, especially that designed to instruct the laity, was replete with graphic images of bodily suffering.

Much of this imagery was incorporated in the late medieval sermon, which in the wake of the development of the itinerant preaching orders in the thirteenth century assumed major importance as a mode of instructing the faithful.[45] Representing a rich convergence of biblical and patristic sources with local mythologies and folklore, the sermon was largely anecdotal and dramatic.[46] One of its chief sources was the vastly influential *Legenda Aurea* compiled by Jacobus de Voragine in about 1260. Assembled from over 100 sources dating from the second to the thirteenth centuries, and extant today in over 1,000 manuscripts, the *Legenda* was an incomparable storehouse of Christian hagiography and was believed to have been more widely disseminated than the Bible.[47] By the fifteenth century, the original 180 saints' legends had expanded to 400, largely in response to their popularity among the laity. Moreover, with the advent of printing in the 1450s, hundreds of editions of the *Legenda* were published in both Latin and the vernacular languages of Europe, including Caxton's publication of *The Golden Legend*, his own translation, in 1483.[48] Thus through the *Legenda* the saints came to represent, as Helen White puts it, 'the very warp and woof of the religious life' (68) for the ordinary Christian. On at least fifty annual feast-days, the vivid and often riveting narratives of the *Legenda* were recounted to the laity as models of Christian conduct.

In terms of the shaping of the popular religious imagination, then, the

Legenda's virtual obsession with extravagant forms of torture, graphically rendered, is noteworthy: 'of the 153 chapters ... devoted to saints' days, at least 75 have dismemberment as a central motif' (Bynum, *F&R*, 290). In most instances, the saints are depicted as impervious to their tortures. As with the mystics, the emphasis on bodily process becomes, paradoxically, a way of denying it, of pointing towards the incorruption awaiting the saint after death. Not surprisingly, many of the mutilated martyrs featured in the *Legenda*, like the mystics, are female virgins, notwithstanding the fact that more men than women were formally canonised as saints in the Middle Ages (Bynum, *F&R*, 188). The traditional association of female virginity with physical incorruption (as with the Blessed Virgin Mary) is, therefore, a major hagiographical motif, but here the emphasis on the physical dis-assembly of the virgin signifies the transformation of the fluid, porous and fertile female body itself – so intimately associated with nature's own reproductive cycle – into an emblem of the Christian defeat of natural process. Thus the pervasive topoi of the *Legenda*'s hagiography insist that martyrdom commandeers the violence of nature by means of a grotesque surrender to it, a capitulation that is simultaneously a usurpation of nature's destructive power.[49]

In submitting to torture, the virgin martyr was, of course, re-enacting the Crucifixion – the ultimate triumph over natural process – in a different register, and the gruesomeness with which such martyrdoms are described in the *Legenda* functioned as a heavy-handed way to establish this con-nection. It would seem that the *Legenda*'s elaborate narratives of torture were designed to inspire horror, notwithstanding the customary assurances that many victims felt no pain, or the predictability of oft-repeated motifs, such as the tearing off of women's breasts with iron pikes. The trials of Margaret and Catherine, two of England's most popular virgin martyrs, demonstrate the *Legenda*'s characteristic fascination with hyperbolic detail:

> By the prefect's [Olybirus of Antioch] order [Margaret] was hung upon a rack and was beaten with rods and then lacerated with iron rakes, so cruelly that her bones were laid bare and the blood poured from her body as from a pure spring ... Refusing again to sacrifice to the gods, she was stripped of her clothes and her body was burned with torches; and all wondered how so delicate a girl could withstand such torture. Then the judge had her bound and put in a tub full of water, in order to increase the suffering by varying the pain; but suddenly the earth shook and the virgin came out unharmed. (I, 369–70)

> Now a certain prefect urged the furious ruler [the Roman Maxentius] to have prepared, within three days, four wheels studded with iron saws and sharp-pointed nails, and to have [Catherine] torn to pieces with these horrible instru-ments, thus terrorizing the rest of the Christians with the example of so awful a death. It was further ordered that two of the wheels should revolve in one

direction and the other two turn in the opposite direction, so that the maiden would be mangled and torn by the two wheels coming down on her, and chewed up by the other two coming against her from below. (II, 338)

Similar dismemberments by rack, pike, nails and other instruments, frequently conducted on naked female bodies, and an equally imaginative variety of tortures by fire – roasting, frying, boiling – are insistently reiterated in the *Legenda*.[50]

But if, on the one hand, the torments of the martyrs served as an analogue to the agony on the cross, they also became, as I noted earlier, virtually indistinguishable from those of the souls in purgatory, because bodily violence was a constituent part of the redemptive experience (and its prolongation the archetypal damnation) for all Christians. It is therefore noteworthy that the *Legenda* modelled its description of purgatory after that of the celebrated twelfth-century visionary work, the *Purgatorium Sancti Patricii*, or *Saint Patrick's Purgatory*, in which the voyager to the underworld (Owein the Knight in the *Purgatorium*; Nicholas in the *Legenda*) cannot distinguish between purgatory and hell.[51] Extrapolated from their context, details from the *Legenda*'s passage on purgatory might indeed serve indiscriminately to describe purgatory, hell or the martyrdom of a saint:

He was led to still another place, where he saw some men being burned alive and having hot iron blades thrust deep into their bodies by the demons … He saw others being bitten by serpents, while demons dragged out their entails with incandescent iron hooks. When Nicholas continued to resist them, they threw him into the same fire and made him feel the same blades, the same pains. But again he called upon Jesus Christ and was freed of the pain forthwith. Then he was taken to a place where men were being fried in great frying pans, and where there was a very large wheel full of flaming iron hooks upon which men were hanging by various parts of their bodies; and the wheel spun so rapidly that it threw off a globe of fire … Next he saw a large building where there were trenches filled with molten metal, into which some men had one foot, some had two, and others were in up to the knees, others to the waist, to the chest, to the neck, to the eyes; but Nicholas called upon Christ and passed safely through all this. (I, 195)[52]

As this passage makes clear, purgatory, notwithstanding its relatively late development as a doctrine in the Middle Ages, was absorbed into an icono-graphical framework of virtually interchangeable metaphors, informed by the generative and originary metaphor of Christ's passion. Homilitic descriptions of the passion itself, to come full circle, were of course them-selves rendered in accordance with this pervasive vocabulary:

Byholde, thanne, that goede lord chyveryng and quakyng, al his body naked and bounde to a pyler; aboute him stondying the wycked men, withouten eny resoun, ful sore scourgyng that blessed body, withouten eny pite. See how they cesse nought fram here angry strokes, tyl they se him stonde in his blode up to the anclees. Fro the top of the hed to the sole of his fote, hole skyn saved they non. His flesch they rase to the bone ... A garland of thornes they thrast on his heved, tyl the blode ran doun in his eyghen, nose and mouth and eeren.

He was betun and buffetid, scorned and scourgid, that unnethis [scarcely] was ther left ony hoole platte of his skyn, fro the top to the too, that a man myghte have sette in the point of a nedil. But all his bodi rane out as a strem of blood. He was crowned with a crowne of thornes for dispite. And whanne the crowne, as clerkis seien, wolde not stik fast and iust doun on his heed for the longe thornes and stronge, thei toke staves and betun it down, til the thornes thrilliden the brayne panne. He was naylyd hond and foot with scharp nailis and ruggid, for his peyne schulde be the more; and so, at the last, he sufferid moost peynful deeth, hanging ful schamefulli on the cros.[53]

It is this *gestalt* of the body – the comprehensiveness of its signification in expressing the foundational concepts of Christianity – that underlies the late medieval veneration of relics. If the body of the saint, like that of Christ, needed to be wracked and tormented prior to its transfiguration, then the saint's purified remains, already guaranteed a brilliant reassemblage, actually contained, at least in *potentia,* the power and mystery of Christian transcendence:

> The relic is ... a fragment of the saint's rejected remains; as such, it is neither noumenal – since by definition the relic preserves the body and not the soul of the saint – nor strictly phenomenal, since its curative properties hallucinatorily suspend the laws of nature, shooting *physis* through with the rays of the divine. (Lupton, 67)[54]

Moreover, if the doctrine of transubstantiation affirmed that every morsel or fragment of the Eucharistic Host – the relic that Christ left of himself – contained the whole of Christ's body, then popular belief assumed by analogy that the saint too '[was] fully present in his or her every part' (Bynum, *F&R*, 285). Hence the concurrent development during the fifteenth and sixteenth centuries of the Feast of Corpus Christi, which reinforced the centrality of the Eucharist to Christian belief, and the so-called 'cult of the saints,' which gave new prominence to shrines, pilgrimages and the veneration of relics.

Many of the most popular shrines were those of female saints, and the laity's devotion to their relics was undoubtedly influenced by the *Legenda*'s emphasis on the sacramental parallels between the bodies of virgin martyrs and that of the crucified Christ. Not only did virgins often submit themselves, as we have seen, to tortures resembling those of Christ, such as the racking of limbs, beating, flailing and impalement, but their wounds, like Christ's own, produced fluids that served as spiritual nourishment. The 'pure spring' of blood that poured from Margaret's lacerated limbs, or the mixture of milk and blood from Faith's severed breasts, functioned in much the same way as the blood from the side of the crucified Christ or the milk from the lactating breasts of Jesus-as-Mother did. In this symbolic economy, Christ's own generative/nutritive functions intersected in specific ways with those of his martyrs: both were associated with restorative fluids – food for the body transformed into food for the soul.[55]

But if the body of the martyr were symbolically linked to that of Christ, there was at the same time no mistaking the differences between the Redeemer's body and all others. Unlike Christ's gratuitous sacrifice on the cross and in the Eucharist, the self-sacrifice of the martyrs of either gender was a purifying ritual: a beatified or incorruptible body was the reward for the violent obliteration of the corrupt earthly body. Accordingly, one of the Church's requirements for canonisation in the late Middle Ages was the absence of ordinary putrefaction in the corpse of the prospective saint, which meant that it must remain 'lifelike and supple' for a prolonged period (Bynum, *F&R*, 187). In a sense the 'jewellike hardness' (*RoftheB*, 108) of the corpse as *bone*, stripped of any remnants of flesh – which, of course, was the relic ultimately preserved and venerated by the faithful – reinforced this concept of radical purification. The sanctified bones of the saints were reminders that their bodies had been wholly cleansed of physical and moral corruption by martyrdom, or by some other penitential means.[56]

Thus the cult of the saints, like so much else in Christian ideology, emphasised the mutually dependent oppositions between corrupt bodies and perfected ones, with the relic negotiating the ideological space between them. In the *Legenda*, the conquest of putrefaction is implicit in Margaret's 'pure springs of blood', and especially in Charity's immunity to immolation: 'the child walked unscathed in the midst of the fire and shone like gold' (I, 186). But it was the miraculous and curative relic, itself believed sometimes to exude oils and other restorative fluids, that served as a tangible emblem of the paradoxical relationship between bones as dessicated remains, the end product of ordinary putrefaction, and bones as the beatified body *in potentia*. Interestingly, as Bynum points out, reliquaries themselves reinforced this paradox by surrounding their contents with gold and precious jewels. Some reliquaries even 'flamboyantly announced that fragments were fragments' by replicating the shapes of the bones they contained (*F&R*, 271, 280), and thereby underscoring the co-extensive relationship between 'dead' body parts and immortality.[57]

But if encasing the saints in imperishable gold was designed to strike awe in the worshipper, to set the saints apart, the Church also took pains to instantiate their presence in the daily lives of the faithful:

> the saints were perceived as part of the economy of grace. They were dispensers of gifts and miracles, and the essence of their cult lay in its assurance of the possibility of rescue from the iron laws of cause and effect, the painful con-

strictions of poverty, disease, and the sometimes harsh ordering of society ... and
the threat of a terrifying reckoning ... (Duffy, 186)

In this context the mythic extravagance of the saints' lives and deaths
was doubly necessary – certainly to their function as exemplars, but also,
ironically, to their transformation into 'kynd neyghbours, and of our
knowyng'.[58] In romanticising and memorialising extraordinary suffering, at
once a distancing and familiarising strategy, the cult of the saints made it
possible for the ordinary Christian to perceive Christian tribulation as a
gateway to happiness as well as a punishment for sin. Purgatory too was
such a gateway, but because few believers could imagine themselves
enduring the pain of martyrdom or purgatory, the saints could also serve
as intercessors, powerful but loving friends who could be depended upon
for solace, protection and assistance in expediting the difficult process of
redemption. It is hardly surprising that the Blessed Virgin Mary, the mother
par excellence, inspired the deepest and most widespread devotion in the
medieval Catholic Church.

The iconographical cataloguing of saints by specialties associated with
their methods of execution was another popular mode of negotiating the
suffering required by Christian teaching. Whereas the Church theoretically
positioned pain as part of a process of spiritual purification, the faithful,
pummelled regularly with the graphic exempla of Catholic doctrine and
legend, focused instead on the dynamics of suffering itself. Thus although
'any saint could be expected to help the sufferer in spiritual distress, or the
soul passing to or already in the pangs of 'purgatory', requests for relief
were customarily addressed to specialists: to St Apollonia for toothache
because her own teeth were supposedly pulled out one by one (she was
portrayed 'with a pair of pincers holding a giant molar'), to St Erasmus for
bowel disorders because he was tortured by having his intestines spun out
on a nautical windlass, and so on (Duffy, 179–80 and *passim*).[59] In this
fashion, horror was not only domesticated but transformed into a form of
intimacy, as shown by the story of Henry Walter, a mariner during the reign
of Richard III who sued to St Erasmas while suffering from a grievous
abdominal wound. After fifteen days of solitary agony in a small boat,
Walter found that 'the holy martyr Erasmus ... lay near him, as if with the
pain of his sufferings renewed, just as he is often represented in churches,
being tortured by his executioners' (Duffy, 180).[60] The great degree of
empathy shown here by a celebrated saint for a lowly petitioner, notwithstanding the bizarre circumstances of their intimacy, is characteristic
of what Duffy calls the 'neighbourliness and homeliness' (161) of English
devotion. By making the fearsome familiar and the familiar communal, the
saints served iconically to neutralise at least partially the perils of Christian
belief.[61]

That the ideal of sanctity in the late Middle Ages presupposed a dramatic intensification of ordinary human suffering should not be surprising, given the centrality of the crucified Christ in Christian ideology and of suffering itself in the Christian redemptive scheme. But at least in the view of early modern reformists, the simplicities and superstitions of medieval piety betrayed a pagan relish in the bodily violence at the core of Christianity, an appetite for the grotesqueries of death deriving from the Church's insistence on an imagery of bodily process in sermon, iconography and liturgical ritual. The reformists believed that the Church had in effect sabotaged itself during the late Middle Ages by promoting the doctrine of purgatory and the cult of the saints, by going too far in foregrounding the dead. It was, after all, easy enough for Protestants to catalogue and ridicule what had already become legendary medieval excesses, especially in conjunction with pilgrimages. At shrines throughout England, for example, the clutter of 'holy' objects around the image or reliquary of the saint, itself bedecked with candles and perfumed with incense, was likely to include wax images of the diseased body parts of the pilgrims, abandoned crutches and other such witnesses to miraculous cures, and on occasion the 'ashes' of the saint specially blended by a local charlatan (Duffy, 197). Even the body parts chosen to emblematise modes of martyrdom in church screens and stained glass windows – St Apollinia's molar, for example – were singled out as ludicrously facile representations of sanctity, and as such, subversive of its mystery.[62]

But for reformists to extrapolate such instances from the *gestalt* of medieval belief was to risk misrepresenting popular recognition of the intimate relationship between the material and immaterial body, in much the same way that focusing on the niceties of scholastic debate risked obscuring a similar recognition. If, to quote Bynum again, 'a sense of the self as psychosomatic unity' was the fundamental principle by which the body – and the corpse – were understood in the Middle Ages, then beneath the excesses and absurdities of popular religious practice lay a stubborn insistence that corporeality was at the heart of the Christian mystery. The quite considerable challenge to Protestantism was to reconstitute this deeply entrenched perception of corporeality itself.

3. Reconfiguring the dead in Reformation England

In early modern England, the categorical distinctions of Cartesian philosophy had not yet come to dominate any sphere of intellectual life, including that of religion. Certainly, Protestant iconoclasm shifted discursive emphasis from the interdependence of body and soul to the priority of the spirit, and in so doing established a prototypical paradigm for mind/body duality. None the less, the development of the reformist movement was hardly linear or univocal, so that the concepts and/or symbolic matrices of the old and new religions often fused in ways that defied categorical description.[63] I wish to stress this point again because the analysis in this section will focus on two texts in the Calvinist tradition – the English homily on idolatry and Foxe's *Book of Martyrs* – which purport to reconceptualise the materiality of the body and of the corpse in self-conscious opposition to Catholic beliefs and practices. I have selected these strongly polemical texts for analysis precisely because they foreground Reformation pressures to *change* modes of perceiving and imaging the body/corpse, and because of their undeniable influence on the development of English Protestantism. In attacking Catholicism's sacramental and hermeneutic uses of the body, the homily attempts to reconstitute the conceptual relationship between the living and the dead. And in establishing a new Reformation model for the martyr, Foxe eschews the exaltation of bodily mutilation and partition in the *Legenda Aurea*.

Both the homily on idolatry ('Agaynste parell of Idolatry and superfluous decking of churches') and the second edition of Foxe's *Acts and Monuments*, popularly known as the *Book of Martyrs*, were published in English in 1563, well into the Reformation and five years after the accession of Elizabeth I. The homily, intended for delivery in churches throughout the country, represented the monarchy's officially sanctioned position on the materiality of anthropomorphic idols and images.[64] Its arguments show the cumulative influence of Calvin's *Institutes*; by mid-century, Calvin's reputation in England was steadily eclipsing that of any other continental reformer.[65] The widespread infiltration of Calvinist ideology is especially apparent in the popularity of the Geneva Bible, translated in 1575, which eventually became the 'household Bible of the English people'.[66] At the same time, Foxe's *Book of Martyrs*, second only to the Bible in popularity, sought to position the Elizabethan Reformation as the apocalyptic culmination of a historic struggle between Christ and the anti-Christ extending back to the early Church. In the service of this ambitious scheme, Foxe fashioned a new kind of distinctively English folklore, which rivalled that of the *Legenda Aurea* and whose narratives, like those of the *Legenda*, were incorporated into sermons.[67] Considered jointly, these propagandistic texts articulated a new and strongly felt Protestant anxiety about the body – put simply, a need to envisage its materiality, like that of the idol, as dead.

The homily's agenda for demystifying the body proceeds from an argument about the corpse which is, in effect, a *tour de force* of circular reasoning. The homilist implies, as we shall see, that only a Catholic sophist would waste time speculating on the mode by which a putrefying body is subsumed into an immortal soul because the corpse is *axiomatically* dead – it is, beyond disputation, the only entity that can demonstrate what 'dead' means. By establishing this status as a self-evident premise, the homilist conjures the corpse with every utterance of the word 'dead', rendering it virtually omnipresent throughout the text, at the same time that he erases the problem that the corpse represented to medieval Catholicism. Whereas formerly the corpse emblematised the Christian mystery that most needed resolution, that is, the relationship of the generative process of putrefaction to that of transfiguration, in the homily the corpse is presented as incontestable evidence that this relationship is not an issue. The homilist's emphasis on the end result of transfiguration brackets off its intervening process as the work of the Spirit – divine and unfathomable, like creation itself.[68] Catholic interrogation of this mystery is castigated accordingly as presumptuous and perverse.

At bottom, it is the indeterminacy of all bodily process as a mode of understanding spiritual transformation that the homily attacks on every front. Thus the brilliance of appropriating the corpse, the most fearsomely indeterminate of material entities, as the standard for *dead*. In medieval ideology, as we have seen, the union of seemingly opposite principles in the person of Christ, and the centrality of his body to the redemptive sacrifice, constituted the heart of the Christian mystery. By foregrounding ambiguity in the relationships between immaterial/material, soul/body, Catholicism affirmed a deity whose spiritual legacy could be transmitted materially, as in the sacrificial blood that flowed from Christ's crucified body, and the Host that preserved the God/man for the consumption of future generations. Even the pervasive misogyny in medieval social attitudes was made to coexist with the concept of redemption as generative (as in the lactating breasts of the bi-gendered Christ), and the recognition that the body of God gestated in that of a mortal and sinless woman. For medievalists, the transformative union of opposites in the matrix of the body enabled all the Christian mysteries, with the putrefying corpse at the centre of this *gestalt*.

But for reformists, Catholicism's excessive preoccupation with the humanity of Christ had succeeded in diminishing his divinity and that of the godhead, and idolatry provided the ideal issue with which to attack the privileging of bodily processes in the interpretation of Christian ideology. The real business of the homily is to harden the distinction between body and spirit in order to emphasise the differences between the Deity and His subjects. Thus the body is described in virtual opposition to the soul, and the bodily properties that make visual representation possible – de-animated materiality and externality – are 'dead'. By extension, then, visual representations, which cannot recreate the sentience, or interior spirit of the body, are themselves 'dead'; further, the harlot with the painted face, and indeed any woman who uses body surfaces as a canvas for carnal purposes, are likewise 'dead'. In the end, and despite the Incarnation, the homily comes close to denying the interdependence of soul/body,[69] and is especially wary of the status of the female body. Distrustful of ambiguity, it points towards categorical clarities, aiming to establish a strong foundation for affirming a non-corporeal God.

The homily's emphatic association of materiality with *in*sentience, which I shall consider in detail shortly, is best understood as the culmination of a historical development in Reformation ideology. The viewpoint espoused by the homily had struggled for ascendancy throughout the reign of Henry VIII, and had made considerable progress under Archbishop Cranmer during the minority of Edward VI. By mid-century, Protestant iconoclasts had rejected, most notably, the doctrine of transubstantiation, the doctrine of purgatory (including its attendant intercessions for the dead and the system of indulgences) and the cult of the saints (including that of the Blessed Virgin Mary), as promulgated by statues, images, shrines, pilgrimages, relics, devotions and the celebration of feast-days.[70] Conversely, they endorsed, after initial resistance, the production of the English vernacular Bible, signalling the priority of the word over the visual image. From 1531 until the death of Henry in 1547, Cranmer steadily and purposefully set the course for reform by adopting continental positions on all these issues, although he never succeeded in extirpating the king's conservative leanings.[71] By the accession of Edward VI, however, Cranmer was well positioned to articulate a full-blown iconoclastic stance through the publication of a series of normative texts, including the first book of homilies (1547) and the 1549 and 1552 editions of The Book of Common Prayer. The 1552 edition of the latter work, in particular, prepared amidst a 'flood-tide of radicalism', attempted 'to break once and for all with the Catholic past' (Duffy, 472–3).[72]

Cranmer's sweeping agenda for reform marks a critical mid-point between the fluctuations of the Henrician monarchy and the post-Marian settlements of Elizabeth.[73] In the context of this trajectory, the 1563 homily on idolatry can be seen as an uneasy resolution of decades of internal disputation, and the homily's reliance on Calvin's *Institutes* itself bears witness to the maturation of the iconoclastic movement in England. Certainly, Cranmer's Edwardian publications accelerated this process greatly, but for England the ideological struggle was initially shaped during the Henrician Reformation by the confrontation between Sir Thomas More and William Tyndale. Their contentious debate set out the key issues that were to dominate subsequent iconoclastic discourse.[74]

By English standards in 1530, Tyndale's radical fervour was suspect, but most of his arguments against idolatry were none the less adopted in due course by the English Protestant establishment. Positioning himself in the tradition of Wycliffe, Tyndale contended that the laity, and especially the ignorant, were likely to confuse their ocular perceptions of material images with the entities they purported to represent, so that veneration of these images was synonymous with the worship of false gods as proscribed by scripture. But Tyndale sought to go beyond conventional reasoning to strike at what he saw as the root problem, that is, the idolatry of man's own imagination' – 'a "blind" imagination' so thoroughly corrupted by the effects of original sin as to become a virtual factory of narcissistic idol-*making*.[75]

For Tyndale, '"blind" imagination' was invariably connected with *visual* perception, and it is of course ironic that Tyndale's continually recurring metaphor for spiritual confusion was itself a visual one.[76] Characteristically, however, Tyndale presents his personal convictions as if their common sense is indisputable:

> Hereby seist thou what is to be thought of all other ceremonies/as holowed water/bred/salt/bowes/belles/wax/ashes and so forth/and all other disgisinges and ape playe and of all maner coniuracions/as the coniuringe of church and church yards and of alter stones and soch like, where no promyse of God is/there can be no faith nor iustifienge/nor forgevenes of synnes./For it is moare then madness to loke for any thinge of God save that he hath promysed ... *To have a fayth therfore or a trust in any thinge/where God hath not promysed ys playne ydolatrye and a worshepinge of thine owne imaginacion instede of God. (Pi)

Tyndale's insistence on the crucial difference between God's promises and the interpretive apparatus of the Church underlay his reformulation of the decalogue, wherein the first commandment as understood by Catholic tradition was divided into two, the first against the worship of false gods and the second against the making of them.[77] By the time the homily appeared in 1563, the two-part commandment was a well-established feature of Protestant belief, and the controversy over idolatry had become at least as concerned with the spiritual dynamics that gave rise to idol-making as with the disposition of material artifacts.

Importantly, however, as More understood early and only too well, Tyndale's case against idols and the idol-producing imagination of man rested on his skill in defending the Bible as the clearly accessible record of God's promises. This meant differentiating between the text's 'literal' meaning and what he termed the 'choplogical' (Ri[v]) hermeneutics of Catholicism. But the metaphoric character of biblical language, which Tyndale acknowledged, forced him into a circular chop-logic of his own:

> Thou shalt vnderstonde therefore that the scripture hath but one sence which is the literall sence. And that literall sence is the rote and grounde of all & the ancre that never fayleth where vnto yf thou cleve thou canst never erre or goo out of

the waye ... Never the later the scripture useth proverbes/similitudes/redels or allegories as all other speaches doo/but that which the proverbe/similitude/redell or allegory signifieth is ever the literall sence which thou must seke out diligently. (Ri[v], Rii)

This allegory proveth no thinge ... For it is not the scripture/but an example or a similitude borowed of the scripture to declare a texte or a conclusion of the scripture moare expressly and to rote it and grave it in the herte ... Moareover if I coulde not prove with an open texte that which the allegory doeth expresse/then were the allegory a thinge to be gested at and of no greater value then a tale of Robyn hode ... Thus doeth the litterall sence prove the allegory and beare it/as the foundacion beareth the house ... God is a spirte and all his wordes are spirituall. His *litterall sence is spirituall ... (Riii, iii[v], vi[v])

The deficiencies of Tyndale's style of argumentation, a form of co-option that is interestingly similar to that of the homily on idolatry, are obfuscated in his assertion of principle here, that the right-minded reader will not confuse God's allegory with that of 'a tale of Robyn hode'.[78]

In presenting the case for Catholicism, More offered a strong and erudite if traditional defence of the function of images as a proper stimulus to devotion, and of the Old Testament prohibition against idolatry as historically directed against the worship of pagan gods.[79] But More understood that Tyndale's emphasis on idol-making was ultimately a mode of dismantling the entire liturgical apparatus of the Church, and further, of denying the legitimacy of any visual representation. More gained little ground, however, in pointing out Tyndale's refusal to acknowledge the representational function of *words* as images, subject to the same mental processes as visual images.

(c4[v])... all the wordes that be eyther written or spoken/be but ymages representing the thynges that the wryter or speker conceyueth in his mynde: lykewyse as the figure of the thynge framed with ymagynacyon and so conceyued in the mynde/is but an ymage representing the very thing it selfe that a man thynketh on ... But nowe as I began to say/syth all names spoken or wrytten be but ymages/yf ye set ought by the name of Iesus spoken or wrytten: why [c5] shold ye set nought by his ymage paynted or caruen that representeth his holy person to your remembraunce/as moche and more to/as doth his name written.[80]

For Tyndale, the divine inspiration of the Bible guaranteed its linguistic clarity as well as its accessibility to the ordinary Christian without benefit of intermediary. Tyndale was in fact contemptuous of what he saw as More's sophistical if not cynical efforts to equate a work of divine origin with a corrupt, man-made artifact. Unfortunately for More, their differences in prose style indirectly supported Tyndale's point: More found it hard to counter Tyndale's colourful, anecdotal expressiveness with his own prolix and erudite argumentation.

In any case, Tyndale circumvented the philosophical subtleties of More's approach by adducing a developmental pattern in Church history that supported his iconoclastic position and that focused on Catholicism's wilful contamination of its own liturgical practices. In so doing, Tyndale was among the first in England to give common currency to the so-called Byzantine precedent, the condemnation of the ecclesiastical use of images by Constantine V in 754 which was decisively rejected by the second Council of Nicaea in 787. According to the reformist argument, the schism between the Greek and Western churches during the reign of Charlemagne, and the subsequent decline of Christianity in the West, were attributable to the Catholic endorsement of the veneration of images at Nicaea. Moreover, the origins of the eighth-century crisis could be traced to a letter issued by Gregory the Great in *c.* 600 promoting the use of such images as instructional tools. In this chronology of church history (which was also that of Foxe's *Book of Martyrs*), the primitive Church – that is, the Church during the first five centuries of its existence – was 'pure' by virtue of its freedom from idolatrous practices. By obliterating such practices, the Reformation would in effect reverse a relentless, degenerative process.[81]

Because Catholic apologists, including More, defended the judgements of the Council of Nicaea,[82] the Byzantine precedent and its implications for early church history became a focal point in the controversy over idolatry, in England and elsewhere. One of the oddities of the Protestant position was its eagerness to claim not only Constantine V as a prototypical iconoclast, but also Charlemagne, who as the first Holy Roman Emperor was, of course, the chief beneficiary of the schism in the Christian church. Ironically, early modern reformists believed that Charlemagne's appointment as Emperor gave credence to his condemnation of the Council of Nicaea in the *Libri Carolini*, compiled by Carolingian theologians in *c.* 794.[83] The 1550 edition of Calvin's *Institutes*, for example, cites several Carolingian arguments, and indeed Calvin's lengthy attack on idolatry, greatly expanded from that of the 1536 edition, may have been prompted by the pseudonymous publication of the *Libri Carolini* in Paris in 1549.[84] The English homily on idolatry, in turn, borrowed from Calvin in developing its own shriller and more sensational version of Byzantine history.

Although the homily purports to set out methodically the entire reformist case against idolatry, the demagogic tone of its attack adduces theological argumentation as part of a heavy-handed programme of indoctrination.[85] Divided into three parts, the homily follows, at least in broad outline, a historical progression. The first part discusses biblical prohibitions against idols and images, with primary reference to Old Testament authorities; the second invokes the support of the Church Fathers prior to an extensive treatment of the Byzantine precedent, which serves as the centrepiece of the homily itself;[86] and the third provides the Protestant rationale for the repudiation of images in contradistinction to the specious arguments of Catholics, past and present. Until the third part (and for most of that as well), the argument is advanced through examples of the disastrous effects of idolatrous practices; attention to the internal dynamics of idol-making is, as it were, folded into the interstices of diatribe. Moreover, the historical progression implied by the three-part structure is frequently disrupted by extensive attention to one or another *bête noir*, such as the role of the Empress Irene in the Council of Nicaea, and to the mantra-like invocation of key phrases and themes that helps to bind the argument rhetorically and emotionally.

Because the ostensible project of the homily is to prove that images and idols are dead,[87] establishing what 'dead' signifies is the *sine qua non* of the text. The homily develops this concept incrementally, chiefly by means of shifting metaphors. The mantra repeated most often throughout the text – 'dead as stocks and stones', or as 'blocks and stocks' – initially identifies insentient materiality as 'dead', so that the chief danger of anthropo- morphic images made from 'stocks and stones' is, as Tyndale argued, their pretence at vitality, or sentience. Inevitably, or so the homily says, the false vitality of bodily representations tempts the viewer to 'spiritual whoredom', or to an acceptance of the image's attractive appearance as alive. This shift in the focus of the argument from the insentient elements that make up the image to the power of its impression on the viewer serves to implicate the body itself, at least indirectly, in the signification of 'dead'. That is, to imagine the bodily image as autonomously alive is to divorce the body from the soul, which alone can vitalise it: without the soul, the body is 'dead'. 'Spiritual whoredom' is thereby conjoined with 'carnal fornication' because to privilege the body as an independent entity over the soul is to privilege its corruption: 'And it was very agreeable (as St Paul teacheth) that they which fell to idolatry, which is spiritual fornication, should also fall into carnal fornication, and all uncleanness ...' (191).

But in warning against the carnality of idolatrous practice, the homily's emphasis is on man's inclination to follow the stimulus of woman in wor- shipping images, or on woman as temptation to both kinds of 'whoredom': 'the nature of man is none otherwise bent to worshipping of images ... than it is bent to whoredom and adultery in the company of harlots' (206). Thus the frequent comparison of the gilded image and the painted woman: 'Doth not the word of God call ... a gilt or painted idol, or image, a strumpet with a painted face?' (206). In this equation, the painted face functions as does an idol in conveying a false vitality, an autonomously external 'self', so that the strumpet – with whom spiritual and carnal fornication are simul- taneously possible – puts man in double jeopardy. Further, the homily suggests (although never overtly) that because both painted face and gilded image are 'dead', fornication with the strumpet can be viewed as a form of necrophilia.

The connection that the homily develops between dead materiality and woman depends, in the first instance, on establishing the principle of material insentience in 'stocks and stones'. The first part introduces this issue as if it were altogether straightforward, betraying the unabashedly literal way in which the homily interprets all visual and textual signifiers:

> And first, that our images and the idols of the Gentiles be all one concerning themselves, is most evident, the matter of them being gold, silver, or other metal, stone, wood, clay, or plaster, as were the idols of the Gentiles; and so being either molten or cast, either carved, graven, hewn, or otherwise formed and fashioned after the similitude and likeness of man or woman, be dead and dumb works of man's hands, *having mouths and speak not, eyes and see not, hands and feel not, feet and go not* ... (187, my italics)[88]

> [Pagan] images have no power to do harm to others, though [some] of them have an axe, some a sword, some a spear in their hands, yet do thieves come into their temples and rob them, and they cannot once stir to defend themselves from the thieves ... (151)

> the dead and dumb idol, the work of man's hand, which never did nor can do any thing ... no, is not able to stir, nor once to move, and therefore worse than a vile worm, which can move and creep? (210)

In its naïve insistence on the transparency of signification, the homily elides the issue of representation: there is no middle ground between the sentient and the insentient, the creations of God and the productions of man. By virtue of God's creative power, even a worm lives, but man is incapable of creating a living creature. On the contrary, his fashioning of 'similitudes' from 'stocks and stones' is a mode of trafficking with the dead: 'What a fond thing is it for man, who hath life and reason, to bow himself to a dead and insensible image, the work of his own hand!' (191).

In progressing from the idea of the insensible image to the proposition that 'spiritual and carnal fornication go together ... [that] the worshipping of images is numbered amongst the *works of the flesh*' (154), the homily turns, significantly, to the monstrous but presumably exemplary career of the Empress Irene. The lengthy, lurid exposé of her history purports to demonstrate the dehumanising effects of idolatrous practices, especially on women who use them as a mode of wielding power. But in rehearsing Irene's contribution to the Byzantine precedent (viewed by reformists as the watershed in Catholicism's history of idolatrous practices), the homily also sets up a series of misogynistic associations in which Irene's taint is connected first to the goddesses of pagan mythology and later to the hierarchy of Catholic saints. The cumulative effect of this strategy is to demonise all women across a spectrum that situates Irene in the centre, with Venus and Diana at one extreme and the Blessed Virgin Mary at the other.[89]

Focusing first on Irene, the homily measures her catastrophic impact on Christianity by reference to early church history: prior to 760, 'in the churches of Asia and Greece there were no images publicly by the space of almost seven hundred years. And there is no doubt but the primitive church next the Apostles' times was most pure' (170). Almost single-handedly, Irene, 'whose ambition and desire of rule was insatiable ... whose wicked and unnatural cruelty passed Medea and Progne' (173) reversed this history by conspiring with Rome to promote the worship of images and by ruthlessly exterminating her adversaries, including, finally, her son, Constantine VI:

> But within a few years after, Irene, the empress, taken again into her son's favour, after she had persuaded him to put out Nicephorus his uncle's eyes, and to cut out the tongues of his four other uncles, and to forsake his wife ... now further to declare that she was no changeling, but the same woman that had before digged up and burned her father-in-law's body, and that she would be as natural a mother as she had been a kind daughter, seeing the images, which she loved so well, and had with so great cost set up, daily destroyed by her own son ... deprived her son of the empire; and first, like a kind and loving mother, put out both his eyes, and laid him in prison, where, after long and many torments, she at the last most cruelly slew him. (172)

The homily also credits Irene with masterminding the work of the Second Council of Nicaea, 'alienating the empire to Charles king of the Francons', and seeking 'a secret marriage between her self and the said king' (173), although Charlemagne himself is claimed as an ally of the iconoclasts:

> the book of Carolus Magnus's own writing [the *Libri Carolini*] ... heweth the judgment of that Prince, and of the whole council of Frankfort also, to be against images, and against the second council of Nice assembled by Irene for images; and calleth it an arrogant, foolish, and ungodly council ... (174)[90]

In its final, sweeping judgement of Irene's 'lewd life', the homily claims that she effected

> an horrible schism between the East and the West church ... Christians against Christians ... at the last, the tearing in sunder of Christendom and the empire into two pieces, till the Infidels, Saracens and Turks ... by God's just vengeance, should in like wise partly murder, and partly lead away into captivity us Christians, as did the Assyrian and Babylonian kings murder and lead away the Israelites ... (173, 176)

Thus the shocking aftermath of Irene's machinations include, finally, the partial suppression of the Christian Church by 'Infidels, Saracens and Turks', pagan powers not unlike those that dominated the world during the pre-history of Christianity. This resurgence of heathen power can be attributed directly to the Church's own paganism:

> What be such saints, to whom, contrary to the use of the primitive church, temples and churches be builded, and altars erected, but Dii Patroni of the Gentiles idolaters? Such as were in the Capitol, Jupiter; in Paphus Temple, Venus; in Ephesus Temple, Diana ... And where one saint hath images in divers places, the same saint hath divers names thereof, most like to the Gentiles. When you hear of our Lady of Walsingham, our Lady of Ipswich, our Lady of Wilsdon, and such other; what is it but an imitation of the Gentiles idolaters? Diana Agrotera, Diana Coriphea, Diana Ephesia, &c. Venus Cypria, Venus Paphia, Venus Gnidia. (188)

Because there is fundamentally no difference between pagan temple and Christian shrine, the idols worshipped in them – Diana, Venus and the Blessed Virgin Mary – are similarly interchangeable. This scathing if rhetorically circumspect attack on *dulia*, or the worship that Catholics believed was owed to the Mother of God,[91] is also implicit in the homily's condemnation of the sexual activity encouraged by pilgrimages: 'But it is too well known, that by such pilgrimage going, Lady Venus and her son Cupid were rather worshipped wantonly in the flesh' (190). Because the most popular shrines for pilgrimages were those dedicated to the Virgin (such as those at Walsingham and Ipswich already mentioned), the wanton worship of 'Lady Venus and her son Cupid' refers not only to 'carnal fornication' among the pilgrims themselves but also to their 'spiritual fornication' with the image of Mary/Venus and Christ/Cupid.

The homily's denigration of the Virgin's exalted position in the Catholic hierarchy of saints foregrounds one of its strongest beliefs, that is, that the distinction between carnal and spiritual fornication itself collapses in the wantonness of bodily images. Indeed, descriptions of 'wantonness' are threaded obsessively throughout the text so that signifiers such as 'harlot', 'paramour' and 'idol' refer interchangeably to body or image in such a way as to confuse or conflate them, as in the following:

> But yet afterword the same Solomon suffering his wanton paramours to bring their idols into his court and palace, was by carnal harlots persuaded, and brought at the last to the committing of spiritual fornication with idols ... (209)

> You would believe that the ... idols of our women-saints were nice and well-trimmed harlots, tempting their paramours to wantonness ... (219)

> Now he that will bring these spiritual harlots out of their lurking corners, into public churches and temples ... (208)[92]

Although 'images of our men-saints [appearing as] princes of Persialand with their proud apparel' (219) are also wanton, the homily almost invariably identifies the wantonness of woman as the subversive threat to 'man's nature'. The gilded image of the female saint, including that of the Virgin, is indistinguishable from the body of the harlot/strumpet with the painted face. Beneath the 'decking' of idol/harlot is material corruption and spiritual death, an all-encompassing 'whoredom' which serves, finally, as metaphor for the Church itself:

> Now concerning excessive decking of images and idols, with painting, gilding, adorning with precious vestures, pearl, and stone, what is it else, but for the further provocation and enticement to spiritual fornication, to deck spiritual harlots most costly and wantonly, which the idolatrous church understandeth well enough. For she being indeed not only an harlot, (as the Scripture calleth her,) but also a foul, filthy, old, withered harlot, (for she is indeed of ancient years,) and understanding her lack of natural and true beauty, and great loathsomeness with of herself she hath, doth, after the custom of such harlots, paint herself, and deck and tire her self with gold, pearl, stone, and all kind of precious jewels, that she, shining with the outward beauty and glory of them, may please the foolish fantasy of fond lovers, and so entice them to spiritual fornication with her: who, if they saw her (I will not say naked) but in simple apparel, would abhor her, as the foulest and filthie harlot that ever was seen: according as appeareth by the description of the garnishing of the great strumpet of all strumpets, the Mother of Whoredom, set forth by St. John in his Revelation, who by her glory provoked the princes of the earth to commit whoredom with her. (216)

By identifying the Catholic idol as a 'gross [material], bodily, and visible similitude' (179), and gendering it as female, the homily sets up the terms by which it will present the Protestant alternative to 'the Mother of Whoredom'. In complete opposition to the idol, the 'incomprehensible majesty' of the Protestant God is *im*material, *dis*embodied and *in*visible:

> How can the infinite majesty and greatness of God, incomprehensible to man's mind, much more not able to be compassed with the sense, be expressed in a finite and little image? How can a dead and dumb image express the living God? ... God is a pure spirit, infinite, who replenisheth heaven and earth ... (180–1)

> And after this [Isiah] crieth out, *O wretches, heard ye never of this? Hath it not been preached unto you since the beginning ... how by the creation of the world, and the greatness of the work, they might understand the Majesty of God, the Creator and Maker of all, to be greater than that it should be expressed, or set forth in any image or bodily similitude?* (150)

> and let us have no strange gods, but one only God, who made us when we were nothing, the Father of our Lord Jesus Christ ... For such worshippers doth our heavenly Father love, who is a most pure Spirit ... (224)

As *'pure* Spirit,' God cannot be comprehended by any corporeal being, so that the conversion of 'the incorruptible God' into the 'similitude of a corruptible man' (181), is, as Isaiah contends, sacrilege.[93] However, the 'pure Spirit' of God is simultaneously paternal: God is the 'heavenly Father' of Christ, the second Person of the Trinity, but also of the worshippers whom He 'loves'. Thus the homily suggests that the qualities of Spirit are, at least by analogy, imbricated in the male principle; by extension, then, whatever is not Spirit – that which is 'gross, bodily, and visible' – is theoretically female. By gendering the Spirit as male, the homily buttresses its attack on the Catholic hypostatisation of the (bi-gendered) body, although obviously a gendered Spirit is itself an anthropomorphic projection. None the less, the homily insists that God the Father cannot be imaged; his 'pure Spirit' has no corporeal correlative.

The chief stumbling block in the homily's attempt to advance the concept of a disembodied deity is of course Christ, the second Person of the Trinity, who as Redeemer 'took upon him flesh, and became man' (181) in order to be sacrificed. For the most part, the homily deals with Christ by erasing him. Indeed, the text consistently refers to the Christian deity as 'God' or 'God the Father', and describes Christ, when he is mentioned, in relationship to the Father: 'but thou art a Christian, and therefore by Christ alone hast access to God the Father' (189). The one passage that directly addresses the issue of imaging Christ, the man/God, either sidesteps the implications of the Incarnation or shifts attention to Christ's divinity:

> Now concerning their objection, that an image of Christ may be made, the answer is easy: for in God's word and religion, it is not only inquired whether a thing may be done or no; but also, whether it be lawful and agreeable to God's word to be done or no ... And the words ... out of the Scriptures are, that images neither ought nor can be made unto God. (181)

> Furthermore, no true image can be made of Christ's body, for it is unknown now of what form and countenance he was. (181–2)

> And yet it appeareth that no image can be made of Christ, but a lying image ... for Christ is God and man. Seeing therefore, that of the Godhead, which is the most excellent part, no images can be made, it is falsely called the image of Christ. Wherefore images of Christ be not only defects, but lies. (181)

Thus, despite the centrality of the Incarnation to Christianity, the homily condemns bodily images of Christ by maintaining its emphasis on Christ's participation in the godhead.[94]

Significantly, this focus on Christ's divinity obviates the need to address the thorny issue of the Eucharist, which, as we have seen, Catholics believed to be a material form in which Christ was bodily instantiated. Although by 1563 Protestantism had rejected the Catholic doctrine of transubstantiation, there was no denying that the Host, a material entity if not an anthropomorphic image, represented Christ in some way. Among the reformists, Calvin argued for the acceptance of the Host as a sacramental image because its designation by Christ himself as a mode of devotion set it apart from other images. None the less, Calvin emphasised the spiritual function of the Host, so that even its bodily ingestion by the faithful was said to enable a communion of the Christian soul with the informing Spirit of the Godhead.[95] In order to de-corporealise the Eucharist in this way, it was first necessary to reformulate the Catholic concept of the hypostatic union – in effect, to distinguish between Christ's humanity and his divinity so as to marginalise Christ the man. The homily's continual subordination of Christ to God the Father (and possibly even its avoidance of the entire issue of the Eucharist) underscores the Protestant preoccupation with this agenda.

In the end, the only 'imaging' that the homily implicitly allows derives from the trinitarian language in which Christ, as the Father's Son, is the Father's 'image', which means that Father and Son are 'identical in their essence' (Pelikan, 2, 109).[96] Thus when the homily affirms that 'the *image* of God is *in* every man … (who has) a godly heart and a pure mind' (222, my italics), it is extending the trinitarian concept metaphorically to imply that the 'true' image of God is man's soul – an interior, invisible and immaterial gift of and from the divine Spirit. Although the text is careful to point out, in accordance with Calvin, that the promise of bodily resurrection for the elect is implicit in Christ's death and resurrection, it none the less expends most of its energy, as we have seen, in detailing the earthly body's moral and physical corruption.

The encapsulating emblem for all that the homily would demonise is, of course, the corpse, the presence of which permeates every page of the text. The image is 'dead as stocks and stones' because it is insentient, a body without a vitalising spirit; the painted face of the strumpet is likewise 'dead' because it conveys a false vitality; and the images of female saints, including those of the Mother of God, are in a sense doubly 'dead' because they are interchangeable with harlots. In the homily's circular mode of argumentation, 'dead' is repeatedly defined at the same time that its meaning is assumed: the corpse always lurks behind the metaphor. Presumably, there is nothing more 'dead' than the corpse itself – the originary, insentient artifact, the body utterly devoid of its soul.

The homily's attack on relics makes clear just how sharp a distinction it would draw between the spirit and the corpse:

> But in this they pas the folly and wickedness of the Gentiles, that they honour and worship the relics and bones of our saints, which prove that they be mortal men and dead, and therefore no gods to be worshipped … (195)

> the souls [of the saints], the more excellent parts of them, can by no images be represented and expressed. Wherefore they be no images of saints, whose souls reign in joy with God, but of the bodies of saints, which as yet lie putrefied in the graves. (181)

Just as Christ's divinity is his 'most excellent part', so too are the souls of the saints, which alone can 'reign in joy with God' prior to the Last Judgement. Until their final transfiguration, the bodies of the saints are dead, and the proof of this is that they are also putrefied. Far from viewing putrefaction, as medieval Catholics did, as itself a mysterious process of generation and transformation, implicit, if in a horrific way, in the beatification of the body, the homily would establish body rot as an indisputable proof of deadness.

The near-absolute distinction between the saint's dead body (including, of course, its bones and body parts) and her living soul is underscored further by the absence of any overt reference to the doctrine of purgatory. Whereas for Catholics purgatory complicated the already vexed question of the relationship between dead and transfigured bodies, for reformists the elimination of the suffering dead greatly simplified the effort to de-animate the corpse. In declining to address this issue, or indeed to speculate at all about the disposition of Christian souls between death and the Last Judgement, the homilist may well have taken his cue from Calvin, who neatly sidesteps what for Catholics was a consuming concern:

> To enquire of their meane state, is neither lawfull nor expedient. Many doe much comber themselues with disputing what place they keepe, and whether they doe now enioy the heuenly glory or no. But it is folly and rashnes, to search deeplier of vnknowen things, than God doth giue vs leaue to know. (Lib. III, Cap. 25, Mm2–2[v][270–1]).[97]

In two particularly compelling instances, the homily emphasises the originary deadness of the corpse by reference to narratives from authoritative sources. The first is a biblical account of the origin of idolatry as corpse worship; and the second is the fabled story of Epiphanius (*c.* AD 390), who wrapped an unholy image around a dead man in order to consign them both to putrefaction. Interestingly, in the biblical account, the first idol was inspired by the need of a grief-stricken father for the revivification of a dead son, and not by an impulse to represent an anthropomorphic deity or saint:

> the origin of images, and worshipping of them, as it is recorded in the eighth chapter of the book of Wisdom, began of a blind love of a fond father, framing for his comfort an image of his son, being dead, and so at the last men fell to the worshipping of the image of him, whom they did know to be dead ... (205)[98]

Although this anecdote has the ironic effect of humanising the idolater, its intention is to demonstrate the direct connection between corpse and idol, without the mediation of 'stocks and stones' or painted faces. The same point is made, conversely, in the insistence of Epiphanius on the dissolution of the idol in the putrefying corpse:

> I entered (saith Epiphanius) into a certain church ... when I did see the image of a man hanging in the Church of Christ, contrary to the authority of the Scriptures, I did tear it, and gave counsel to the keepers of the church, that they should wind a poor man that was dead in the said cloth, and so bury him.' ... [Epiphanius] did not only remove [the image] out of the church, but with a vehement zeal tare it in sunder, and exhorted that a corse should be wrapped and buried in it, *judging it meet for nothing but to rot in the earth* ... (158–9, my italics)

The dead belong with the dead, the idol with its source; in the absence of spirit, both are 'meet for nothing but to rot in the earth'.

Whereas the homily seeks to drive a wedge between the living Spirit of God and the dead corporeality of man by means of heavy-handed remonstrances, Foxe's *Actes and Monuments* de-centres the body from another direction. Because martyrologies axiomatically focus on heroically exemplary deaths, one might assume an uncomfortable fit between the homily's disavowal of the body and Foxe's detailed accounts of bodily torment. But reformers in England were able to use the homily, Foxe's narratives and Cranmer's 'sombrely magnificent prose' (Duffy, 593) inter-dependently and to great effect in the effort to extirpate Catholic habits of thought because, despite their generic and stylistic differences, these texts provide strong reinforcement for one another.[99]

If the homily's polemic continually returns to the *bête noir* of the Byzantine precedent, *Actes and Monuments* depends on a less overt but equally pervasive negative standard for the construction of its argument – that is, the *Legenda Aurea*. Although Foxe never overtly recognised the *Legenda* as inspiration, his commemorative text sets out to 'supplant medieval hagiographies' and establish martyrdom 'as an act of witnessing to religious faith'.[100] Unlike the myriad torments of Catholic martyrs, virtually everyone in Foxe's narrative burns, and despite the fact that singed, blackened and liquefied body parts appear in abundance, the collective impression is that Protestant martyrs are immolated.

According to Janel M. Mueller, immolation is fundamental to Foxe's intention: it serves 'as an entry into bodily relation with divinity' (177), a reversal or 'shifting [of] transubstantiation from the domain of miracle to that of natural law' (171). Unlike the Catholic preoccupation with Eucharistic ingestion of the God/man, Foxe would focus on God's plan 'to ready the faithful in their bodies for incorporation with his *heavenly* body' (172, my italics). The terrible agony of burning dissolves the corrupt body so that its glorified form may be subsumed into the godhead, a 'heavenly body' conceived of as a spirit. In this framework, there is a 'negligible quotient of eroticism as metaphor for bodily relation with divinity. In place of images of embrace or coition, the body is conceived as raw stuff for processing into an entity of a *qualitatively different kind* (my italics) ... organic matter feeds fire with its vital substances'.[101] Thus the clean, purifying process of immolation supersedes that of putrefaction, fore-grounding the *destination* of the glorified body/soul. In contradistinction to the *Legenda*, Foxe's martyrology stakes out 'a rival ontology in which analogical relations bind with the force of physical connections' (178).

Foxe advances his ideological agenda by the masterful use of a straight-forward prose style: unapologetically polemical, Foxe would none the less give the impression that in serving as historical witness he adheres to the facts. Because his standard for 'truth' (even in invention) is a moral one, Foxe would no doubt have viewed the pseudo-documentation of descriptions which include 'manifestly fictionalized detail' (King, 14–15) as accurate.[102] The careful crafting of Foxe's martyrological model is further evident in his effort to democratise, at least to some degree, the heroism of Protestant resistance by deliberately juxtaposing ordinary 'craftsmen, traders, labourers and housewives' (O'Day, 16)[103] with celebrated Henrician and Marian martyrs such as John Frith, Nicholas Ridley, Hugh Latimer and Thomas Cranmer. Even when describing group executions, Foxe's approach to portraiture is essentially the same for all the actors in his saga: that is, he prefaces the account of each death with a biographical sketch that establishes the identity of the martyr and his or her contribution to the reformist cause. Often, these lengthy sketches tend to marginalise or even eclipse the death scene itself.

Not surprisingly, the fullest biographical accounts focus on 'the great Protestant heroes who have advanced the cause of religion in England ... and secured its victory' (White, 147), such as Archbishop Cranmer and George Wishart, a Scotsman and friend of Foxe who taught at Cambridge for many years. Foxe domesticates the significance of both men's lives through anecdotal description, praising Wishart, for example, for his generosity to students and for the kindness of his temperament, never more in evidence than when he kissed the cheek of his executioner. Cranmer's history is rehearsed at greater length, particularly his public disavowal at St Mary's Church of his notorious recantation, a surprising reversal im-mediately prior to Cranmer's execution which represented a great triumph for the Protestant cause. Importantly, Foxe depicts the actual martyrdoms of these men with an eloquent succinctness that subordinates their suffering to their function as religious symbols. Wishart

> by and by ... was put vppon the Gibbet and hanged, and there burnte to pouder. When that the people behelde the greate tormentinge, they mighte not with hold from piteous mourning and cõplaining of this innocent Lambes slaughter. (PP3[v])

Cranmer, also depicted as a lamb led to slaughter, is memorialised for the dramatic gesture of self-repudiation during his death throes:

> And when the wodde was kindled, & the fyre began to burn nere him, stretching out his arme, he put his right hand in the flame, which he held so stedfast and immouable (sauing that once with the same hande he wyped his face) that all men might see his hand burned before his body was touched. His body did so abide the burning of the flames, with suche constancie and stedfastnes, that standing always in one place without mouing of his members, he semed to moue no more then the stake to whiche he was bound: his eyes were lifted vp into heauen, & oftentimes he repēted his vnworthy right hand, so long as his voyce would suffer him: & vsing often the words of Stephane, Lord Jesus receiue my spirite, in the greatnes of the flames he gaue vp the ghoste. (SSSs1ᵛ)

By building incrementally on such heroic moments in individual deaths, Foxe develops an overriding impression of a heterogeneous army of the elect courageously confronting the stake.

For Mueller, this emphasis on the triumph of constancy over cruelty challenges the transhistorical validity of the proposition recently elaborated by Elaine Scarry that 'torture ends in the breaking-down of a tortured person's self, world, and voice' (161).[104] Mueller argues that Foxe was concerned to demonstrate the opposite proposition, to constitute the 'truth' of Protestant martyrdom as 'a spiritual self-possession at total odds with the judicially imposed restraint of the body' (161, 165). Thus the Catholic authorities, by first allowing the Protestant martyrs the right to speak in their own defence, and then publicly subjecting them to one of the worst of bodily extremities, death by fire, ironically provided Foxe with the ideal framework for his purposes. What Foxe was determined to convey had less to do with the victims' torment *per se* than with the way in which this torment was subsumed in the courage and integrity of their last public performances.[105]

Although I find Mueller's summation of Foxe's ideological aims convincing, she does not differentiate, as Cynthia Marshall has recently argued, between Foxe's rhetorical schematic for the martyr and the often inadvertent but powerful effects of his text on the reader. This distinction is crucial, as Marshall makes clear, in understanding how the sado-masochistic pleasures of Foxe's descriptions work against his recuperative strategies.[106] The structure of Foxe's work would organise these 'readerly pleasures' according to the requirements of Protestant polemic:

> Foxe proceeds by renaming as martyrs those condemned as heretics under Marian rule, thereby redirecting the passionate condemnation of those executed toward those who prosecuted them. In other words, the thrill of watching or imaginatively participating in a scene of tortured death was reassigned from affiliation with the tormentors (sadistic pleasure) to sympathetic identification

with the victim (masochistic pleasure), with hatred of the Papists supplying further opportunity for sadism. (89)

According to Marshall, these conflicting enticements were strongly reinforced by Foxe's attention to the sensuous details of death by fire, which sought to 'excite and horrify' readers so as to provide (in Lacanian terms) 'the radical, unsettling textual interaction of *jouissance*':

> a reader who truly identified with a martyr would feel herself undone, the structuring terms of identity shattered. Foxe presumably worked for this effect in order to encourage shaken readers to dedicate themselves to a sustaining structure of religious faith. His aim … was to recuperate for the church the loss of selfhood provoked in readers by their contemplation of martyrological horrors. (94)

In this view of Foxe's *aim*, Marshall seems to be in agreement with Mueller. But Marshall believes that whereas Foxe's textual strategies guarantee the 'secure placement' of the martyr within his recuperative scheme, his iconographic violence leaves a decidedly unsecured reader in the decentring ambiguities of the sado-masochistic dynamic.[107]

Marshall's deconstruction of Foxe demonstrates the ways in which *Actes and Monuments,* like the homily on idolatry, implicitly refutes its own ideology by certain kinds of rhetorical insistences. But Mueller's point is also well taken: fire *is* the appropriate metaphor for a hagiography that would obviate the putrefying body by 'disappearing' it, thereby eliminating the Catholic preoccupation with the corpse as problematic agent/channel to Christian transcendence. Moreover, martyrs (of whatever stripe) cannot claim that title without physical suffering of some sort, and in a great many, if not most, of Foxe's accounts, as I have suggested, the horrors of immolation are subordinated to the testimony of the martyr's life. The considerable slippage between Foxe's ideological controls and his actual narrative is telling: these excesses suggest the near impossibility of erasing the body in a martyrological model of transcendence, as do the graphic detailing of the text's accompanying woodcuts.[108] But although Foxe's relentlessness in promoting a new kind of martyrology is precisely what betrays the gaps in his rationale, there is still a collective impression in the consistency of his individual descriptions that exerts considerable power in the text.

I think it also important to remember that many early modern readers of Foxe would have viewed the burnings of martyrs or heard firsthand accounts of them, and that at least in some cases these executions were not likely to have coincided with Foxe's idealisations. The goriness of Foxe's descriptions may, in fact, have seemed *less* terrible to such readers than the images stored in their memories. If such disparities formed part of the mythologising work of *Actes and Monuments*, then to the degree to which readers recognised and accepted Foxe's discursive transformations, they participated, perhaps consciously, in the fictionalising of their own experience.

I would argue, then, that even those sensational agonies for which Foxe provides a litany of graphic details serve his larger scheme as martyrologist. The excruciating death of Bishop John Hooper, certainly one of the most famous passages in Foxe's testament, is a case in point and worth demonstrating at length:

> Anon commaundement was geuen that fire should be set to: so it was. But because there wer put to no fewer grene faggottes, then two horses could carry vpon theire backes, it kindeled not by and by: and was a prety while also before it tooke the reedes vpon the faggotes. At length it burned about him: but the wind hauing full strength in that place (it was also a louring and a cold morning) it blewe the flame from him: so that he was in maner nothing but touched by the fire. Within a space after, a fewe drie faggots wer brought, & a new fire kindled with faggots,(for ther wer no more redes): & that burned at the nether partes, but had smal power aboue bicause of the winde, sauing that it did burne his heare, & as wel his skin a little. In the time of the which fire, euen as at the first flame he prayed, saying mildely and not very loud (but as one without paines:) O Jesus the sonne of David haue mercy vpon me, and receaue my soule. After the second was spent he dyd wype both his eyes with his handes, and beholding the people he said with an indifferent loude voice: For gods loue (good people) let me haue more fire: and all this while his nether partes did burne. For the faggots were so fewe, that the flame did not burn strongly at his upper partes. The thirde fyre was kindled within a while after, which was more extreme then the other two: and then the bledders of gonnepowder brake, which did him small good, they were so put, and the wind had such power. In the which fire he praied, with somwhat a loud voice: Lord Jesu haue mercy vpon me: Lorde Jesu haue mercy vpon me. Lord Jesus receaue my spirite. And they were the last wordes he was herd to sound: but when he was blacke in the mouth, and his tonge swollen, that he could not speake: yet his lippes went, till they wer shrounke to the gommes: & he did knocke his brest with his hands vntill one of his armes fel of, and then knocked still with the other, what time the fat, water, and bloud dropped out at his fingers endes, vntil by renewing of the fire, his strength was gonne; and his hand did cleaue fast in knocking, to the the [*sic*] yron vpon his brest. So immediately bowing forwardes, he yelded vp his spirite.
>
> Thus was he thre quarters of an hower or more in the fire, euen as a lambe: patiently he abode the extremity therof, neither mouing forwards, backwardes, or to any of the sides: but hauing his nether partes burned, and his bowels fallen out, he died as quietly as a child in his bed, & he now reigneth I doubt not as a blessed martir in the ioyes off heauen ... (CCC3ᵛ)

Foxe's startling summation of this brutal scene – 'he died as quietly as a child in his bed' – would assimilate Hopper's burning nether parts and cascading bowels in an image of serenity and security. An outrageous rhetorical move, it nevertheless encapsulates Foxe's insistent agenda: to refute the Catholic presumption that the martyr's identity as heretic will be broken down and destroyed along with his body. Instead, the slow and visible dissolution of Bishop Hopper, whose wasting he himself fervently but patiently anticipated, testifies to a transcendent spiritual integrity that turns even the horror of the Catholic death apparatus against itself.[109]

Foxe's representation of the martyr's suffering body differs greatly, then, in both style and function from that of the *Legenda Aurea*. In the *Legenda*, the fixation on varieties of bodily torture and fragmentation connect, however naïvely, with the notion of the inextricability of the body and soul: martyrdom signifies as an honorific corollary to the Crucifixion of the incarnated deity; bloodied bodily fragments testify to the horror and wonder of sacrificial nurture. In Foxe, as well as in the homily on idolatry, the marginalising of Christ axiomatically marginalises His crucified body as sacrificial archetype. In this very different context, Foxe represents the body of the Protestant martyr as a kind of envelope that literally melts away, albeit piecemeal, in the purifying flames, releasing the soul for instant communion with the godhead. In effect, the self-possession of the martyr at the stake is a spiritual quality that the body is privileged to reveal by means of its own disappearance.

Foxe's martyrology also differs from the *Legenda* in that it purports, at least in its accounts of contemporary martyrs, to be a form of documentation rather than a narrative of mythic proportions transmitted orally over the centuries. Nobody in Foxe is impervious to torture, no naked virgin bodies are thrown on red-hot gridirons and emerge unscathed and no flames leap from the stake, as they did from the fiery furnace in Charity's martyrdom, to kill the victim's persecutors. Foxe would have his readers believe that he sticks to the facts, eschewing phantasms and fictions; that fire kills, although bodies reduced to cinders after prolonged agonies none the less 'sweetly slept in the Lord Jesus' (212, 232). Foxe would not presumably have viewed his propagandistic idealisations as a form of fiction because for him they illustrated a truth of inestimable importance: that the interior, invisible soul is the entity that connects with the antecedent, transcendent godhead. The suffering body functions as redemptive agent, and will be fully reconstituted at the Last Judgement, but what the martyrology seeks to dramatise is a purification ritual in which corporeal materiality is ultimately eliminated. That which is left is, at best, a skeleton: clean bones and no rot.

Considered jointly, Foxe's martyrology and the homily on idolatry may be seen as complementary exercises in demystification or, as better befits their polemical tone, exposé. Both would strip the body of its inordinate claims to parity with the soul, and no doubt the rhetorical power of these texts advanced the iconoclastic agenda in England more effectively than did the assaults against churches and shrines. But because for centuries Catholic traditions had permeated English culture, efforts by the faithful to come to terms with the Reformation's devalued body were unavoidably conflicted. More than any other physical entity, the corpse gave definition to this conflict. However disembodied the new ideology might wish to appear, it could not deny the necessity of transfiguration in the Christian redemptive scheme. The corpse, an integral part of this process, presented a conundrum – that is, a 'dead' body whose liminality was somehow inscribed in its very materiality. Notwithstanding the homily's denunciation of materiality, and Foxe's 'disappearing' of the body itself, the corpse encapsulated the challenge that most would-be Protestants faced in reformulating the relationships of body/spirit, material/immaterial, visible/invisible, living/dead.

Some version of this challenge was enacted every time the English public theatre, which flourished during the period of the Reformation, 'performed' a corpse for a large and heterogeneous audience. In the next chapter, my aim is to reflect on the relationship between the ideology of the body produced by the Reformation iconoclasts, and representations of the corpse as idol in Jacobean plays by Middleton and Massinger. As I shall demonstrate, this relationship was shaped by a complicated and reciprocal tension: if the corpse, or the paradox of its signification, lay at the heart of Protestant dilemma, its representation on the stage challenged both the ideological function and the performative agency of the theatre itself.

Notes

1. Because it evolved with the spread of Christianity, theological discourse was, of course, disparate and multi-vocal, inflected with the social and political pressures of particular cultures and locales. None the less, the central doctrines of the new religion established the body as its symbolic matrix. See Peter Brown, *The Body and Society: Men, Women and Sexual Renunciation in Early Christianity* (New York: Columbia University Press, 1988).
2. In referring to English 'Protestants' and 'reformists' for the purposes of this conceptual summary, I do not mean to imply homogeneity among sects in either doctrine or social agenda, nor to minimise the ideological contestations among Anglican and Puritan leaders. Because I focus on religious controversy with respect to its modes of imaging and of perceiving the body/corpse, the term 'anti-popery' is perhaps better suited to my purposes than 'Protestant'. According to Peter Lake, this 'polemically ambiguous' concept was appropriated by Protestant sectarians of many stripes:

   the ambiguity of anti-popery operated at deeper levels than the conscious polemical and political manipulations of contemporaries. Arguably the power of anti-popery as a source of ideological leverage and explanatory power was based on the capacity of the image of popery to express, contain and, to an extend, control the anxieties and tensions at the very center of the experience and outlook of English Protestants ... the popish threat provided an unimpeachably 'other' ... the Protestant image of popery allowed a number of disparate phenomena to be associated to form a unitary thing or force. (79–80, 82)

See 'Anti-popery: the Structure of a Prejudice', in *Conflict in Early Stuart England: Studies in Religion and Politics 1603–1642*, eds. Richard Cust and Ann Hughes (London and New York: Longman, 1989), 72–106 (but see also note 63.) For a perceptive analysis of the importance of recognising, on the one hand, Protestant pluralism in England, and, on the other, the limited usefulness of sectarian distinctions, see Debora Kuller Shuger, *Habits of Thought in the English Renaissance: Religion, Politics, and the Dominant Culture* (Berkeley: University of California Press, 1990), 1–16 and *passim*. For an investigation of the effects of anti-Catholic sentiment on the early modern English imagination (and also for a corrective to recent critical tendencies to categorise Catholics in the period), see Alison Shell, *Catholicism, Controversy and the English Literary Imagination* (Cambridge: Cambridge University Press, 1999). For a discussion of Calvinist influence in England, see notes 65 and 66.

3. The Church's venery was, of course, a major preoccupation of reformists eliciting strong condemnation, if not outrage, as in the following indictment by Tyndale, which serves as the conclusion to a much lengthier diatribe:

> The mother chyrch and the hie altare must have some what in every testamete. Offeriges at prestes fyrst masses. Ite no man is professed/of whatso ever religion it be/but he must bringe some what. The halowinge or rather coniuringe of chirches/chapels/altares/superaltares/chalice vestimentes and belles. Then boke/bell/candelsticke/organes/chalice/vestimentes copes/altare clothes/syrpleses: towels basens/euars/shepe[incense boat]/senser and all maner ornamentes must be founde them frely/they will not geve a myte therevnto. Last of all what swarmes of bedginge freres are there The person shereth the vicare shaveth/the perish prest polleth/the frere scrapeth and the perdoner pareth we lacke but a bocher to pole of the skynne.

See *The obediēce of a christen man*, 1528 (STC 24446), Bᵛ. In quoting from this text here and elsewhere, I have silently altered long ʃ to 's',   to ampersand (&), : to 'r', 3 to 'gh', ~ to 'm' or 'n', ẏ to 'the', and ẏ to 'that'. I have also failed to note hyphenation.

4. The denunciation of the cosmeticised woman and her proclivity to promiscuity was a time-honoured motif in the Judeo-Christian tradition which Protestant iconoclasts were able to exploit in drawing parallels between two kinds of 'paint' (see section 2 below). Shell emphasises that Catholicism shared the Protestant opposition to cosmetics (*Catholicism, Controversy and the English Literary Imagination*, 30).

5. Bynum would differentiate between the centrality of the body to medieval concepts of the soul/self and what Le Goff identifies as the Pauline repudiation of pleasure in the social ethic: see Jacques Le Goff, *The Medieval Imagination* (Chicago and London: University of Chicago Press, 1988), and note 19 below. Further, she would contextualise the presumed misogyny implicit in the Thomistic/Aristotelian association of the concepts of male/form with those of female/matter. Fundamentally, Bynum's cross- disciplinary studies of the body, which traverse 'scholastic discourse, hagiography, poetry, and art', contest the philosophical tradition that examines systems of thought in the Middle Ages primarily in terms of an opposition between Platonism and Aristotelianism: see Caroline Walker Bynum, *Fragmentation and Redemption: Essays on*

Gender and the Human Body in Medieval Religion (New York: Zone Books, 1996), 254ff., fns. 45 and 46, 401, 222–3; and her *The Resurrection of the Body in Western Christianity, 200–1336* (New York: Columbia University Press, 1995), 319.

6. Miri Rubin points out that 'the gash made by the lance, from which flowed water and blood ... determined the liquid of the chalice as a mixture of wine and water, which became that sacrificial blood and water ... Thus the Chistocentric fascination with sacrifice and bloodied passion was conflated with the eucharistic drive ...'. See *Corpus Christi: the Eucharist in Late Medieval Culture* (Cambridge: Cambridge University Press, 1997), 303, 306.

7. In *The Sexuality of Christ in Renaissance Art and in Modern Oblivion* (New York: Pantheon, 1983; rev. Chicago and London: The University of Chicago Press, 1996), Leo Steinberg argues, I think persuasively, that the fore-grounding of Christ's penis in early modern art was a mode of emphasising the humanisation of Christ by means of his sexuality. Steinberg takes exception to Bynam's tendency to subordinate the sexual to the generative in her interpret-ation of late medieval portraiture, and also to what he sees as her undue emphasis on the feminising of Christ. In a response to Bynam's critique of his work (see *F&R*, 79–117, esp. 85–93), Steinberg clarifies his position as follows:

> To me, the *ostentatio genitalium* in the paintings discussed did not seem posed as male versus female. I read the new genital emphasis as an imaginative reintegration of the sexual into the ideally human, the projection upon Christ of a sexuality which in him – in him as in the first Adam anterior to sin – exists without guilt. And because Christ was born male, and because the male body's status as paradigm remains axiomatic for Renaissance culture, I suggested that the penis restored to the sacred body after centuries of denial signified the sexual potential as such – not to exclude the female, but to acknowledge sex as participant in that human nature which the Incarnation espoused. (365, second edition)

Although there are significant differences in the critical approaches of these scholars, I have focused on their joint emphasis on Christ as *bi*-gendered, that is, on the ways in which foregrounding either a male Christ *or* a female Christ ultimately serves to implicate both genders in Christ's humanisation. It is interesting in this connection to compare Kristeva's discussion of Hans Holbein the Younger's (1497–1543) *The Body of the Dead Christ in the Tomb*, in which the unvarnished agony on the face of the corpse suggests utter, wholly human dereliction. Holbein depicts Christ as 'strangely athletic, brawny and tensed'; in another painting, Christ holds a 'spasmic' right hand 'curled up before the sexual organ'. Kristeva queries: 'From what passion did such a pain arise? Woud the man-God be distressed, that is, haunted by death, *because* he is sexual, prey to sexual passion?' See *Black Sun: Depression and Melancholia*, trans. Leon S. Roudiez (New York: Columbia University Press, 1989), 107–38, esp. 112.

8. The paradox of the bi-gendered Christ was at least indirectly reinforced by Galenic medical theory, which privileged blood as the primary concoction resulting from the transmutation of food and drink. As a porous, fungible concoction, blood stimulated the production of other life-sustaining bodily fluids, including those that enabled the body's reproductive agency. See Thomas Laqueur, *Making Sex: Body and Gender from the Greeks to Freud*

(Cambridge, MA: Harvard University Press, 1990), 38–42, *passim*; and Gail Kern Paster, *The Body Embarrassed: Drama and the Disciplines of Shame in Early Modern England* (Ithaca, NY: Cornell University Press, 1993), 68–84, *passim*. The transformative agency of blood thus contributed to the breakdown of borders between imperfectly differentiated sexes, as well as between the bodily functions of a single sex: for example, 'breast milk was the purified form of menstrual blood' since both derived from 'the same essential substance' (Paster, 39–40).

9. The close association of Christ's reproductive agency with that of the Virgin is further evident in the medieval iconography of marriage, in which gender representations are notably unstable. Thus Christ appears as bride of *humanitas*, and of the Church, and Mary, analogously, appears as bride of the Church; however, the Church also appears as the bride of Christ (see *F&R*, 93–108, 205–22). The dual function of the Church as both bride of Christ and, as we have seen, his offspring (as in the 'delivery' at the Crucifixion) symbolically parallels that of Adam, forerunner of Christ, whose spouse, Eve, was likewise created from Adam's flesh or rib. Taken collectively, the sexual inversions of this iconographic pattern suggest that Christ, like Adam, was 'one-in-flesh' with a woman, although in Christ's case Mary was mother, not wife, and it was Christ himself who emerged from the flesh of his own original creation. Interestingly, this kind of gender-shifting can also be found in Talmudic accounts of the Old Testament God, particularly in metaphors of marriage used to describe God's jealous response to Israel's idolatries. See Moshe Halbertal and Avishai Margalit, *Idolatry*, trans. Naomi Goldblum (Cambridge, MA and London: Harvard University Press, 1992), 9–36; see also Julia Reinhard Lupton, *Afterlives of the Saints: Hagiography, Typology, and Renaissance Literature* (Stanford, CA: Stanford University Press, 1996), 188–96, *passim*. I am grateful to Ramie Targoff for the reference to Halbertal's book.

10. 'In the Eucharist there was a powerful assimilation of eating, the most common of human functions, into the economy of the supernatural ... The promise of being one with God in a bodily sense could hardly be surpassed ... communion [was] an enormous event' (Rubin, 26, 45).

11. Peter Bowe, *Die eucharistischen Wunder des Mittelaters* (Breslau: Muller & Seiffert, 1938). Quoted by Bynum, in *F&R*, 185.

12. Perhaps the most famous dramatic treatment of this theme is the fifteenth-century *Croxton Play of the Sacrament*, in which a group of disbelieving Jews perform successive sacrileges on a Host and are horrifically chastised (see *Non-Cycle Plays and Fragments*, ed. Norman Davis, Early English Text Society, 1970). For a commentary on the play, see Eamon Duffy, *The Stripping of the Altars: Traditional Religion in England c. 1400–c. 1580* (New Haven, CT and London: Yale University Press, 1992), 102–7; see also Rubin, 187.

13. Bynum's judicious analysis of this phenomenon sees female mysticism as an alternative to clerical authority, including supervisory authority in convents, and to clerical monopoly of sacramental power: the mystics' emphasis on union with the Eucharistic Christ may be partly attributed to the infrequency with which most nuns were allowed to receive – rather than simply view – the Host. Bynum does not, however, consider female mystics solely in terms of a proto-feminist agenda. She argues that institutional Catholicism also benefited

from sanctioning and even encouraging mystical experience. See *Jesus as Mother: Studies in the Spirituality of the High Middle Ages* (Berkeley and Los Angeles: University of California Press, 1984), 170–262, esp. 250–1, 256–62, and *F&R*, 119–50, esp. 122–5, 134–9. For an analysis of Eucharistic piety among the faithful as a visual phenomenon (dating from the elevation of the Host in the late twelfth century), see Duffy, 95–107. For an excellent summation of the development of the ritual of the Mass prior to and including the decision to elevate the Host, see Rubin, 12–82, esp. 49–63.

14. Bynum and Shugar are both concerned with the frequent failure among contemporary scholars to distinguish between the sublimation of sex in religion and the expression of religious experience by means of sexual or erotic images. See *F&R*, 79–117, esp. 85–8; and *Habits of Thought*, 193–4, 254, and *passim*. Their caveats are especially apt in connection with the mystics, whose erotic language is easily extrapolated, often reductively, from a medieval religious to a modern psychoanalytical context. However, I would argue that it is possible to affirm the inextricability of all forms of desire (in particular, the imbrication of sexual desire in the death drive) without predetermining or simplifying the modes by which desire manifests itself in historically specific symbolic systems.

15. It is noteworthy in this connection that transvestism and sexual inversions are recurrent motifs in medieval hagiography as well. For example, St Theodora and St Pelagia(ius) cross-dressed in order to become monks; in addition, St Theodora was expelled from the monastery for seven years for supposedly having fathered a child. St Uncumber, another popular saint in England, miraculously grew a beard on her wedding day in order to safeguard her virginity, and was subsequently crucified by her father. See Jacobus de Voragine, *The Golden Legend: Readings on the Saints*, trans. William Granger Ryan (Princeton, NJ: Princeton University Press, 1993), I, 324–5, 365–8; and II, 232–3; and *The Oxford Dictionary of Saints* (New York: Oxford University Press, 1987), 437–8. For a more extended treatment of the *Legenda*, see pp. 39–44. I am indebted to Carole Levin for calling my attention to these saints.

16. James of Vitry, 'Life of Mary of Oiginies', in J. Bollandus and G. Henschenius, eds., *Acta sanctorum … editio novissima*, ed. J. Carnandet *et al.* (Paris: Palme, etc., 1863–), June, vol. 5 (1867), 568; and Hadewijch, vision 7, in *Hadewych: Visioenen*, ed. J. Van Mierlo, 2 vols., Leuvense Studien en Tekstuitgaven (Louvain, 1924), vol. 1, 74–9; trans. Columba Hart in *Hadewijch: The Complete Works* (New York: Paulist Press, 1980), 280–1. See Bynum, *F&R*, notes 1 and 2, p. 343.

17. Catherine of Siena, *Le Lettere de S. Caterina de Siena, ridotte a miglior lezione e in ordine nuovo disposte con note di Niccolo Tommaseo a cura di Piero Misciatelli*, 6 vols. (Siena: Giuntini y Bentivoglio, 1913–22), letter 86, vol. 2, 81–2; and Marguerite of Oingt, *Les Œuvres de Marguerite d'Oingt*, ed. and trans. Antonin Duraffour, Pierre Gardette and P. Durdilly, Publications de l'Institut de Linguistique Romane de Lyon, 21 (Paris: Belles Lettres, 1965), 77–9. See Bynum, *F&R*, notes 39 and 43, 335–6 (Bynam's translation).

18. It was common to differentiate between two kinds of incorruptibility in the resurrected Christ: the body at the harrowing of hell (which bore the wounds of the Crucifixion) and the physically perfect, transfigured body that ascended

into heaven. See Jaroslav Pelikan, *The Christian Tradition: A History of the Development of Doctrine*, Vol. 3, *The Growth of Medieval Theology (600–1300)* (Chicago and London: The University of Chicago Press, 1978), 33; for representations of the harrowing of hell in the mystery plays, see Rosemary Woolf, *The English Mystery Plays* (Berkeley and Los Angeles: University of California Press, 1972), 269–74. Mary's dispensation from corruption was implicit in the doctrine of the Immaculate Conception, which established Mary's freedom from original sin from the moment of her conception (but did not become dogma until 1854).

19. In *The Body and Society*, Brown describes the disposition of the early Church to focus increasingly on sexual continence and virginity as modes of establishing a distinctive identity, one that would differentiate the new religion from the pagan and Judaic traditions with which it had much in common. For example, although Christianity shared with Judaism and Islam a repressive misogyny, only Christianity eventually established virginity, or the complete renunciation of sexual experience, as an ideal. This shift of emphasis had profound ramifications for the theological status of the body in relationship to the soul, as well as for the Christian view of death, since sexual continence became 'linked on a deep symbolic level with ... man's ability to undo the power of death' (86). In *The Medieval Imagination* (93–103), Le Goff stresses the repressive measures by which the Church ultimately repudiated sexual pleasure itself during the period of the Gregorian Reform (1050–1215, the year of the Fourth Lataran Council). These measures included new proscriptions against fornication and sodomy, both broadly defined, and even against passion in conjugal relations.

20. Mary's exemption from putrefaction is explained in two lengthy narratives about the Assumption in the *Legenda Aurea*. The dominating image for the Assumption is matrimonial, like that of the mystics' union with Christ:

> Then the Saviour spoke and said: 'Arise, my dear one, my dove, tabernacle of glory, vessel of life, heavenly temple! As you never knew the stain of sin through carnal intercourse, so you shall never suffer the dissolution of the flesh in the tomb.' Thereupon Mary ... was assumed into the heavenly bridal chamber ... she was assumed integrally in soul and body ... (II, 82)

The *Legenda* also invokes Augustine's claim that '"Putrescence and the worm are the shame of the human condition. Since Jesus has no part in that shame, Mary's nature, which Jesus, as we know, took from her, is exempt from it"' (83).

21. There are interesting affinities between the mystics' ambivalence towards the organicism of bodily process and that of St. Augustine, for whom redemption signified a triumph over natural process, expressed best, paradoxically, in terms of metaphors of nourishment:

> The bodies then that the righteous will have at resurrection will need ... [no] material nourishment to keep them immune from suffering of any kind from hunger and thirst. The reason is that they will be endowed with a sure and absolutely inviolable gift of immortality, and hence they will eat only if they wish, having power, but no compulsion, to do so ... For it is not the ability, but the need to eat and drink that will be removed from such bodies. Hence they will also be spiritual, not because they will cease to be bodies, but because they will have a life-giving spirit to sustain them. (*The City of God Against the Pagans*, Loeb Classical Library, Vol. IV (Cambridge, MA: Harvard University Press, 1988), trans. Philip Levine, Book XXII, 221, 223)

22. The iconographical associations of worms with putrefaction were especially pervasive in the fourteenth and fifteenth centuries: see Philippe Ariès, *Western Attitudes toward Death from the Middle Ages to the Present*, trans. Patricia M. Ranum (London: Johns Hopkins University Press, 1974), 39–46; and Duffy, 303–10. The most sensational example of this preoccupation is the so-called transi tombs of northern Europe (discussed more fully in Chapter 4), which sculpted the putrefying body in graphic detail.

23. See Heinrich Denzinger, *Enchiridion symbolorum definitionum et declarationum de rebus fidei et morum*, 31st edition, ed. Karl Rahner on basis of C. Bannwart and J. Umberg (Freiburg: Herder, 1957), 200, 216. Quoted by Bynum in *RoftheB*, 155 (Bynum's translation).

24. The problematic relationship between corpse and resurrected body was frequently formulated in terms of the question: 'Can God make the body of Peter out of the body of Paul?' One 'elegant solution' to this question, originating with Aquinas, argued for a distinction between corpse and cadaver corresponding to that between soul and secondary matter. Thus 'God can make the body of Peter out the *dust* that was once the body of Paul' (*F&R*, 259–60, 61–2, my italics; see also *RoftheB*, 259–60). Not surprisingly, this 'solution' generated new problems, such as whether it was the cadaver or the corpse of Christ that lay in the tomb for three days, or whether the relic was identical with the body of the saint.

25. Aquinas's body of work, which underwent revision throughout his lifetime, can, in Bynum's phrase, 'be read both as eclipsing and as guaranteeing the ontological significance of the body'. For example, his appropriation of Aristotle's hylomorphic paradigm is usually understood as a rejection of Platonic dualism, but at the same time it can be argued that his emphasis on the soul as substantial form establishes the resurrected body as an expression of the glory of the resurrected soul, and the soul as guarantor of self: 'It is more correct to say that soul contains body [continent corpus] and makes it to be one, than the converse' (*ST*, ia, q. 76, art. 3, vol. II, pp. 60–1 [Bynum's translation]; see *RoftheB*, 259; also, 268–9 and *passim*).

26. Bonaventure, *Sentence* commentary, bk. 4, dist. 43, q. 5, conclusio, p. 462. Quoted in Bynum, *RoftheB*, 244.

27. The common analytical distinction between scholastic and non-scholastic (e.g. Franciscan, Augustinian) theological systems should not obscure their interdependence. Augustine was a major influence on Aquinas; moreover, much of Augustinian philosophy was mediated for both Bonaventure and Aquinas by Peter Lombard, whose *Sententiae in IV libris distinctae* was used as a textbook in medieval universities. Lombard's work is itself 'a patische of borrowings', with most of the Augustinian passages taken from his late works. See Bynum, *RoftheB*, 8–9, 121–32 and *passim*; for Lombard's *Sentences* as a 'reintegration of the Catholic tradition', see also Pelikan, vol. 3, 270–84.

28. During the thirteenth and fourteenth centuries, quodlibetal disputations, or 'debates by university students and masters on freely chosen rather than set topics', were common and therefore 'an excellent index to which issues excited contemporary interest' (Bynum, *F&R*, 224). Rubin describes the circuitous mode by which this learning, primarily meant for the upper clergy, sometimes reached the parishes (85–6).

29. In *The Resurrection of the Body*, Bynum structures her detailed examination

of medieval discourse about the corpse from the twelfth to the early fourteenth centuries in terms of the two persistent metaphors for bodily transformation: that of germination and growth (the seed) and that of reassemblage (as, for example, in the Augustinian image of the broken statue). Bynum contends that the organicism implicit in the seed metaphor (cited in I Corinthians 15 and elaborated by St Paul) was generally distrusted, chiefly because metamorphosis implied a non-material continuity (that is, the seed and the sheaf share a spatio-temporal continuity but not necessarily a continuity of material particles); and because metaphors of natural process tended to diminish the supernatural agency through which the dead body was reconstituted. Metaphors of reassemblage, on the other hand, usually implied material and structural continuity between corpse and glorified body, but left open the question of how this process was effected, as well as the extent to which these bodies resembled each other. Bynum's strategy in employing this metaphoric framework as a means of threading the maze of theological debate – and also of demonstrating the contradictions to be found in any single position – is, to my mind, inspired. For example, by focusing on the seed metaphor, she is able to draw parallels between Aquinas's discomfort with biological process (as evident in his response to Aristotle's *On Generation*) and that of Augustine. At the same time she invites consideration of the seeming contradiction between Augustine's dynamic model for the soul and his proclivity to associate growth with dissolution and rot. See especially 237–47.

30. Jacques Le Goff, *The Birth of Purgatory*, trans. Arthur Goldhammer (London: The University of Chicago Press, 1986), 13.

31. Patrick J. Geary, *Living with the Dead in the Middle Ages* (Ithaca, NY and London: Cornell University Press, 1996), 4. Duffy shares this assumption: 'there was a remarkable degree of religious and imaginative homogeneity across the social spectrum, a shared repertoire of symbols, prayers, and beliefs which crossed and bridge [*sic*] even the gulf between the literate and the illiterate' (3). The writings of the mystics, replete with images of bodily process that informed the entire Catholic sacramental system, is a case in point.

32. The theological rationale for purgatory relied primarily on four ambiguously related biblical texts: II Maccabees 12: 41–6, which describes the sacrifice of Judas Maccabeus to redeem the sins of his soldiers; Matthew 12: 31–2, which refers to the remission of sins; I Corinthians 3: 11–15, which suggests that sinners may be purified after death by a fire-like substance; and Luke 16: 19–31, which recounts the story of Lazarus and the rich man. See Le Goff, *The Medieval Imagination*, 67. Judeo-Christian apocalyptic writings, especially the Apocalypse of St Paul, were also influential, notwithstanding the controversial origins of most of these texts. See Le Goff, *The Birth of Purgatory*, 29–41.

33. Le Goff argues that 'Parisian theologians gave [purgatory] a name and a definite location some time between 1170 and 1180'; this dating has been challenged as premature. (For a summary of recent scholarly objections to Le Goff's argument, see Bynum, *RoftheB*, 280, fn. 2). The first doctrinal definition of purgatory was by Innocent IV in 1254, twenty years prior to the Second Council of Lyons. The doctrine was reconfirmed in subsequent centuries by the Council of Florence (1438) and during the Counter-

Reformation by the Council of Trent (1563). See *The Medieval Imagination*, 67–8; and *The Birth of Purgatory*, 82–3.

34. Le Goff finds it significant that the birth of Purgatory coincided with the invention of the clock, a rival to the liturgical calendar that had regulated ordinary life for centuries under the jurisdiction of the Church. He argues that the clock eventually subordinated the circular and repetitive cycles of the liturgical calendar to a concept of linear time divided into equal intervals; this new system of quantification influenced learned and popular conceptions of purgatorial time. See *The Medieval Imagination*, 70–2; *The Birth of Purgatory*, 6–7, 290–5 and *passim*.

35. Le Goff identifies Augustine and Gregory the Great as 'the true fathers of Purgatory ... Augustine influenced primarily the theology of the subject, including the notion of purgatorial time, whereas Gregory contributed to the imagery of purgation' (*The Medieval Imagination*, 68; see also Pelikan, Vol. 3, 32–3). For a detailed examination of the views of Augustine and of Gregory, respectively, see *The Birth of Purgatory*, 68–87, 88–95.

36. Bynum expresses a similar view somewhat differently. Theologians conceptualised the purgatorial body 'as a manifestation or flowing out [of the soul] that appear[ed] almost timeless'; prior to the Last Judgement, the soul 'already in some way possessed, or expressed itself in, its body' (*RoftheB*, 283).

37. Theologians were aware of the dangers implicit in popular responses to the doctrine. Aquinas, for example, was wary of pagan overtones in the concept of *revenants*, or purgatorial ghosts who visited the living. See *The Birth of Purgatory*, 266–78, esp. 269, 273, 277.

38. It was not until 1336 that the Church endorsed the view that individuals sentenced to Purgatory might enjoy the Beatific Vision immediately after they were cleansed of their sins. See Le Goff, *The Medieval Imagination*, 72; and Bynum, *TheRoftheB*, 282.

39. *Ars Moriendi*, a hugely popular fifteenth-century tract, appeared sometime between 1414 and 1418 and was translated and printed by Caxton shortly thereafter; in 1505, it was incorporated into another popular work, *The arte or craft to lyve well and to dye well*, published by Wynkyn de Worde (RSTC 793). One well-known chapter in *Ars Moriendi* focused on deathbed temptations and was illustrated by woodblock prints. Both text and prints portrayed an 'epic struggle' between infernal and heavenly forces during the last agonies of the dying. See Duffy 313–18, esp. 317. According to Paul Binski, the dying Christian might also have reason to dread his final sacramental anointing, 'a ritually transformative act from which there was no return. Those who were anointed and yet lived were latter-day Lazaruses, walking corpses. Hence anointing was the most fearful of death rituals.' See *Medieval Death: Ritual and Representation* (Ithaca, NY: Cornell University Press, 1996), 29–47, esp. 29; also Peter Marshall, *Beliefs and the Dead in Reformation England* (Oxford: Oxford University Press, 2002), 13. For a comparison of the medieval *ars moriendi* with Reformation tracts on dying, see Ralph Houlbrooke, *Death, Religion and the Family in England 1480–1750* (Oxford: Oxford University Press, 1998), 147–82.

40. It was commonplace long before the emergence of Purgatory as a controversy to depict a 'soul' as a homunculus, or little man or woman, and to represent

the 'souls' awaiting the Last Judgement as bodies or disassembled body parts. But purgatorial images of this kind could easily be misleading. Peter Marshall emphasises the difficulty of finding an appropriate visual code: 'the failure of the Church to establish a fixed and universally accepted set of iconographic conventions for the representation of purgatory must surely also have been a reason for the doctrinal dissemination in primarily aural and textual contexts' (12).

41. See Stephen Greenblatt, *Hamlet in Purgatory* (Princeton, NJ: Princeton University Press, 2001). Greenblatt discusses two vision poems at length: *The Vision of Tondal, c.* 1580 (61–7), and *Saint Patrick's Purgatory, c.* 1180 (73–101).

42. Greenblatt points out other psychological benefits, which were no less real, if 'murkier':

> ... the church could find in Purgatory a way to enable mourners to work through, with less psychological distress than they otherwise might experience, their feelings of abandonment and anger at the dead. To imagine the dead in great pain no doubt caused alarm, fear, and pity, but it also served other, murkier needs, needs that could be resolved in organized acts of mercy or even in the delay or withholding of organized acts of mercy. (103)

43. As Geary points out, only the Church had the power to stabilise this new communality by 'assur[ing] perpetual prayers for the departed' after the disappearance of one's biological descendants (91–2). Hence the importance of the parish bede role, which secured 'the perpetual recollection of one's name in the course of the worship of the parish' and represented a 'social map of the community' (Duffy, 334–5).

44. For an examination of late medieval and early modern funerary rites as they pertain to this phenomenon, see Chapter 4.

45. See G. R. Owst, *Literature and Pulpit in Medieval England* (Oxford: Basil Blackwell, 1961); and *Preaching in Medieval England: An Introduction to Sermon Manuscripts of the Period, c. 1350–1450* (Cambridge: Cambridge University Press, 1926). Owst's work has subsequently been refined and expanded: see, for example, H. Leith Spencer, *English Preaching in the Late Middle Ages* (Oxford: Clarendon Press, 1993). Spencer focuses on sermons of the marginalised 'radicals and reformers' (especially those of Wycliffe) rather than the 'conservative and orthodox preaching traditions' that were Owst's principal concerns (14). He also expands the framework of analysis signifi-cantly by consulting Latin writings which were particularly influential on English preaching. For commentary on the *exempla,* or brief and salutary narratives incorporated into sermons, see also Le Goff, *The Medieval Imagination,* 78–80.

46. Owst's emphasis in *Literature and Pulpit in Medieval England* is on the graphic quality of medieval imagery and on the performative links between preaching and the drama. Owst argues that these instructional media were competitive, but also mutually reinforcing: entire sermons were sometimes incorporated into the Corpus Christi plays. See esp. 471–547.

47. For the documentary history of Christian hagiography, see Helen C. White, *Tudor Books of Saints and Martyrs* (Madison: University of Wisconsin Press, 1963), esp. 1–66. Among sources for the *Legenda* that were particularly important in Britian were Bede's *The Ecclesiastical History of the English*

People, composed *c.* 731 but widely disseminated during the Middle Ages, and Eusebius's *Ecclesiastical History*, *c.* AD 300–25, on which Bede's work was largely modelled. See also Owst, 110–48, and *passim*.

48. Caxton added fifty-nine legends found in English and French versions to his translation of the Latin *Legenda*, as well as a series of biblical lives that had not been incorporated elsewhere. The last printing of *The Golden Legend* by Wynkyn de Worde was in 1527, shortly after the first printing of Tyndale's New Testament in Worms *c.* 1525–6, and approximately three years before Tyndale's version of the Pentateuch. See White, 31–67, esp. 32–3, 67.

49. It is well to remember in this connection that although the problematic status of the female body in the Middle Ages may have rendered it a more encompassing signifier of the transcendent potential of martyrdom, male martyrs, although less numerous in the *Legenda*, formed part of the same symbolic matrix.

50. Its account of the ancient and popular story of Saint Sophia and her three young daughters, Faith, Hope and Charity (aged eleven, ten and eight, respectively), is a virtual compendium of these motifs:

> Faith was punished, first, by being beaten by thirty-six soldiers, secondly, by having her breasts torn off, and all saw milk flowing from the wounds and blood from the severed breasts ... Thirdly, she was thrown on a red-hot gridiron but was unharmed, then, fourthly, was put in a frying pan full of oil and wax, and fifthly, was beheaded. Her sister, Hope ... was first put into a caldron full of pitch, wax, and resin, drops from which fell on some unbelievers and cremated them: finally she was killed with a sword. Charity [was ordered] to be stretched on the rack until her limbs broke and her joints parted; secondly, to be beaten with clubs; thirdly, she was scourged with lashes. Fourthly, she was thrown into a fiery furnace, out of which the flames leapt over sixty yards and killed six thousand idolaters while the child walked unscathed in the midst of the fire and shone like gold. Fifthly, she was stabbed with white-hot nails and thus, with a martyr's dancing step, passed gladly by the sword to the crown ... As for Hadrian [the persecutor], his whole body rotted and he wasted away to death ... (I, 185–6)

51. The visionary tradition to which the *Purgatorium* belongs drew variously from Judeo-Christian apocalyptical literature, from a wide range of writings by the Church Fathers (with those of Augustine and Gregory the Great figuring largely), and from classical texts such as Plutarch's *Moralia*. The most important precursor for the *Purgatorium* was the Vision of Drythelm from Bede's *Ecclesiastical History*, but it was the widely disseminated vision of the *Purgatorium* itself, written in Ireland *c.* 1190 by a Cisterian monk, translated into French by Marie de France and incorporated into several medieval histories, that Le Goff calls purgatory's 'literary birth certificate' (*The Birth of Purgatory*, 181). In a preamble to the vision, the author introduces a legend about St Patrick discovering the 'fossa', or hole leading to purgatory; the main narrative focuses on the fearsome journey to this underworld undertaken by Owein the Knight. See Le Goff, 193–201; and especially Greenblatt for an extended and illuminating discussion of the vision (73–101). For an excellent analysis of the roots of the medieval dream vision in neo-Platonic and patristic writings, see Steven F. Kruger, *Dreaming in the Middle Ages* (Cambridge: Cambridge University Press, 1992). For the Vision of Drythelm, see *The Ecclesiastical History of the English People*, trans. Leo Sherley-Price, rev. R. E. Latham (London: Penguin Books, 1990), 284–9.

52. Le Goff stresses the difference between this Celtic rendition of purgatory and Dante's vision of it as 'a place of hope, of initiation into joy, of gradual emergence into light' (*The Birth of Purgatory*, 346, 334–55), a view strongly supported by Bynum (*RoftheB*, 291–305). Duffy also argues for 'English perceptions of Purgatory in the late Middle Ages ... [as] altogether grimmer' than Dante's (344, *passim*).

53. From MS Harl. 2398, fol. 186b, and MS St Albans Cath. fol. 20 (= MS. Land. Misc. 23), respectively. Quoted in Owst, *Literature and Pulpit in Medieval England*, 508, notes 2 and 5.

54. Geary contends that for most people, 'relics *were* the saints, continuing to live among men'; they served as 'security deposits' (202) that confirmed the principle of transcendence animating the corpse. Thus their value had to do with their dual status as 'prestige objects' or commodities, and as 'persons': as such, 'they demonstrated that the boundaries between object and subject are culturally induced and semipermeable' (215–16).

55. As I have already suggested, blood as an emblem in medieval hagiography and in the Christian sacramental system worked to dissolve gender distinctions. None the less, although the blood of male martyrs such as St Sebastian carried many of the symbolic valences of female martyrs, the inviolate body of the female *virgin* martyr (like that of the Blessed Virgin Mary) called attention to the contaminating power of female sexuality.

56. The crucial distinction between Christ-as-relic and the relics of the saints was that the Host, as a material extension of Christ Himself, the uncontaminated man/God, might be eaten.

57. For an analysis of the aestheticism of church art, and especially of the association of gold with curative powers and with the immortality of the 'heavenly habitat', see Margaret Aston, *England's Iconoclasts: Laws Against Images*, Vol. I (Oxford: Clarendon Press, 1988), 20–34, esp. 26–7.

58. Julian of Norwich, in *A Book of Showings to the Anchoress Julian of Norwich*, eds. Edmund College and James Walsh, II (Toronto: University of Toronto Press, 1978), 447. Quoted by Duffy, 161.

59. Iconographic emblems for saints were frequently connected with 'the means of their bodily affliction ... the knife or skin of Bartholomew, the wheel of Catherine', and the breasts of Agatha, for example. In her Lacanian analysis of this phenomenon, Lupton usefully invokes Lacan's imaginary as a hermeneutic framework for this emphasis:

> The images of the saints reconstituted in the portrait gallery of divine history are marked – both identified and marred – by the singular traits of mutilation that ensured their place therein. In such portrayals, the visual integrity of the saints as forms or *Gestalten* coalesces around the piecemeal hieroglyphics of their attributes ... In *Seminar II* (1954–55), Lacan sets forth the imaginary order as the mode of representation that psychically configures the body at once as a beautiful form or unifying *Gestalt* and as an entity prone to morcellation and dissolution. (45–6)

60. Duffy recounts the story as told in *The Miracles of King Henry VI*, eds. Ronald Knox and Shane Leslie (Cambridge: Cambridge University Press, 1923), 77–84.

61. Duffy also delineates the many ways in which saint worship served to bind communities, as witnessed by miracles of healing after 'concerted acts of intercession to the saint ... by friends, neighbours, and even passing strangers'

(188); by the proliferation of guilds for the corporate worship of particular saints; by the custom of taking subscriptions to augment parish expenses or to provide ornamentation for churches; and, of course, by the popularity of pilgrimages (142–54). This social cohesiveness was of a piece with the linkages that saint worship provided with the next world – links between Christ and the unworthy sinner, and between the living Christian and the suffering souls in purgatory.

62. No less a theologian than Thomas More found himself defending this practice against the scorn of early reformists:

> [o6] Nowe as touchynge the thyrde point of superstycyous maner of worshyppynge/ or unlaufull petycyons desired of sayntys/as one sample may serue bothe/yf women offer otys to saynt Wylgefort to haue her vncomber them of theyr housbandys/ somewhat is it in dede that ye say/and yet not all thynge to be blamyd that ye seme to blame. For as to pray to saynt Appolyne for the helpe of our tethe is no wytchecrafte/consyderyng that she had her tethe pulled out for Crystys sake. Nor there is no superstycyon in suche other thyngys lyke. And peraduenture syth saynt Loy was a ferrour/it is no great faute to pray to hym for the help of our horse.

See *A dyaloge of syr T. More. Wherin be treatyd dyuers maters, as of the veneration & worship of ymagys*, 1529 (STC 18084); see also *The Complete Works of St. Thomas More*, eds. Thomas M. C. Lawler, Germain Marc'hadour and Richard C. Marius, Vol. 6, Part I (New Haven, CT and London; Yale University Press, 1981), 232.

63. Perhaps the most celebrated instance of a religious sensibility that resisted classification is that of John Donne, an especially prominent figure in the late English Reformation by virtue of his appointment as Dean of St Paul's in 1621. Donne's last sermon, *Death's Duel*, delivered at Whitehall before Charles I in 1631 (six days before Donne's death), is characteristically reformist in its preoccupation with the doctrine of justification by faith, the moral corruption of man and the infinite distance between a powerful God and his unworthy subjects. At the same time, however, there is an extravagant sensibility in Donne's poem that is reminiscent of the medieval mystics, as in its emphasis on the relationship between the fragmented and resurrected Christian body and on Christ's blood as salvific nurture. Donne's emotional identification with the violence of the Crucifixion is, moreover, strikingly similar to that found in medieval sermons. In saying this, I am not arguing for Donne's sensibility as Roman Catholic, despite his religious background, but rather for an originality of style that escapes such labelling. For 'Death's Duel', see *The English Sermon, Vol. 1, 1550–1656*, ed. Martin Seymour (Old Woking, Surrey: Unwin Brothers, 1976), 354–90. In *Habits of Thought* (159–217), Shuger provides an excellent analysis of Donne's religious orientation; in *Death, Desire and Loss in Western Culture*, 71–7, Dollimore focuses on Donne's attraction to death, drawing provocative parallels with Freud's death drive, and examining the proposition that Christ's Crucifixion was itself a kind of suicide.

64. The first edition of *Certayne sermons, or homilies* was published in 1547 (STC 13639), six months after the death of Henry VIII and under the direction of Cranmer. *The seconde tome of homelyes*, published in 1563 (STC 13663), included the homily on idolatry. Although issued with her approval and after a partial revision at her hands, the homily on idolatry did not represent

Elizabeth's more moderate views on the issue. These are more accurately reflected in the Acts of Supremacy and Uniformity of 1559, and in the injunctions of the same year, which attempt in numerous ways to mitigate the severity of the earlier Edwardian injunctions by safeguarding 'meet ornament' (for example, vestments, reliquaries, altar furnishings and stained glass windows) for the Church. According to Aston, Elizabeth did not believe that images were proscribed by scripture, and despite her approval of an injunction in 1561 prohibiting crosses in English churches, she refused to remove the cross from her own chapel (to the great consternation of the iconoclasts). See 294–342, esp. 306–14.

65. For an analysis of the dominance of Calvinist thought in the English reformed Church from the Elizabethan era to the Civil War (but with close attention to variations among sects and among Anglican spokesman such as Hooker and Whitgift), see P. G. Lake, in 'Calvinism and the English Church 1570–1635', *Past and Present*, 114 (February 1987), 32–114. For a consideration of the complex relationships between English conformists and Puritans in connection with the Admonition Controversy, a debate about the relevance of the Geneva model of church government to English Protestantism, see Peter Lake, *Anglicans and Puritans? Presbyterianism and English Conformist Thought from Whitgift to Hooker* (London and Boston: Unwin Hyman, 1988). For a discussion of William Perkins' adaptation of Calvinism in his hugely influential catechism, *The Foundation of Christian Religion* (1590), see Christopher Haigh, *English Reformation: Religion, Politics, and Society under the Tudors* (Oxford: Clarendon Press, 1993), 285–95, esp. 292–3. For a concise summary of Calvinist principles, the channels of Calvinist influence in England and English responses to the doctrine of predestination, see Alan Sinfield, *Literature and Protestant England 1560–1660* (London and Canberra: Croom Helm, 1983), 7–19. Marie Aston has pointed out that the homilist also borrowed directly from Bullinger's *De origine erroris, in divorum ac simulachrorum cultu*, and from Bucer's *Das einigerlei Bild* (which appeared in the mid-1530s in an English edition), in particular with respect to Bucer's call for 'the removal and destruction of *all* images'. See *Faith and Fire: Popular and Unpopular Religion, 1356–1600* (London and Rio Grande: The Hambledon Press, 1993), 292, 296.

66. Charles C. Butterworth, *The Literary Lineage of the King James' Bible, 1340–1611* (Philadelphia, 1941), 163–5; quoted in Helen C. White, *Tudor Books of Saints and Martyrs,* 92. Patrick Collinson also emphasises the importance of the Geneva Bible in shaping 'the religious imagination' of the English people; see 'Biblical Rhetoric', in *Religion and Culture in Renaissance England*, eds. Claire McEachern and Debora Shuger (Cambridge: Cambridge University Press, 1997), 17. In the same collection, David Scott Kastan provides a useful analysis of the politics of earlier Henrician editions of the Bible in English, from royal opposition to Tyndale's translation of the New Testament in 1525, to the publication in 1540 of the Great Bible, supposedly free of 'the insistent Lutheranism of earlier versions' (see '"The noyse of the new Bible": Reform and Reaction in Henrician England', 46–68).

67. In exile on the continent during the reign of Mary Tudor, Foxe published a Latin edition of his martyrology in six books at Basel in 1559. It included a reprint of a 1554 edition of early church history, descriptions of the Henrician

and Edwardian martyrdoms and three books on the Marian persecutions, ending with the death of Cranmer. When Foxe returned to England in 1559, he was able to obtain firsthand accounts of the Marian martyrs, which he incorporated in the greatly expanded English edition of 1563 (STC 11222), published by John Day and accompanied by fifty woodcut illustrations; see Rosemary O'Day, *The Debate on the English Reformation* (New York and London: Methuen, 1986), 19, 16–30. The second English edition, in 1570, was expanded further, with 1,500 woodcuts; other editions, some with new additions, were published in 1576, 1583, 1596, 1610 (which included an account of the St Bartholomew Day's Massacre) and 1632 (a folio in three volumes): see STC 11223–8. Timothy Bright published an abridgement of the martyrology in 1589 (STC 11229). For a review of the editing history of *Actes and Monuments*, see David Loades, 'John Foxe and the Editors', in David Loades (ed.), *John Foxe and the English Reformation* (Aldershot: Scolar Press Hants: 1997), 1–11. Citations in this essay are taken from the 1563 edition. I have silently altered black-letter ſ to 'r', and have eliminated hyphenation.

68. Calvin also emphasises the inimitable power of God in raising the dead:

> Shall we say that soules rest in the graues, that they lying there may heare Christ? and not rather that at his commaundement the bodies shall returne into the liuelinesse which they had lost? ... But for as much as God hath all the elements ready at his becke, no hardinesse shall hinder him, but that he may command both the earth & waters & fire, to render that which seemeth to be consumed by them.

See *The Institution of Christian Religion, written in Latine by M. John Caluine, and translated into English ... by Thomas Norton* (London, 1599, STC 4423), Lib. 3, Cap. 25, Mmvi (271), viᵛ (272).

69. Calvin's deconstructive distinctions between the body and the soul, in both man and Christ, are like those of the homilist:

> Now if the soule were not a certain thing by it selfe seuerall from the body, the Scripture would not teach that we dwell in houses of clay, that by death we remoue out of the Tabernacle of the flesh, that we do put of that which is corruptible ... the Image of God is in the Soule ... (Lib. I, Cap. 15, G2 [42]) ... Now where it is saide, that the Worde was made flesh: that is not so to be vnderstanded, as though it were either turned into flesh, or confusely mingled with flesh, but because he chose him a temple of the Virgins wombe to dwell in, he that was the sonne of God, became also the sonne of man, not by confusion of substance, but by vnitie of person ... If any thing in all worldly things may be found like to so great a mysterie, the similitude of man is most fit, whom we see to consist of two substances, whereof yet neither is so mingled with other, but that either keepeth the propertie of his owne nature ... We therefore do determine that Christ, as he is both God and man, consisting of both natures, vnited, though not confounded ... (Lib. II, Cap. 14, Rvᵛ, 6ʳ)

70. The shape of each of these transformations was, of course, hotly debated within contesting groups of reformers, ensuring that remnants of the old order were appropriated (if reformulated) into the new. Peter Marshall's excellent analysis of the devolution of the doctrine of purgatory in Henrician England is a case in point. See *Beliefs and the Dead in Reformation England*, 47–93, and *passim*.

71. Until his downfall in 1539, Cromwell worked with Thomas Cranmer to promulgate opinions that were considerably to the right of Henry's own. For example, both men sidestepped objections to the publication of *Pyctures and*

other ymages (STC 24238–9), a translation by William Marshall (a client of Cromwell) of Bucer's *Das Einigerlei Bild*. Bucer's iconoclastic tract, first published in 1530, defended Zwingli's notorious destruction of images at Strasbourg in 1524–5 (in 1528, Henry had denounced image-breaking in Paris) and also attacked the Mass (which Henry strongly supported). See Duffy, 386, 421; and Aston, 203–10. Cranmer's later differences with the king on the issue of idolatry are readily apparent in the rival editions of the so-called *Bishops' Book* (*The institution of a christen man*, 1537 [STC 5163–7]) and the *King's Book* (*A necessary doctrine and erudition for any christen man*, 1543 [STC 5168–77]). Although Cranmer believed that the *Bishops' Book* did not go far enough in condemning the veneration of images, Henry found its views too drastic and revised it accordingly. For a discussion of these texts, see Duffy, 379–447; and Aston, 223–46. For Cranmer's influence on the English Bible and the Anglican homilies, see John N. King, *English Reformation Literature: The Tudor Origins of the Protestant Tradition* (Princeton, NJ: Princeton University Press, 1982), 122–37.

72. Cranmer had made considerable inroads in eliminating Catholic practices in a series of injunctions issued in 1536, 1538 and 1547. Injunction 28, for example, countenanced the destruction of images in stained glass windows, although even Zwingli had spared these in Zurich. See Duffy, 451; and Aston, 257; also 226–33, 254–8 (Images before the law). Chief among the targets for reform in the 1549 and 1552 editions of The Book of Common Prayer were the Mass as sacrificial re-enactment of the Crucifixion, the cycle of feast-days in the liturgical calendar and the Catholic cult of the dead, including, for example, sacramental rituals for the dying, funerary practices and chantries. Among the proscriptions in the second, more radical edition of this work were a ban on Eucharistic prayers of consecration which served to buttress the Catholic concept of transubstantiation, together with a directive to curates to consume leftover bread and wine at home; and a ban on intercessions on behalf of the dead at funerals, so that 'the oddest feature of the 1552 burial rite is the disappearance of the corpse from it' (Duffy, 475, 448–77). Peter Marshall notes further that 'the corpse was now spoken of by the minister in the third rather than the second person ... a subtle shift of register, but one that was designed to minimize any suspicion that the Church was engaged in plea-bargaining with God with respect to the soul of the departed'. See *Beliefs and the Dead in Reformation England*, 111. For another view of the 'momentous alteration' made by The Book of Common Prayer in the sacramental significance of the Mass, see Janel M. Mueller, 'Pain, Persecution, and the Construction of Selfhood in Foxe's *Acts and Monuments*', in *Religion and Culture in Renaissance England*, 178; see also White, 87–9.

73. For an incisive assessment of the power struggles between Cranmer and his adversaries, both Protestant and Catholic, during the reign of Edward VI, see Cristopher Haigh, *English Reformation: Religion, Politics, and Society under the Tudors* (Oxford: Oxford University Press, 1993), 168–83.

74. See especially More's *A dyaloge of syr T. More. Wherin be treatyd dyuers maters, as of the veneration & worshyp of ymagys*; *The cofutacyon of Tyndales answere*, 1532 (STC 18079), and *The second parte of the cofutacion of Tyndals answere*, 1533 (STC 18080); and Tyndale's *The obediēce of a christen man*, 1528 (STC 24446), and *An answere vnto Sir T. Mores dialoge*,

1530 (STC 24437). For a valuable assessment of ideological differences between More and Tyndale on a range of issues, which includes analysis of the relationship between temperament and rhetorical style in each writer, see Stephen Greenblatt, *Renaissance Self-Fashioning from More to Shakespeare* (Chicago: University of Chicago Press, 1980), 74–114.

75. Although Tyndale's early writings were heavily influenced by Luther (the chief cause for suspicion of his works in the Henrician court), his view of the human mind as an idol-making 'factory' is virtually identical to that of Calvin in *The Institutes*. For an analysis of Calvin's theory of the human mind as a 'labyrinth' perpetually 'boiling up' false – that is, material – images of God, see Carlos M. N. Eire, *War Against the Idols: The Reformation of Worship from Erasmus to Calvin* (Cambridge: Cambridge University Press, 1986), 195–233. Eire contends, however, that Calvin perceives materiality itself as 'neutral' or 'indifferent', condemning only the uses to which man's corrupt imagination puts it in his effort to 'harness divine power' and diminish God: in Calvin's 'psychology of idolatry', 'men are inherently idolatrous' (207, 217, 232). In a fascinating study of Calvin's concept of mimesis, Adrian Streete points out the contradiction in Calvin's condemning, on the one hand, images of the Deity ('*Every figurative representation of God contradicts his being*'), and requiring, on the other, that the sinner acknowledge reflections of the divine 'Artificer' in the material world. Further, if, as Calvin claims, corrupt human perception has no access to God's own order of being, then the 'mirror' of the world can only be *mis*recognised in the mirror of the mind: 'Staring at the statue of God or gazing into the interior mirror becomes, strangely and almost inexplicably, *the same action*.' See 'Reforming Signs: Semiotics, Calvinism and Clothing in Sixteenth-century England', *Literature and History*, 3rd Series, 12: 1 (Spring 2003), 1–18. For an analysis of Tyndale's association of false imagination with 'the mummery and poetry' of Catholicism, see Greenblatt, 112–13.

76. In *The obediēce of a christen man*, 'blind' may be the most prevalent adjective, modifying a wide range of Catholic attitudes and practices, e.g. 'blind hearts', 'blind ceremonies', 'blind disputes', 'blind reason', and even 'blind scripture' when used 'as it hath done oure scoleme and oure sotle disputers' (Siiii).

77. Tyndale was following the example of the Greek Orthodox Church (as did Bucer, Bullinger and Calvin, although not Luther) in dividing the first commandment and combining the two precepts against covetousness (the ninth and tenth commandments in the Western tradition). Justification for this approach was found chiefly in Exodus 10: 1–17 and Deuteronomy 5: 6–21, passages which Tyndale foregrounded in his own English translation of the Pentateuch, which appeared in 1530. By 1537, the reformist decalogue was affirmed by its inclusion in *The Bishops' Book*. See Aston, 343–91.

78. In attacking the 'blind imagination' of literature elsewhere in his argument, Tyndale once again obfuscates the issue of metaphor in his outrage at the immorality of these texts:

> Fynally that this thretenynge and forbiddynge the laye people to reade the scripture is not for love of youre soules (which they care for as the foxe doeth for the gysse) is evidente & clerer then the sonne /in as moch as they permitte & sofre you to reade *Robyn hode & bevise of hampton/hercules/hector and troylus with a tousande histories & fables of love & wantones & of rybaudry as fylthy as herte can thinke/to

corrupte the myndes of youth with all/clene contrary to the doctrine of christ & of his apostles. (Ciiii)

79. See, for example, *A Dialogue concernynge heresyes & matters of religion*, in *The Complete Works of St. Thomas More*, Vol. 6, Part I, eds. Thomas M. C. Lawler, Germain Marc'Hadour and Richard C. Marius (New Haven, CT and London: Yale University Press, 1987): I xix, 110–13; II vii–xii, 209–46.

80. See *A Dialogue*, in *The Complete* Works, Vol. 6, Part I: I ii, 46–7. In this passage More proleptically sets out what might be described as a Saussurean theory of language:

> As for ensample yf I tell you a tale of my good frende Your mayster/the ymagynacyon that I haue of hym in my mynde/is not your mayster hym selfe but an ymage that representeth hym. And when I name you hym/his name is neyther hym selfe/nor yet the figure of hym/whiche figure is in myn ymagynacyon/but onely an ymage representynge to you the ymagynacyon of my mynde. Now yf I be to farre from you to tell it you/then is the wrytyng not the name it selfe/but an ymage representing the name. And yet all these names spoken/and all these wordes written/be no natural sygnes or ymages but onely made by consent and agrement of men/to betoken and sygnyfye suche thynge ...

81. For a summary of the Byzantine precedent as it pertains to the English Reformation, see Aston, 47–61. For eighth- and ninth-century commentary on the crisis, see Pelikan, Vol. 2, *The Spirit of Eastern Christendom (600–1700)* (Chicago: University of Chicago Press, 1974), 91–133, 170–83.

82. More's *Dialogue* may have been influenced by the publication in 1522 of John Eck's *De non tollendis Christi et santorum Imaginibus, contra haeresim Faelicianam sub Carolo magno damnatam, et iam sub Carolo V renascentem decisio*, which blamed the schism in the Church to the impious treatment of images by the Greek emperors (Aston, 51).

83. Charlemagne presumably supervised the preparation of these books for the Synod of Frankfort, which he convened in 794. Although the *Libri Carolini* provided Protestants with considerable ammunition for their cause, these books were also (but not equally) critical of the ruthless iconoclasm of Constantine, a feature conveniently ignored in many reformist commentaries.

84. Catholics suspected the *Libri Carolini* to be a forgery 'of either Carolingian or Protestant iconomachs', and were especially sceptical of the anonymity of the 1549 edition; in 1586, Cardinal Bellarmine attempted to discredit its authenticity. Although Calvin was influenced by this edition, he was none the less aware of the problematic status of the Byzantine precedent itself, since the Greeks allowed icons, if not statuary, in their churches, and approved the veneration of relics. See Aston, 56, 52–7.

85. The homily's arguments are, for the most part, considerably less complex than those of Calvin or Tyndale; still, as products of an emerging print culture, there is a much closer affinity in style and tone between reformist theology and its popular redactions than between medieval theology and, for example, the *Legenda Aurea*. Quotations from the homily are taken from the fourth facsimile edition of *Sermons or Homilies* (Oxford: Clarendon Press, 1816), 146–225; sigs. K8ᵛ-Q1.

86. The homily provides extensive documentation for its argument that 'the old primitive church ... was most uncorrupt and pure' (156), citing a roster of Church Fathers, including Tertullian, Origin, Athanasius, Lactantius,

Epiphanius, Jerome, Ambrose, Eusebius, and particularly Augustine, who is quoted at length. In preparation for its treatment of the Byzantine precedent, the homily also traces the gradual introduction of ecclesiastical images from about AD 460.

87. The homily does not distinguish between images and idols: ' that although in common speech we use to call the likeness or similitudes of men or other things, images, and not idols: yet the Scriptures use the said two words (*idols* and *images*) indifferently for one thing alway' (145–6). Lupton comments tellingly on the advantages of this conflation:

> The Protestant rendering of *eikon* as 'idol' was not a mistranslation; it exacerbated a fundamental duplicity inherent in *eidolon* … Whereas the Decalogue's emphasis on the idol focuses on the danger of concretizing and localizing the divine in physical receptacles that would 'represent' God in a political or hieratic sense, the Protestant inflection of the idol as icon generalizes and escalates the danger of mimetically visualizing God. (183)

88. Calvin's *Institutes* also stress materiality as dead, as in the following passage:

> In the mean time, sith this brutish grossenes hath possessed the whole world, to couet visible shapes of God, and so to forge themselues gods of timber, stone, gold, siluer, and other dead and corruptible matter, we ought to holde this principle, that with wicked falshood the glorie of God is corrupted, so oft as any shape is fained to represent him … Of the Prophets onely *Esay* [Isaiah] shall be enough, which speaketh oft and much hereof, to teach that the maiestie of God is defiled with vncomely and foolish counterfaiting, when he being without bodie, is likened to bodily matter: being inuisible, to a visible image: being a spirit, to a thing without life: being incomprehensible, to a small lumpe of timber, stone or golde … nothing is lesse allowable, than gods to be made of dead stuffe. (Lib. I, Cap. 11, D2[18], 2ᵛ, D3[19])

89. The homily's conflation of Catholic and pagan practices is a characteristic stratagy for asserting the ascendancy of the Reformation movement. See Lupton's investigation of the proposition that Protestantism 'institutes itself as the cancellation of all ceremony and imagery in order to implicate Catholicism as the vestigial afterlife of both classical paganism and Jewish legalism' (180, 178–85, and *passim*).

90. Calvin refers to the *Libri Carolini* in like manner:

> They that at this day maintaine the vse of images, alledge the decree of that *Nicene* Synode for their defence. But there is extant a booke of confutation bearing the name of *Charles* the Great, which by the phrase [style] we may gather to haue beene written at the same time. (Lib. I, Cap. 11, D6[22])

91. The second Council of Nicaea distinguished between *latria*, or the worship owed to God alone, and *dulia*, or the reverence due to God's creatures, such as the saints, citing Augustine as authority for these terms. *Hyperdulia*, introduced later but current by the time of Wycliffe, was the worship due to Christ as both creature and creator, but became associated as well with the Blessed Virgin Mary. See Aston, 48–9, 102–3. The homily, of course, rejects such distinctions: 'and herewithal is confuted their lewd distinction of Latria and Dulia; where it is evident, that the saints of God cannot abide, that as much as any outward worshipping be done or exhibited to them' (191).

92. Calvin's language is equally strong:

> The pictures and images that they dedicate to saints, what are they but examples of extreme riot and vncleannesse, whereunto if any woulde fashion him elfe, he were

woorthie to be beaten with staues? Surely, the brothelhouses can shew harlots more chastely and soberly attired, than their temples shewe images of these whom they would haue called virgins. (Lib. I, Cap. 11, D4[20])

93. Calvin is eloquent on this issue:

God indeede, I graunt, sometime in certaine signes hath giuen a presence of his godhead, so as he was saide to be beholden face to face, but all these signes that euer he shewed, did aptly serue for meanes to teach, and withal did plainly admonish men of an incomprehensible essence ... not *Moses* himselfe ... obtained by praier to see that face, but receiued this aunswere, that man is not able to sustaine so great brightensse ... For the Cherubins with their wings stretched abroad did couer it [the mercy seat of God], the veile did hide it ... for as much as they were made for this purpose, that hiding the mercie seat with their wings, they should not onely keepe back the eies of man, but also all his senses from the beholding of God ... For this purpose maketh it, that the Prophets described the Seraphins shewed them in a vision, with their face vncouered: whereby they signifie, that so great is the brightensse of the glorie of God, that the Angels themselues are kept from direct beholding it, and the small sparkes thereof that shine in the Angels are withdrawen from our eies. (Lib. I, Cap. 11, D2ᵛ, D3[19])

94. Again, Calvin set a strong precedent for this focus. Although he is careful to avoid both Gnostic and Manichean heresies, he none the less connects Christ's assumption of bodily form to the sin of Adam, and insists that Christ himself 'openly distinguisheth the day of his manifestation [as man] from his eternall essence', that is, his existence in the godhead as anterior to his function as Redeemer (Lib. 2, Cap. 14, Rᵛ[126]). Calvin's interpretation of the hypostatic union as two natures 'vnited' but not 'confounded' or mingled (see note 69) supports this emphasis. In a related issue, Calvin also stresses Christ's submission to his Father:

For such prerogatiues had the sonne of God, when he was hewed in the flesh, which although he enioyed with his father before the world was made, yet hee had them not in the same maner nor the same respect, and which could not be giue to such a man as was nothing but man ... Christ after the iudgement ended, shal yeeld vp the kingdome to God & the Father: Euen the kingdome of the sonne of God, which had no beginning, nor shall haue any ending: but euen as he lay hid vnder the basenes of the flesh, & abased him elfe, taking vpon him the forme of a seruant, and laying aside the port of maiestie, he shewed himselfe obedient to his father: and hauing performed all such subiection, at length is crowned with honor and glory, & aduanced to the highest dominion, that all knees shall bow before him: so shall he then yeelde vp to his father both that name and crowne of glorie, and whatsoeuer he hath receiued of his father, that God may be all in all. (Lib. 2, Cap. 14, Rvi [126], vi[v])

Debora Kuller Shuger offers another, intriguing perspective on Calvin's privileging of God the Father in her analysis of Calvin's description of the Crucifixion in *Harmony of the Evangelists* (1558, translated into English in 1584). Shuger argues that although the crucified Christ 'slips to the margins of English Protestantism' (89), Calvin analysed the Crucifixion as a psychological crisis in which Christ felt abandoned by a wrathful Father to whom he was none the less enjoined to submit without loss of 'inner autonomy' (110). See *The Renaissance Bible: Scholarship, Sacrifice, and Subjectivity* (Berkeley: University of California Press, 1994), 89–127.

95. For the differences between Protestant alternatives to transubstantiation, specifically, consubstantiation (the position of Luther), virtualism (that of Calvin) and memorialism (that of Zwingli), see Pelikan, Vol. 4, 183–203; see

also Huston Diehl, *Staging Reform, Reforming the Stage: Protestantism and Popular Theatre in Early Modern England* (Ithaca, NY: Cornell University Press, 1997), 94–109. Calvin's virtualism (or some variation thereof), a *via media* between the affirmation of Christ's presence in the Eucharist and the idea of the sacrament as purely symbolic, was widely adopted by English Protestantism. Diehl summarises it well: virtualism viewed 'the Lord's Supper as a promise and a memorial, not a sacrifice or a miracle', although 'the sacrament depends on the correspondence between earthly bread and Christ's body, between physical eating and spiritual nourishment' (101, 106). The Last Supper 'therefore invites its worshippers to remember, receive, and rise up to a transcendent God who cannot be seen, eaten, or touched' (103).

96. This concept was, ironically enough, used by the Byzantines to argue that 'the Eucharist could be, and in fact was, a true image, for only it was identical in essence with Christ' (Pelikan, 109). The acceptance of transubstantiation in the Eastern Church was yet another factor that rendered the 'Byzantine precedent' considerably more muddied than reformist propaganda would have it.

97. Throughout this chapter, Calvin addresses eschatological issues, but he maintains an incurious approach to questions that Catholic theologians prefer to probe. Several times he inveighs against unseemly curiosity, once citing the exhortation of St Paul to 'bridleth the libertie to dispute like Philosophers' (Mm3ᵛ). In *The obediēce of a christen man*, Tyndale issues the same caveat:

> As pertaynge to our ladyes body/where it is or where the body of Elyas/of John the Evangeliste and of many other be/perteyneth not to vs to know. One thinge are we sure of/that they are where God hath leyde thē. *Yf they be in hevē/we have never the moare in Christe: Yf they be not there/we have never the lesse. Oure dutie is to prepare oure selves vnto the commaundmentes and to be thankefull for that which is opened vnto vs/and not to sherch the vnsherchable secretes of God. (S3ᵛ, S4)

98. Interestingly, Calvin gives short shrift to this biblical explanation:

> As concerning the beginning of idols, that is by common consent thought to be true which is written in the booke of wisedome, that they were the first authors of them, which gaue this honor to the dead, superstitiously to worship their memory. And truly I grant that this euill custome was very ancient, and I deny not that it was the firebrand wherewith the rage of man being kindled to idolatrie, did more and more burne therein. Yet doe I not graunt that this was the first originall of this mischiefe. For it appeereth by *Moses* that images were vsed before that this curiositie in dedicating the images of dead men, whereof the prophane writers make often mention, were come in vre [*sic*]. When he telleth that *Rachell* had stolen her fathers idols, hee speaketh it as of a common fault. Whereby we may gather that the wit of man is, as I may so call it, a continuall worship of idols ... The mind of men ... presumeth to imagin god according to hir own coceit: ... Thus the minde begetteth the idoll, & the hand bringeth it foorth. (Lib. I, Cap. 11, D4ᵛ)

Calvin's notion of man's corrupt imagination as the source of idolatry is of course similar to that of Tyndale (see note 75).

99. In discussing the permutations of the 'apologetic' and 'apocalyptic' traditions in early modern English Protestantism, Richard Helgerson distinguishes between the 'Churches' of Foxe and Hooker, the former 'identified with a scripturally inspired and sometimes disruptive movement of God's word through time', and the latter with 'a particular institutional order and a particular order of service'. The Foxian Church 'relied for its maintenance

on printing, preaching, and tales of persecution. Its Hookerian rival depended on ritual performance and official coercion.' See *Forms of Nationhood: The Elizabethan Writing of England* (Chicago and London: The University of Chicago Press, 1992), 284.

100. See John King, 'Fiction and Fact in Foxe's *Book of Martyrs*', in Loades (ed.), *John Foxe and the English Reformation*, 15. For an analysis of the relationship of *Actes and Monuments* to the *Legenda* (and in particular, the organisation of their calendars), see White, 132–68, esp. 135–9.

101. See 'Pain, Persecution, and the Construction of Selfhood in Foxe's *Acts and Monuments*', in *Religion and Culture in Renaissance England*, eds. Claire McEachern and Debora Shuger (Cambridge: Cambridge University Press, 1997), 170.

102. White argues that the combination of 'the triumphant' and 'the macabre' (164) in Foxe's style is a function of the polarity of his values; his is 'the classic psychology of the crusade' (146).

103. O'Day here draws from the evidence provided by Elizabeth Eisenstein in *The Printing Press as an Agent of Change*, Vol. 1 (Cambridge: Cambridge University Press, 1979), 423.

104. See Elaine Scarry, *The Body in Pain: The Making and Unmaking of the World* (Oxford: Oxford University Press, 1985).

105. Diehl's study focuses on the theatricality that Foxe exploits in *Actes and Monuments*. She argues that Foxe sought to establish a new, anti-idolatrous and communal mode of perception that was assimilated into the dramaturgy of the burgeoning public theatre. See *Staging Reform*, esp. 9–40, and *passim*.

106. For me, Marshall's methodology represents an unusually intelligent application of psychoanalytical theory to literary/historical criticism. Interested in the 'self-canceling' dynamic of human subjectivity, Marshall would 'use modern terminology ... not to pathologize the desires of the Renaissance but to bring them into focus and demonstrate their historical contingency'. Her focus on 'the theoretical concept of sadomasochism ... in uncovering the early modern impulse to undo or negate the emergent self' is inspired:

> the theoretical construct of sadomasochism ... works against established [psycho-analytical] models of subjectivity. From Freud's early struggles with the concept onward, sadomasochism has been the barbarian within the gates of psychoanalysis, troubling established models by confirming what they imply but have rarely embraced: the contradictory, self-canceling nature of subjectivity. (7)

See Cynthia Marshall, *The Shattering of the Self: Violence, Subjectivity, & Early Modern Texts* (Baltimore, MD: Johns Hopkins University Press, 2002).

107. Interestingly, Streete argues that the relationship of Calvinist Christology to the concept of selfhood also involves a sado-masochistic dynamic. Streete contends that by emphasising the ascendancy of Christ's spirit over his body, and at the same time offering Christ as a mimetic model of selfhood, Calvin in effect sets up a paradigm in which the elect must 'imitate' Christ's own sacrificial expiation while simultaneously recognising 'an irreducible difference between model and copy' (153). This 'radical self-abandonment' replicates, in one sense, Christ's own estrangement from his Father (the point at which Christ becomes 'fully human' according to Slavoj Žižek), but the subject's 'imitation' is itself so debased that she ends up, as it were, doubly estranged:

Therefore, the attempted appropriation of Christological mimesis by the subject in early modern culture might well be read as a pathological drive towards a masochistic 'union' with the deity that the subject knows s/he will not achieve. (154)

Enjoined to 'internalize the desolation of death as a prerequisite of selfhood' (147), and finding absence rather than presence at the center of this desolation, the sinner takes refuge in sado-masochistic violence. See '"*Consummatum Est*": Calvinist Exegesis, Mimesis and *Doctor Faustus*', *Literature and Theology*, 15: 2 (June 2001), 140–58. The quote from Žižek is from *On Belief* (London: Routledge, 2001), 146, quoted by Streete in an unpublished essay, '*Ecce homo*: Imitation and the Early Modern Subject'. I am grateful to Streete for sharing with me several essays from his forthcoming book.

108. The relationship of text to woodcuts has yet to be adequately explored and may in fact provide further evidence for Marshall's argument. In a fascinating introduction to 'The Iconography of *Actes and Monuments*', Margaret Aston and Elizabeth Ingram argue that between the 1559 publication of the *Ecclesia Gestarum* and the 1563 edition of *Actes and Monuments,* there was a decided shift from stylised to realistic representation in the woodcuts. The figure of Hooper, for example (see quoted passage on p. 64 of this text), stood 'rock-like in the fire' in the 1559 illustration, whereas that of 1563 foregrounded 'the dreadful effects of [the] fitful fire of deficient green faggots … No detail is spared – even the hand and arm fallen into the fire' (86). See *John Foxe and the English Reformation*, 66–142. If, as J. H. Plumb suggests, *Actes and Momuments* was one of the few Elizabethan books 'which the illiterate, the semiliterate, and the literate poor ever knew in any detail', then the visual text may have been as important as the literary one in disseminating Foxe's influence. See *The Death of the Past* (Boston: Houghton Mifflin, 1970), 84; quoted in Helgerson, 287. The significance of pictorialism in Foxe has recently come under renewed scrutiny in a collection edited by Christopher Highley and John N. King, *John Foxe and his World* (Aldershot: Ashgate, 2002). See especially Andrew Pettegree, 'Illustrating the Book: A Protestant Dilemma' (133–44), which argues for the 'polemical power' (133) of Foxe's woodcuts, situating them within European traditions of illustration prior to the Genevan strictures against it; Thomas Betteridge, 'Truth and History in Foxe's *Acts and Monuments*' (145–59), which views Foxe's text and images as a single ideological design; and David Kastan, 'Little Foxes' (117–29), which discusses the relationship of Foxe's burgeoning readership to the successive abridgements of his book. In 'John Foxe and National Consciousness' (10–34), Patrick Collinson identifies the considerable historical and methodological difficulties in determining the influence of Foxe's martyrology, and, in the first instance, of identifying what represents 'Foxe' in a work that ultimately passed through many hands.

109. Another often quoted sequence from Foxe describes the sensational death of 'Iohn Hullier Minister and martyr, burned at Cambridge'. Here Foxe contrasts the gory effects of insufficient fire with Hullier's remarkable reading from a Communion book, intended as fuel, that he rescues from the flames. Foxe insists that Hillier is 'joyfull' throughout his ordeal, subordinating even the stark image of the standing skeleton that remains after Hillier's death to the counter-spectacle of his unswerving joyfulness (see RRRRr3[v]; iiii). One of

the curiosities of this passage is Foxe's inclusion of the relic-hunting activities of the spectators after Hillier's demise:

> Of the people some tooke as they could get of him, as peeces of bones. One had his hart, the which was distributed so farre as it would go: one tooke the scalpe and looked for the tong, but it was consumed except the very roote.

Chapter 3

Animating Matter: The Corpse as Idol in *The Second Maiden's Tragedy* and *The Duke of Milan*

Because theatrical illusion is produced principally through the agency of actors, it is in large part about the body: the body as constitutive in the formation and expression of human ideas and emotions, the body as object of the spectator's gaze, the body as subject to the transformations of impersonation. Notwithstanding significant differences in theatrical traditions, the actor's body none the less constitutes the primary locus of performance. Yet in early modern England, at the same time that a burgeoning secular theatre was fast becoming a new staple of public life, Protestant reformers were castigating those uses of the body that made such performance possible. As we have seen, the homily on idolatry – one of the most important polemical productions of the English Reformation – effectively precluded the performative agency of the actor as part of its larger attack on material, and especially anthropomorphic, images. The new theatrical industry did not, of course, repudiate itself in response to religious polemic, nor did it shrink from examining the issue of idolatry in its own right by means of corporeal representations. But in an important sense this theatre developed *as theatre* in continual tension with a pervasive Protestant ideology that sought to revise the conceptual framework for apprehending the material body.

My project in this chapter is to examine the repercussions of this tension in two plays that directly address the issue of idolatry – Thomas Middleton's *The Second Maiden's Tragedy* (1610–11), and Philip Massinger's *The Duke of Milan* (1621–2). These plays, based on well-known legends of Herod the Tetrarch, are unusual in that they feature sustained and sensational representations of necrophilia, the most taboo form of idolatry. I argue that by focusing on the transgressive desires of protagonists who insist on the re/generative potential of the corpse, both plays are implicated importantly in the core concern of Protestant iconoclasm: that is, the question of what 'dead' means in relation to materiality. If the corpse, or the paradox of its signification, can be said to lie at the heart of the Protestant case against materiality, then its representation on the stage simultaneously challenged both the ideological and performative agency of the early modern theatre. Inevitably, this theatre evoked its own problematic relationship to the body/soul conundrum every time it 'performed' a corpse for a large and heterogeneous audience, and particularly when it attempted to represent the corpse as idolatrous object of desire.

1. Performing idols

In one sense, of course, to speak of idolatry in connection with the theatre is an oxymoron. All theatrical representation depends on artifice: performance, or play-acting is a self-conscious pretence. But if artifice is the *sine qua non* of any performance, the new secular theatre in England pointedly called attention to the conventions that shaped its fictions, to the inner workings, as it were, of the fantasy machine. The distinctiveness of this theatre was its meta-theatricality: the representation of illusion in a mode that foregrounded representation *as* illusion.

Such meta-theatricality precluded drama that we have come to associate with the later tradition of realism – that is, drama constructed on the premise that the illusion must seem 'real'.[1] On the contrary, performances on the early modern public stage were at mid-day, whatever the supposed time of a play's action, with most of the elevated platform stage open to the elements; scenery was minimal and for the most part symbolic; and the arrangement of the audience around a three-sided stage precluded a comprehensive view of the action for many spectators. Further, in both public and private theatres, poetic language, including soliloquies and asides, emblematic and stylised modes of acting, unlocalised settings, anachronistic costuming, the mixing of dramatic genres and tonalities, and disparities of time and place all contravened illusionistic representation. By showcasing such gaps between fiction and performance, early modern drama encouraged the audience to maintain a double perspective, that is, an identification with the fiction and a simultaneous recognition that this fiction was a pretence, an artificial construct.

On the one hand, the self-consciousness of meta-theatricality would seem to have protected the theatre, at least to some degree, against the charge that its artifice was designed to deceive. But the dual perspective required of the theatrical spectator was notably akin to that of the Catholic worshipper before the statue, and reformers, among other critics, were acutely aware of this affinity. Moreover, theatrical performance, which fundamentally depended on the blurring of categorical divides through the agency of impersonation, posed its own, independent danger to viewers. Each instance of impersonation enacted some convergence of actor/fictional figure, disguise/identity, and it was the actor's business to proliferate such confusions, to multiply roles. As fragmenters or disintegrators of the 'self', actors could be seen as idol-makers, and spectators who invested such impersonations with any measure of credibility, or false substantiality, seen as idol-worshippers.

In addition, the idolatrous ambience of impersonation was significantly compounded by the centuries-old tradition of transvestite acting, or the impersonation of women by boy actors. Transvestism foreclosed the possibility of representing women apart from the agency of male bodies, which meant that no female figure in an early modern play could be represented as unproblematically gendered, nor could the representation of erotic desire be unproblematically differentiated by sex. By virtue of this division or conflation of conventional gender and sexual distinctions, transvestism enabled the theatre to interrogate the viability of the male/ female divide and explore fluid and shifting erotic valances – from an iconoclast's viewpoint, a kind of free-floating concupiscence.[2]

This sexually ambiguous ambience, as Peter Stallybrass has persuasively argued, was a function of the cross-dressed boy actor staging two contradictory fixations or fantasies of sexuality: what was visible and prosthetically suggestive of the 'essential' marks of female sexual identity: breasts, vagina; and what was absent and imagined: the body beneath the prosthetic fantasy, which might be imagined as male or female.[3] Transvestism thereby required the simultaneous awareness of contradictions: it was a presence, like other kinds of meta-theatricality, that spoke of absence. To 'stage' such contradiction, to call attention to gaps in signification, was in these instances to 'play' in an enticingly open fashion with the liminalities of gender and sexuality. As Catherine Belsey puts it, the cross-dressed boy actor provided opportunities for 'multiple sexual identifications ... in the *margins* of sexual difference, those margins which a metaphysical sexual polarity obliterates' (188–9, my italics).[4] That is, in addition to inviting spectators to fantasise erotically about either or both genders, transvestism stimulated confusedly pleasurable erotic feelings which seemed to have no proper object at all.

Anti-theatrical polemicists, who heatedly denounced the theatre as idolatrous, were especially exercised about what they saw as the shamelessly overt way in which stage performances linked idolatry and lust. John Rainolds, one of the most learned and alarmed of these critics, levelled a sustained attack against the temptations of transvestism in a disputatious correspondence between 1591 and 1594 with two Oxford scholars, William Gager and Alberico Gentili.[5] In one instance, he compared the erotic power of cross-dressed 'beautifull boyes' to that of a bi-gendered, animated idol:

> can you accuse your selfe, or anie other, of anie wanton thought stirred vp in you by looking on a beautifull Woman? If you can; then ought you beware of beautifull boyes transformed into women by putting on their raiment, their feature, lookes, and facions. For men may be ravished *with loue of stones, of dead stuffe*, framed by cunning grauers to beautifull womens likenes ... [so also] the cladding of youthes in such attire is an occasion of drawing and provoking corruptlie minded men to most heinous wickedness ...[6] (my italics)

Presumably, Rainolds would not have included himself among his group of 'corruptlie minded men', but the passion with which he condemned transvestism bears eloquent witness to his fear of the theatre's seductive power. To lose oneself in multiple, unlocalised desires was to risk losing, at least momentarily, the spiritual integrity of a centring self.

Despite their deep distrust of impersonation as idolatrous, however, Rainolds and his fellow polemicists did not specifically address the implications of the *corpse* on stage. In a sense, their preoccupation with the allure of transvestism precluded attention to the more profoundly unsettling signification of the dead body: none the less, the corpse was the ultimate site of the problem of idolatry *and* of impersonation. If, as Elizabeth Bronfen has argued in the context of the visual arts, every image of death is fetishistic in that it suggests 'a severing of the body from its real materiality',[7] then the image of the theatrical corpse is especially complicated in that the material body itself serves as agent for the image: theatre is, in Greenblatt's phrase, 'illusory *embodiment*' (22, my italics).[8] Thus the representation of the corpse on the early modern stage entailed the meta-theatrical recognition not only of an illusion, but also in effect of a double illusion – an illusion of an illusion. That is, a material, sentient body was supposed to signify an insentient one, severed from 'its real materiality' – a *dis*embodied body. Further, because death was outside the experience of actor and theatre-goer alike, the illusion of death could not be evoked through the prism of memory: 'corpseness' itself was unsignifiable. As a disembodied body *in potentia* only, the body of the actor was thereby enjoined to represent the unrepresentable on several levels, in what might be called the consummate instance of meta-theatricality.

Yet another complicating set of valences came into play whenever a boy actor was enjoined to impersonate a female corpse, especially if this corpse were an object of infatuation. Certainly, the erotic charge of gender ambiguity, as Rainolds argues so cogently, was an integral part of the early modern theatre's ambience. But the eroticism of the cross-dressed corpse was distinctive in that this corpse purported to blur both male/female and body/spirit divides; further, as idol, it interrogated the nature of desire in the absence, as it were, of these categorical structures. As an erotic object configured without the securities of gender distinctions, one in which sexual attractiveness and 'deadness' were presumably indistinguishable, the corpse/idol invited the audience to a voyeuristic engagement, if only on a subconscious level, with the furthest reaches of erotic desire.

Or such, at least, was the potential of the corpse as erotic object on the early modern stage. But, as I suggested in Chapter 1, the difficult conjunction of artifice, sensationalism and psychological complexity that is the hallmark of Benjamin's fully developed *Trauerspiel* was uncommon, and the dramaturgy of *The Second Maiden's Tragedy* and *The Duke of Milan* – although certainly sensational and meta-theatrical – attempted a less complicated set of effects. For example, both plays feature a climactic scene in which a female idol/corpse is ostentatiously propped up in a chair and cosmeticised in full view of the audience, pointedly calling attention to the many layers of artifice in the figure's multiple makeovers: to the artifice of the living actor inhabiting the 'corpse', the male actor inhabiting the 'female' body, the compounded artifice of the corpse/idol, and finally, of course, the corpse/idol itself in the process of having its 'putrefaction' painted over.[9]

I would argue that the unvarnished exhibitionism of this scene accords with the tendency of both plays to represent idolatry and its erotic complications in a more or less literal fashion. Thus, for example, the representation of the female protagonist in *The Second Maiden's Tragedy* is split into a convenient binary: the virtuous Lady, whose death supposedly renders her living body a dead artifact, embraced as idol by the play's Tyrant; and the Lady's Ghost, the living spirit that transcends the death of the Lady's body. For reasons that will soon become apparent, this body/soul opposition is implicitly contravened by the deconstructive mechanisms of the early modern stage. But the ideological stance of the play insists on the Lady's corpse as a literal emblem of an idol, a dead thing whose final painting unequivocally confirms its sacrilegious status. Thus, in Middleton's play the psychological and erotic possibilities in the representation of idolatry are shortcircuited by heavy-handed symbolism. Indeed, dramatic tensions arise primarily as accidents of ideological inconsistencies, as fallout from the play's untenable polarities.

Massinger's representation of Marcelia, the female protagonist of *The Duke of Milan*, also divides into a binary – that of goddess/whore – but this division is considerably more fraught than that of the Lady. In an interesting variation on her predecessor, Marcelia herself is both idol and idolater, that is, for most of the play she is not only alive, but fully complicit in the Duke's misguided apotheosis of her as goddess. However, to the Duke's soldiers, courtiers and family, Marcelia's high-mindedness is a fraud, masking the moral anarchy of her lust. Marcelia's contradictions (like those in the representation of the Lady) serve as the organising principle, or nub, of the play's dramatic action. But as a woman whose power as idol originates in her own self-worshipping surrender to pleasure, Marcelia (unlike the Lady) bears a close resemblance to the female who is doubly demonised in the homily against idolatry – as transgressor and as contaminant.

Given this darkening of the sexual themes in Massinger's play, it is noteworthy, especially in the framework of Benjamin's *Trauerspiel*, that corpse desecration ends up besting even necrophilia as the ultimate sacrilege. Francisco the corpse-painter may be seen as a type of *intrigrant*: a charlatan with an edge of 'devilish mirth' (Benjamin, 227) and 'bitingly provocative scorn' (126). Unlike Govianus, his counterpart in *The Second Maiden's Tragedy*, Francisco enjoys cosmeticising Marcelia: he is tempted by 'the illusion of freedom – in the exploration of what is forbidden; the illusion of independence - in the secession from the community of the pious; the illusion of infinity – in the empty abyss of evil' (230). At the end of the play, and in the midst of its exposé of the Duke as necrophiliac, Francisco unexpectedly emerges as a far more disturbing and formidable presence, a demonic magus who takes a sinister pleasure in toying with the dead.

Despite such important correspondences with Benjamin's paradigm, however, neither *The Duke of Milan* nor *The Second Maiden's Tragedy* has enough of what might be called the Francisco element to strike a chord of deep human dread. Not only is the dramatic potential of the subject matter undercut by the aforementioned staging techniques, but also on occasion by interpolations that verge on the farcical, especially (as we shall see) in *The Second Maiden's Tragedy*. Hence the indeterminate fearsomeness of the corpse surfaces, as it were, erratically, as if by accident. In this respect, both plays may be compared to the homily on idolatry in that their particular style of reductive overstatement draws unwanted attention to their textual repressions, so that in the end the corpse makes its presence felt, if only indirectly.

From another angle, of course, it is possible to argue that the theatre's willingness to dramatise necrophilia in *any* mode suggests its recognition of contemporary audience interest in death-related taboos and in the communal expression of deeply transgressive impulses. To be sure, Middleton's and Massinger's plays ostensibly adopted the official iconoclastic stance of the Protestant establishment. Vetted and approved by the Master of the Revels, they borrowed from medieval Catholic legend to satirise Catholic practices, basing their protagonists on the Biblical Herod, King of Judea, made famous in England by his prominent position as self-aggrandising Tyrant in the Catholic mystery cycles. But in the early seventeenth century, what made Herod a compelling target for iconoclastic attack had more to do with his reputed infatuation with the corpse of his dead wife than with his campaign against the infant Christ. By enacting this necrophiliac legend under a formal sanction, the theatre (not unlike Francisco) had its own rationale (or pretext) for trafficking in the taboo. This is not to assume that the subversive undertones in these plays were designed to decentre their attack on idolatry. But it is to suggest that theatrical interventions in the controversy over idol worship were, deliberately or not, performances in which discourses of the time were doubly and problematically reinscribed: as commentary on the issues, and as commentary on the theatre's singular relationship to these issues.

2. The Second Maiden's Tragedy (c. 1610–11)

Over a period of centuries in medieval England, the popular reputation of Herod, King of Judea at the time of Christ's birth, became increasingly larger than life.[10] Repeatedly featured in biblical commentary and vernacular sermons, and dramatised in the Corpus Christi cycles, Herod emerged as an Antichrist, a would-be god who slaughtered rather than saved, his secular career a perverse inversion of Christ's redemptive sacrifice. Herod's savagery in ordering the massacre of Judean male infants under the age of two was associated with his paganism, his birth as a Saracen outside the Judeo-Christian tradition. But Herod's monstrous otherness was not wholly comprehended by his pagan roots. As Antichrist, he was presumed to be impervious to all civilised restraints, defiant of taboo – in Benjamin's phrase, 'a mad autocrat and a symbol of disordered creation' (70). His necrophiliac attachment later in life to the corpse of his wife Mariamne represented an insane autonomy, that is, a refusal to recognise his subservience to the laws of nature and a reckless assertion of his own power over death. In view of such unnatural aggression, the Christian faithful considered Herod's epileptic frenzies and gruesome demise (usually described as consumption by worms) as symbolically suitable punishments.[11]

The chief sources in England for the Herod legend were the gospels, particularly the Vulgate version of Matthew, and two works by the Jewish historian Flavius Josephus (translated into English by Thomas Lodge in 1602): *The Jewish War*, 69–79 AD, and *Of the Antiquities of the Jews*, c. 93 AD.[12] Matthew's accounts of Herod's interrogation of the Magi and his subsequent Massacre of the Innocents became popular staples of the mystery plays and vernacular sermons. Josephus mentions neither of these incidents, but provides detailed and sometimes conflicting descriptions of Herod's political career (including his three-year siege of Judea and bloody defeat of Jerusalem), his marriage to Mariamne, the slaying of Mariamne and her presumed lover, Herod's passionate lamentation after her death and his own horrible end.[13] The only direct reference to Herod's necrophilia is found in the *Babylonian Talmud*, where Herod is said to have worshipped Mariamne's corpse, preserved in honey, for seven years.[14]

Because the medieval mystery plays focused on Herod's challenge to Christ as narrated by Matthew, they emphasised Herod as a self-appointed idol, ruthless rival to his infant competitor. This royal and fearsome Herod, sumptuously dressed and fitted with the accoutrements of kingship, was by all accounts a visually compelling image on stage.[15] But the melodramatic posturings that increasingly became a staple of Herod's stage persona, the rantings and temper tantrums, rendered the figure of the Antichrist, at least some of the time, as farcical – a secular version of the medieval Vice.[16] The inclusion of comic elements in scenes of brutality or tragedy was, of course, a distinctive feature of English native drama (as in the jesting of the soldiers in scenes of the Crucifixion). But the *doppelgänger* approach to Herod's representation (and that of the Vice as well, for that matter) served the particular purpose of diminishing Herod's display of power by trans-forming him into a kind of grotesquerie.[17] In this curious posture, Herod's puissance – his credibility as an adversary of Christ – was indistinguishable from his status as fool.

Middleton's Herod-like Tyrant in *The Second Maiden's Tragedy* (1610–11)[18] is also a grotesquerie, a melodramatic posturer whose behaviour undercuts his grandiose claims, but here he appears in the context of the Talmudic story of Herod's fixation with the corpse of Mariamne. On two occasions, the Tyrant invites a direct comparison between his idolatrous intentions and those of Herod. In 4.3, a scene with a probable antecedent in a passage from Josephus which describes Herod desecrating the tomb of David,[19] the Tyrant breaks into the tomb of the Lady (object of his obsession) and addresses her corpse:

> I once read of a Herod, whose affection
> Pursued a virgin's love, as I did thine,
> Who for the hate she owed him killed herself
> (As thou too rashly didst), without all pity.
> Yet he preserved her body dead in honey,
> And kept her long after her funeral. (115–19)

Later, in another apostrophe to the Lady's corpse, the Tyrant vows to match the duration of Herod's necrophilia: 'I love thee yet, above all women living, / And shall do sev'n year hence' (5.2.25–6).[20] By thus re-enacting Herod's hyperbolic persona not only as tyrant but also as necrophiliac, Middleton's protagonist signifies as both quasi-comic overreacher (Herod as would-be idol) and as worshipper of the dead (Herod as idolater), a combination that underscores the iconoclastic connection between overvaluation of the self and overvaluation of the material body. It is this ideological emphasis that Massinger's play, based directly on a narrative from Josephus, replicates ten years later.

Because of the sensational manner in which he exercises power, the Tyrant dominates the main action of *The Second Maiden's Tragedy*. After usurping the throne, he claims as his Queen a chaste Lady, betrothed to the rightful King, Govianus. The Lady kills herself rather than submit to the Tyrant's will; the Tyrant, refusing to accept the Lady's death and vowing to reverse it, violates her tomb, steals her corpse and threatens to make love to it. The Ghost of the Lady, through the agency of Govianus, orchestrates the rescue of her corpse before the Tyrant can carry out his design; and, in a spectacular dénouement, the Tyrant dies after kissing the cosmeticised corpse whose lips have been poisoned by Govianus. The final passages of the play restore Govianus to the throne.[21]

Traditionally, the central conflict between the Lady (via her surrogate, Govianus) and the Tyrant has been interpreted allegorically as the triumph of chastity over lust.[22] To be sure, the Lady represents herself as a saint with Govianus as her holy avenger, and virtually everyone at the court identifies the Tyrant as obsessed and depraved. Further, the death of the Tyrant in the final scene, the reintegration of the Lady's body and soul, and the restoration of Govianus to the throne would appear to reinstate the moral order the Tyrant has usurped. But because, wittingly or unwittingly, the play itself deconstructs its own ideological oppositions, this allegorical framework serves as a template for a much less straightforward representation of idol worship, and the supposed resolution seems awkward and formulaic.[23]

Much of the ideological confusion in the play derives from dividing the figure of the Lady into two irreconcilable personae: her sainted spirit or ghost, and her desecrated corpse.[24] These divisions make clear that the Lady's corpse is without spirit, or, from an iconoclast's perspective, dead. Yet the desperation with which the Lady's spirit seeks to rescue this corpse and the intense jealousy that Govianus feels at the prospect of its violation by the Tyrant confuse the boundaries between good and evil, living and dead, saint and strumpet. The play may demonise the Tyrant as monster, but the presumed forces of virtue ultimately prove complicit in his transgression.

As ostensible foil to the Tyrant, Govianus, the rightful King, is also committed to the worship of a material idol. Interestingly, the sexual competition that initially links these adversaries is exacerbated when the Lady's suicide removes her body, the object of rival desires, from the scene. Shortly after her death, Govianus addresses the Lady's dead body as 'thou

delicious treasure of mankind' (3.1.244), and in a curious anticipation of
the Tyrant's own final embraces, caresses it: 'I will kiss thee / After death's
marble lip' (3.1.250–1). Later, his exaltation in the Lady's ghost is not
unlike that of the Tyrant in her corpse. Upon first viewing the ghost,
Govianus feels a 'fever' worth more than 'all the pleasures of ten thousand
ages' (4.4.52–3); moreover, he seems unmoved by the fate of her corpse
until the Lady goads his sexual jealousy:

> Is it thy mind to have me seized upon
> And borne with violence to the tyrant's bed,
> There forced unto the lust of all his days? (94–6)

>   I am now at court
> In his own private chamber. There he woos me
> And plies his suit to me with as serious pains
> As if the short flame of mortality
> Were lighted up again in my cold breast:
> Folds me within his arms and often sets
> A sinful kiss upon my senseless lip ... (4.4.66–72)

To a significant degree, then, Govianus's attachment to a spirit he envisages
in material terms and to whom he has an overtly sensual devotion com-
promises his outrage at the Tyrant's necrophilia. Ultimately, it is not in the
interests of the Tyrant or Govianus to forfeit his sexual claim to the Lady
by accepting the consequences of her death: neither a mouldering corpse
nor a decorporealised ghost serves their respective purposes.[25]

But the function of Govianus as mirror/foil is most striking in the
dénouement, when (in disguise) he would redeem the Lady's corpse by
desecrating it. While obeying the Tyrant's command to 'hide death upon
her face' (5.2.81) by painting the Lady's features, Govianus acknowledges
that his act is sacrilegious: 'A religious trembling shakes me by the hand /
And bids me put by such unhallowed business, / But revenge calls for't'
(5.2.91–3). Still, he is willing to risk his own spiritual integrity in order
to prevent the Tyrant from despoiling, and thereby possessing, the Lady's
body. His final taunt is that of the tainted avenger who rationalises sacrilege
in terms of his proprietary claim on the Lady's ghost:

>   Doom me, Tyrant.
> Had I feared death, I'd never appeared noble
> To seal this act upon me, which e'en honours me
> Unto my mistress' spirit. It loves me for't. (5.2.146–9)

But if Govianus is implicated in the unholy desire of the Tyrant, it is
the Lady herself who stokes their passion by establishing her dead body
as a kind of trophy. In her first appearance as ghost, the Lady stresses to
Govianus the urgency of rescuing her corpse from rape, although it is un-

clear how the status of the corpse can affect the salvation (and presumably the sainthood) that she has already won:

> *On a sudden, in a kind of noise like a wind, the doors clattering, the tombstone flies open, and a great light appears in the midst of the tomb; his* LADY, *as went out* [that is, as she last appeared], *standing just before him all in white, stuck with jewels, and a great crucifix on her breast.* (S.D. 4.42.1–4)

Inexplicably, at least from an iconoclastic perspective, the Lady implies that defilement of her corpse is capable of cancelling her self-sacrificial suicide[26] and of disturbing the tranquillity of her afterlife:

> The peace that death allows me is not mine;
> The monument is robbed. Behold, I'm gone;
> My body taken up. (60–2)
>
> My rest is lost; thou must restore't again. (79)

Even Govianus is initially puzzled that the Lady's spirit needs defending:

> Welcome! Who wrongs the spirit of my love?
> Thou art above the injuries of blood;
> They cannot reach thee now. (55–7)[27]

By the end of the play, however, Govianus has adopted the Lady's premise as his justification for murdering the Tyrant: 'thy abuser falls, and *has no pow'r / To vex thee farther now*' (5.2.162–3, my italics).

The Lady's overvaluation of her corpse unavoidably evokes the Catholic fixation with materiality so inimical to reformists, an association reinforced in the play by references to purgatory, Sanctus bells, Latin prayers and rosaries, as well as to the Lady's own 'jewels' and 'great crucifix'. To be sure, the play's Catholic ambience is hardly surprising considering its subject matter. None the less, the spirit 'all in white', who represents the supernatural antidote to the Tyrant's transgression and who orchestrates his downfall, should not, theoretically, be infected with his sin. Fundamentally at issue here is whether it was possible for Jacobean drama to address the contentious issue of idolatry without seeming to conflate conflicting ideologies through its use of Catholic trappings.[28]

But the morally ambiguous representations of Govianus and the Lady develop primarily as a function of their responses to the Tyrant's annihilating autonomy,[29] the benchmark against which idolatrous and anti-idolatrous stances must be measured in the play. From the outset, the Tyrant fixates on the Lady as the sole signifier of his desires: 'There was but one / In whom my heart took pleasure (amongst women), / One in the whole creation ...' (1.1.10–12). Without her, 'If it were possible to be less than nothing, / I wake the man you seek for' (141–2). The intensity of the Tyrant's longing prompts him to configure his sexual conquest of the Lady as a form of religious commitment – she is his 'heart's saint' (2.3.109), his 'blessed object' (4.3.59). But her resistance and subsequent suicide challenge this idealising fantasy, and the Tyrant retaliates by establishing, through violent means, a fetishistic surrogate for the Lady's living body over which he has absolute power. Initially, he would transcend the limitations of his humanity through an erotic investment in a material icon; by the time of his death, he has hypostatised materiality itself as antecedent to spirit and his own erotic energy as a life-giving force.

Throughout the play, the Tyrant's fixation is continually betrayed by his dependence on the sensory perception of external forms – he must always have his Lady in *sight*:

> Methinks the day e'en darkens at her absence.
> I stand as in a shade, when a great cloud
> Muffles the sun … (1.1.212–14)

> I must not miss her; I want her sight too long. (2.3.3)

> I've lost the comfort of her sight forever. (4.2.30)

> I cannot keep from sight of her so long.
> I starve mine eye too much. (5.2.6–7)[30]

To be deprived of 'her sight' is tantamount to standing 'upon a frozen mountain, / Without the confines' of the promised 'kingdom' (1.1.144–5, 142), a kind of death-in-life. Paradoxically, the Tyrant seeks deliverance from this torturous alienation in the disinterment of the Lady's cold and lifeless body, and he welcomes the pale light that fills the darkened crypt as a resurgence, albeit in a less resplendent form, of her influence:

> O, the moon rises! What reflection
> Is thrown about this sanctified building
> E'en in a twinkling! How the monuments glister,
> As if death's palaces were all massy silver
> And scorned the name of marble! Art thou cold?
> I have no faith in't yet; I believe none. (4.3.80–5)

In the absence of the Lady, the Tyrant is 'less than nothing'; his 'new joy' (4.2.33) is to find that her lost presence remains visible to him in her corpse:

> O blessed object!
> I never shall be weary to behold thee;
> I could eternally stand thus and see thee. (59–61)

The pleasure of spiritual fornication, of beholding the 'blessed object', is not, however, enough for the Tyrant: living or dead, the Lady-as-idol incites his carnal appetites as well. For him, the pleasures of sight and touch are, in fact, indivisible, as seen earlier in his violent response to the Lady's rejection ('Force shall help nature' [2.3.74]), and in the mode of punishment that he devises for his sexual rival:

> Nay, more, to vex his soul give command straight
> They [Govianus and the Lady] be divided into several rooms,
> Where he may only have a sight of her,
> To his mind's torment, but his arms and lips
> Locked up like felons from her. (1.1.232–6)

By 'resurrecting' the Lady, the Tyrant has condemned himself to a similar fate so long as he acknowledges the taboo against necrophilia. That he will not do so is already apparent in the grim resolve with which he addresses the soldiers who accompany him to the crypt: 'Death nor the marble prison my love sleeps in / Shall keep her body locked up from mine arms' (4.2.48–9).[31]

As the Tyrant's desire intensifies, so do his fantasies of power. He would pursue his idolatrous passion through a godlike aggrandisement of himself: the corpse will come alive through an act of his will. Alluding to Herod's example ('Yet he preserved her body dead in honey, / And kept her long after her funeral' [4.3.119–20]), he first appropriates external artifice as a means of validating his fantasy:

> But I'll unlock the treasure house of art
> With keys of gold, and bestow all on thee ... (4.3.121–2)

> I can see nothing to be mended in thee
> But the too constant paleness of thy cheek ... (5.2.27–8)

> And as in such a season men will force
> A heat into their bloods with exercise,
> In spite of extreme weather, so shall we
> By art force beauty on yon lady's face
> Though death sit frowning on't a storm of hail
> To beat it off. Our pleasure shall prevail ... (107–12)

Unlike the gilded surface of the painted statue, however, the cosmeticised face of the corpse will not be lifelike 'sev'n year hence' (5.2.26), and the Tyrant's continued 'sight' of the Lady ultimately will require the intervention of a more powerful kind of art.

Although the question that roils the play is whether the Tyrant will have sexual intercourse with the Lady's corpse, as the Lady's spirit fears, this threat is not imminent until the Tyrant moves to resuscitate the corpse with his own libidinal – or, as his fantasy would have it, creative – energy.[32] At the outset of this final desecration, with the corpse 'decked / In all the glorious riches of our palace' (5.2.8–9) and seated in a chair, so that the court may '*make obeisance*' (S.D. 13.4–5), the Tyrant acknowledges that paint can neither reverse the body's corruption nor permeate the 'everlasting frost hangs now upon her' (106). Nevertheless, in an about-face that is also a reprise of his earlier threat to rape the living Lady ('Force shall help nature' [2.3.74]), the Tyrant resolves to suborn art to his implacable will:

> Keep her up;
> I'll have her swoon no more; there's treachery in't.
> Does she not feel warm to thee?
> *Gov.*   Very little, sir.
> *Tyr.* The heat wants cherishing, then. Our arms and lips
> Shall labour life into her. Wake, sweet mistress!
> 'Tis I that call thee at the door of life. (115–20)

In this travesty of divine creation, the soul no longer signifies: as the Tyrant claimed earlier, 'The house is hers; the soul is but a tenant' (5.2.3). He would thus 'renew heat / Within her bosom' (96–7), regenerate her corporeal form with the fire of his own passion, insisting that whereas ordinary fire cannot 'burn back again ... hard, tough bodies' from 'dead ashes' (101–2), desire can. It is not, finally, the awareness of his impending death from the poisoned kiss that will bring the Tyrant to despair, but the appearance of the Lady's invincible spirit as witness to the insubstantiality of her tenant-less corpse: '*Tyr.* I called not thee, thou *enemy to firmness, / Mortality's earthquake!*' (153–4, my italics).

By exposing the Tyrant's belief in the primacy of materiality as delusional, this final sequence supports the homily's charge that for a man to engage in sexual relations with a woman whose artifice masks spiritual emptiness (that is, a strumpet) is to surrender to corruption, both moral and physical. The Tyrant's necrophiliac transgression is distinctive, however, in that he would possess a strumpet of his own making, a contaminated version of a dead body others regard as saintly and that he himself would bring to life. Further, whereas the incipient death that lurks beneath the mask of the living strumpet exists only *in potentia*, the Tyrant's strumpet, represented as dead, is already, as it were, unmasked. There is, then, a curious inversion of the homily's exemplum in the play's dénouement: the Tyrant purports to transform the Lady's corpse *back* into the living body of the painted strumpet.

The verbal and visual imagery of the scene underscores the horror of this inversion. When the Lady's corpse is carried on stage '*dressed up in black velvet which sets out the paleness of the hands and face*' (S.D. 5.2.13.1–2), it already appears unnatural, and the *Song* which accompanies this entrance urges the audience to think of the body as putrefying:

> O, what is beauty, that's so much adored?
> A flatt'ring glass that cozens her beholders.
> One night of death makes it look pale and horrid;
> The dainty preserved flesh, how soon it moulders. (14–17)

The Lady's 'dainty preserved flesh' (probably whitened with lead powder or paint) is thus described as 'horrid' *before* Govianus desecrates her face with yet another layer of artifice. After the completion of this 'unhallowed business', the supposedly mouldering corpse, falsely vivified with poisonous and corrosive cosmetics, would, one assumes, look ghoulish – the Tyrant's corpse-strumpet reconstructed as primordial death-mask.[33] Significantly, when the Tyrant kisses the poisoned lips of the Lady, he is unable to distinguish the 'evil scent' (122) of the poison from that of the corpse.

In the production of the play by the King's Men (1611–12?), the symbolic status of the corpse was further destabilised as a result of doubling the roles of Richard Robinson, a boy actor who played both the Lady and the Lady's spirit, dressed, respectively, in black and in white.[34] Prior to her suicide, the Lady appears 'clad in black' (S.D. 1.1.111.1–2) to protest the usurpation of Govianus, so that the brilliant white of the apparition attests to the primacy of her living spirit over that of her dead body. But the point of this contrast would have been at least partly subverted in the King's Men's production by spectator recognition of Robinson's shift, and more seriously disturbed by the confused colour-coding of the dénouement, where the Lady's spirit appears 'in the same form as the Lady is dressed in the chair' (S.D. 5.2.152.1–2), which is to say, the corpse, spectacularly decked 'in *black* velvet' (S.D. 13.1, my italics). Here, the black costuming connects the spirit not only to the former body of the Lady, but also to its depraved transformation into the Tyrant's idol. Thus although the final visual emblem of the play suggests the reunification of the divided Lady ('*The Spirit … stays to go out with the body, as it were attending it*' [S.D. 205.1–3]), it also implicates the ghost in the wanton and unnatural degradation of the now murderous corpse.

These ideological confusions are, in fact, exacerbated throughout the scene by the strategies of its staging. For the Tyrant's court to pay homage to his enthroned idol, as he commands, the corpse must occupy a prominent position on stage that would help fix the audience's full attention on the sensational business of painting its face.[35] During this process, antithetical visual images of the Lady, as saint and strumpet, blur or converge, finally coming to rest, as it were, in the indeterminacy of the ghoulish mask. But although these turns and shifts provide a stunning visual metaphor for the categorical confusions of idolatry, it is, after all, the Lady's body that has become the emblem of the strumpet, and the Lady's corpse that the Tyrant is on the cusp of violating. The homily against idolatry may conflate the statues of the Blessed Virgin Mary (saint) and the goddess Venus (strumpet) as equally whorish in their function as idols, but here the Tyrant's *delusion* of the corpse as idol is represented by the same body – the saint's body – that is in league with the saint's soul to vanquish this delusion.

In addition, the meta-theatrical effects of the transvestite convention, coupled with the Tyrant's explicit love-making, invest the corpse with complicated sexual nuances at both the conclusion of the play and in the earlier tomb scene. The Tyrant crosses a sacrosanct boundary when he enfolds the dead Lady in his arms in 5.1. and kisses her, imposing, as it were, his contaminating imprint on her body. But in 5.2, this invasive act is immediately preceded by the visually compelling painting of the corpse – or more precisely, the painting of a boy actor already made up to resemble a woman. By evoking the role of cosmetics in the theatre's own construction (and displacement) of gender categories, this sequence emphasises the artificiality of the corpse's supposed sexual allure – the boy beneath the saint, the strumpet and the woman. When the Tyrant fondles a body in which the distinctions among these images are blurred, a body that is also represented as dead, he generates an erotic *frisson* with cross- and trans-gendered, as well as transgressive, valences.

But the most obtrusive of the meta-theatrical interventions in this climactic sequence of events is the representation of the dead body itself through the agency of the sentient actor. As necrophiliac lover in the tradition of Herod, the Tyrant represents the undisguised desire to unite one's being directly with death – a kind of ur-idolatry. That is, rather than confusing the dead image for the living being, as would an ordinary idolater, the Tyrant *recognises* the manifest presence of death in his idol but defiantly seeks to subsume and transform it. From this perspective the poisoned kiss signifies, quite literally, the originary moment in which the Tyrant fails to overwhelm – or in the imagery of the scene, to rape – death. But because the theatrical corpse can be 'performed' only by a living body, layered in artifice that cannot be disassembled, what should serve as the ultimate expose of the horror of idolatry – the literal embrace of putrefaction – looks more like an enactment of its dynamics.

Thus it would seem that the ideological confusions of *The Second Maiden's Tragedy* foreclosed the possibility of doctrinal orthodoxy despite the play's ostensible condemnation of idolatry. At the same time, however, these confusions, legitimated by the play's purported iconoclasm, greatly enlarged the possibilities of affective experience for spectators. For example, the monstrosity (and foolishness) of the Tyrant served to distance the horror of necrophilia at the same time that Govianus's erotic investment in a corporeal corpse brought it closer. So too the multiple personae of the (cross-dressed) Richard Robinson, by subverting the allegorical opposites he represented, served up a titillating compound of holiness, eroticism and ghoulishness. Throughout the play, in fact, the monochromatic represen-tation of the Tyrant provides an ideological constant that in effect obfuscates the play's many invitations to spectators to identify vicariously with the transgressive and the taboo.

Still more fundamentally, as I suggested earlier, early modern theatricality unavoidably foregrounded the absence of those indeterminate phenomena that escape the parameters of any system of signification. The Lady might announce herself as spirit, but the actor's body was all too visible (and possibly the same body as that of her corpse). The Song that described the corpse in the chair might warn of putrefaction, but the living body of the boy actor could not pretend to rot. Yet the other-worldly and the generative dead terrify *because* they are unrepresentable, and this underlying recognition or intuition resonates compellingly in the human subject. By performing its own failure to represent the corpse as idol, *The Second Maiden's Tragedy* affirmed, however indirectly or unwittingly, the failure of signification itself to harness the unknown.

3. The Duke of Milan (c. 1621–2)[36]

Like its predecessor, Massinger's play examines the dynamics of idolatry through necrophiliac transgression, but does so directly only in the last scene, which is modelled after the dénouement of *The Second Maiden's Tragedy*. The prior action of the play comprises a selection of incidents from two accounts by Josephus (in *Antiquities* and *The Jewish War*) of Herod's relationship with his second wife, Mariamne. Specifically, the play features Herod's besotted devotion to Mariamne, his secret injunction that his wife be killed in the event of his own death, his rage at learning of the revelation of his injunction and of her reputed adultery, Mariamne's defiant denial of wrongdoing and Herod's distraction in the aftermath of her execution.[37] Although Josephus makes no overt reference to necrophilia, his description of Herod's 'madness' is not inconsistent with the Talmudic legend, nor with Massinger's adaptation of Middleton's last scene.[38]

Rather than allegorising aspects of the Herod legend as *The Second Maiden's Tragedy* did, Massinger's play resituates the Herod/Mariamne narrative in sixteenth-century Italy and substitutes contemporary political rivalries for those of the Romans.[39] As Duke of Milan, Ludovico Sforza, the Herod figure, is involved in a threatening territorial war with Charles V, King of Spain and Holy Roman Emperor, which he neglects in the interests of his personal pleasure.[40] During one scene (probably inspired by an incident in Josephus), Sforza does show himself the superior statesman in a confrontation with Charles.[41] But his briefly glimpsed nobility only underscores the play's emphasis on his habitual estrangement from public responsibility and his acquiescence in a kind of sexual enslavement.

Unlike the solipsistic obsession of Middleton's Tyrant, however, Sforza's passion is reciprocated, at least initially, by his idol, Marcelia (Mariamne).[42] Marcelia is thereby implicated in Sforza's idolatry not as a passive or helpless object (such as a statue or as the corpse that she will become) but as partner and would-be goddess. Indeed, Marcelia is more supercilious and intractable than Josephus's Mariamne,[43] qualities that underscore her presumption in believing herself worthy of idolatry, as well as her later stubbornness in resisting Sforza's jealous despotism. Because the pride of both the lovers is as excessive as their passion, Marcelia's ultimate destruction at the hands of the more powerful Duke seems foreordained, the inevitable consequence of idol-making 'turn[ed] backwards' (5.1.22).

Prior to the unravelling of their illusion, however, the lovers idealise their sexual desire as a holy excess – rare, transcendent and inaccessible to ordinary mortals. Their glorification of desire is repeatedly conveyed in metaphors of feasting / consumption that conflate bodily appetites with transcendent experience. Sforza's first lines establish this trope: 'You are the mistress of the feast, sit here; / O my soul's comfort!' (1.3.11–12). Certainly, neither Marcelia nor Sforza has any inclination to 'feed / On those gross cates' (76–7) that satisfy the earth-bound appetites of the attendant courtiers. Rather, in an idolatrous inversion that attempts to dematerialise sensory experience, Sforza boasts that he (and, by inference, Marcelia) 'banquets with / *Immortal* viands ta'en in at his eyes' (77–8), '*immortal* nectar' taken from 'those sweet lips' (205, my italics).

Further, it is Marcelia's 'amorous heat' (3.3.116), another kind of bodily sensation, that indisputably establishes her sanctity in the eyes of Sforza. For him, the sensory excess of the feast reenacts their wedding night and the initial discovery of their uncommon passion:

> No night to me
> But is a bridal one, where Hymen lights
> His torches fresh, and new; and those delights,
> Which are not to be cloth'd in airy sounds,
> Enjoy'd, beget desires as full of heat,
> And jovial fervour, as when first I tasted
> Her virgin fruit. Blest night! And be it number'd
> Amongst those happy ones, in which a blessing
> Was, by the full consent of all the stars,
> Conferr'd upon mankind. (42–51)

If Sforza here presumptuously recasts his sexual 'fervour' as 'a blessing ... / Conferr'd upon mankind', Marcelia's passion is likewise reified as a cleansing force: 'Never wife met with a purer heat her husband's fervour' (1.3.22–3).[44] Indeed, Sforza boasts that '[Marcelia's] goodness doth disdain comparison' (4.3.29), that 'had angels sexes, / The most would be such wom[a]n' (53–4) and that ordinary women 'are not worthy / To fall as sacrifices to appease her' (160–1). Sforza's encapsulating metaphor for his wife, put to an unanticipated test in the play's final scene, would inscribe her passion as generator and guarantor of immortality: Marcelia is a 'phoenix of perfection' (26), with superhuman power to renew herself, and him, in the 'fire' or ecstasy of their physical union.

Marcelia herself contributes to Sforza's image-making. Elevating her 'strong desire' (58) to the status of divine gift, granted in response to 'vows, and prayers' (61), she would stamp her sexuality with a heavenly imprimatur. Even Marcelia's overt displays of passion are accompanied by protestations of piety:

> *Marcelia.*   By these lips,
> Which, pardon me, that I presume to kiss –
> *Sforza.* O swear, for ever swear!
> *Marcelia.*   I ne'er will seek
> Delight, but in your pleasure; and desire
> When you are sated with all earthly glories,
> And age and honours make you fit for heaven,
> That one grave may receive us.
> *Sforza.*   'Tis believ'd,
> Believ'd, my blest one. (68–75)

When the 'libidinous beast' Francisco attempts to seduce her ('I am no monster, and you but a woman' [2.1.288, 283]), Marcelia is self-righteously intent on pointing out the moral chasm between them: 'I am yet / Pure and unspotted in my true love to him [Sforza]; / …For thyself, thou art / A thing, that equal with the devil himself / I do detest, and scorn' (411–13).[45]

The view of Marcelia in Sforza's court, however, is entirely different. To the courtiers, Marcelia is a bewitching whore who has entrapped Sforza in a degrading and effeminising dotage: 'he is her creature, / For never man so doted' (1.1.102). Repeatedly, critics of the lovers use the term 'dotage' – which could signify (singly or in combination) excessive affection, stupidity or mental impairment due to age – to describe Sforza's passion.[46] In a display of contrariness, Marcelia herself begins to echo the judgements of her enemies after she learns of Sforza's injunction:

> And something I may do to try his temper;
> At least to make him know a constant wife
> Is not so slav'd to her husband's doting humours,
> But that she may deserve to live a widow
> Her fate appointing it. (3.3.78–82)

>   Was I born
> T'observe his humours, or, because he dotes,
> Must I run mad? (4.2.3–5)

Marcelia's most severe denunciation of her lover evokes her description of Francisco as 'libidinous beast', inferring, if unwittingly, that their own idealised passion must have been bestial:

in troth, you are too great a doter;
And there is more of beast in it than man.
Let us love temperately; things violent last not,
And too much dotage rather argues folly
Than true affection. (4.1.127–31)

Sforza himself is keenly aware of his loss of autonomy[47] and occasionally recognises his need to 'shake off / The fetters of fond dotage' (3.3.148–9),[48] but for the most part Sforza defines dotage (as he does transcendence) in narrowly sexual terms. Presumably exempt from the twin threats of impotence and cuckoldry, commonly associated with aged dotards, Sforza is none the less careful to maintain a strong image of virility. Indeed, at one point he castigates an old courtier (who has supposedly slandered Marcelia) as contemptible because sexually impotent:

> Let me go,
> I scorn to touch him; he deserves my pity,
> And not my anger. Dotard! …
> Lock up thy own wife, fool, that must take physic
> From her young doctor – physic, upon her back,
> Because thou hast the palsy in that part
> That makes her active. (4.3.89–91, 97–100)

When confronted with Marcelia's presumed adultery and his own cuckoldry, however, Sforza in his rage is acutely conscious of a helplessness that is not unlike that of the sexually castrated courtier:

> No wise man ever – taught by my example –
> Hereafter use his wife with more respect
> Than he would do his horse that does him service;
> Base woman being in her creation made
> A slave to man. But like a village nurse
> Stand I now cursing … (4.3.230–5)

Still, by focusing his scorn chiefly on the perfidy of women, Sforza elides the connection between idolatry and sexual enslavement – the dynamics of his own dotage.

Further, Sforza's fury is murderous, however feminised and enfeebled he may appear in his own descriptions. Interestingly, his directive to 'drag [Marcelia] hither by the hair' (243) resonates ominously and ironically with the language of the rapacious soldiers of Charles V, who earlier routed his army. With grim relish, these would-be pillagers fantasised about raping the Milanese noblewomen who scorned them:

> *Hernando.*   I would be tousing [pawing]
> Their fair madonnas … I have seen 'em stop
> Their scornful noses first, then seem to swoon
> At sight of a buff jerkin, if it were not

Perfum'd, and hid with gold; yet these nice wantons,
Spurr'd on by lust, cover'd in some disguise,
To meet some rough court-stallion, and be leap'd,
Durst enter into any common brothel,
Through all varieties of stink contend there;
Yet praise the entertainment.
Medina.   I may live
To see the tatter'd'st rascals of my troop
Drag them out of their closets, with a vengeance,
When neither threat'ning, flattering, kneeling, howling,
Can ransom one poor jewel, or redeem
Themselves from their blunt wooing. (3.1.30–1; 35–48)

Such brutal revenge is precisely the fate that Sforza had most feared for Marcelia after first receiving news of his military defeat:

The city ta'en, the kennels running blood,
The ransack'd temples falling on their saints;
My mother, in my sight, toss'd on their pikes,
And sister ravish'd … (1.3.184–7)

But now Sforza would enact a similar retribution on his own 'fair madonna', destroying her ascendant status through physical assault and public humiliation.[49] After stabbing Marcelia, Sforza, like the soldiers, is 'flesh'd with spoil' (1.3.181) – the once incomparable body of his lover, mutilated and degraded by his own hand.[50]

As visual emblem, Marcelia's bloodied body on stage gives the lie to Sforza's apotheosis of her sexual passion – her 'fervour' or 'amorous heat' – as transcendent. Prior to the murder, Sforza imagines Marcelia's desire as eternally regenerative, like the fire of the phoenix; later in the play he attempts desperately to retrieve this ideal by insisting once again that 'Cupid's fire-brand' can never be extinguished:

I confess [to be] far, far unworthy)
To touch this snow-white hand. How cold it is!
This once was Cupid's fire-brand, and still
'Tis so to me. How slow her pulses beat too!
Yet in this temper she is all perfection,
And mistress of a heat so full of sweetness,
That blood of virgins in their pride of youth
Are balls of snow or ice compar'd unto her. (5.2.62–9)

But if as idol and as corpse Marcelia is 'mistress of a heat' that even un-contaminated virgins cannot match, not so Marcelia the wanton, whose sexual excess bears witness to the common belief that sexual intercourse results in a substantial loss of blood, and consequently heat, in the body:

Impudence!
How ugly thou appear'st now! Thy intent

> To be a whore leaves thee not blood enough
> To make an honest blush ... (4.3.270–3)[51]

Sforza's idolatrous logic affirms that if the blood of Marcelia the sex goddess is paradoxically virginal, then the blood of Marcelia the whore is fit only for the soldiers' 'kennels', to run with that of other 'nice wantons' in an indiscriminate confluence of contamination.

By stabbing Marcelia, Sforza the 'Fury' (251) also collapses the tenuous distinction between lust as 'holy' passion and lust as untempered rage, exposing sexual excess and slaughter as intimately related modes of violence. Significantly, this same linkage is represented in a minor register through the figure of Eugenia, Francisco's sister and Sforza's former mistress, whom he has rejected for Marcelia and who appears in the play (in Act 5 only) cross-dressed as a man. As a despoiled virgin, Eugenia lives 'branded / In the forehead for his [Sforza's] whore, the scorn and shame / Of all good women' (5.1.47–9), but she has refused to accept her social stigma. Having converted her passion for Sforza into hatred, Eugenia describes her fantasy for revenge in a twisted image of gestation and delivery that emphasises her cross-dressing as an assumption of male perogative:

> There's no passion that
> A maid so injur'd ever could partake of
> But I have dearly suffer'd. These three years,
> In my desire, and labour of revenge,
> ... I have endur'd the throes
> Of teeming women, and will hazard all
> Fate can inflict on me, but I will reach
> Thy heart, false Sforza! ... Vengeance, arm'd with fury,
> Possess me wholly now! ... the scandal ... can never
> Be wash'd off from our house but in his blood. (5.1.54–61, 65–6, 70–1)

Berating Francisco for 'base, unmanly fears' (68) and exalting in her own 'strange metamorphosis' (67), Eugenia would, like Sforza, transform the blood of passion into a lust for blood, and empty or bleed the contaminated veins of her lover in a supposedly purgative ritual.

The final scene of the play, a macabre inversion of the Eucharistic feast, consolidates the governing conceits of feasting/consumption and of blood/heat in the ceremonially enthroned corpse of Marcelia. Her lifeless but painted lips, as in a Black Mass, become the 'cup' or chalice from which Sforza, 'carousing deeply' (5.2.240–1), seeks sustenance: 'These lips invite too. I could ever feed / Upon these roses, they still keep their colour / And native sweetness' (210–12). Earlier, in another conjunction of pagan and Christian allusions, Sforza had begged his physicians ('you earthly gods' [49]), to restore Marcelia as Aesculapius did Hippolytus, performing 'a work / The saints will smile to look on, and good angels / Clap their celestial wings to give it plaudits' (57–9).[52] Appropriately enough, Sforza's challenge is answered by the *intrigant* Francisco, disguised as a Jewish doctor versed in the necromantic, or demonic arts, who offers to officiate, as it were, at a feigned resurrection:

> I am no god, sir,
> To give a new life to her; yet I'll hazard
> My head I'll work the senseless trunk t'appear
> To him as it had got a second being,
> Or that the soul that's fled from't, were call'd back,
> To govern it again. I will preserve it
> In the first sweetness, and by a strange vapour,
> Which I'll infuse into her mouth, create
> A seeming breath. I'll make her veins run high too,
> As if they had true motion. (140–9)

Francisco's cosmetic handiwork, what Pescara calls a 'miracle' (167),[53] is instead a pseudo-creation wrought by the transgressive transformation of Marcelia's 'senseless trunk' into a grotesque but inviting caricature of regenerated life – a caricature of Marcelia as phoenix.

Like the Tyrant, Sforza will die by embracing the double-death of corpse and poison, but here the contrast between Sforza's idealisation of Marcelia's dead body and Francisco's contemptuous insistence on its putrefaction serves to desecrate the corpse twice over. To the solicitous Sforza, who in his distraction would reinstate the murdered Marcelia as saint, the corpse is 'my good angel' (168), a precious and fragile cargo: 'Carefully, I beseech you; / The gentlest touch torments her, and then think / What I shall suffer' (47–9). But Francisco takes pleasure in ridiculing the 'trunk' as repugnant in its putrefaction, and in challenging Sforza's dotage in gross and unsparing language:

> [during the painting of the face]
> Your mouth smells sour too,
> But here is that shall take away the scent:
> A precious antidote old ladies use
> When they would kiss, knowing their gums are rotten. (188–90)

> [to Sforza] I am Francisco ...
> That would have whor'd this trunk when it had life,
> And after breath'd a jealousy upon thee
> As killing as those damps that belch out plagues
> When the foundation of the earth is shaken. (222, 225–8)

In an ugly demonstration of the inextricability of perfumed and putrefying flesh, Francisco reveals his reconstituted idol as an indecent version of Sforza's own – material proof, as it were, of Marianna's earlier summation of Marcelia: 'howsoe'er / She seems when she's made up, as she's herself, / She stinks above ground' (2.1.170–2).

Even in his death throes, however, Sforza refuses fully to relinquish his image of Marcelia as phoenix and Eucharistic cup. Instead, he turns the phoenix imagery against himself, so to speak, by offering the ashes of his own poisoned entrails as fiery, expiatory sacrifice: 'O now I feel / An Aetna in my entrails! ... / I burn, I burn! ... When I am ashes / Perhaps she'll be appeas'd ...' (245–6, 248, 261–2). Sforza's extreme self-abnegation is, of course, the obverse of his fury, which earlier in this scene he directed first towards the absent Francisco (who has not yet conducted his necromantic ritual), and then towards himself:

> And for that dog Francisco that seduc'd me,
> In wounding her, to rase a temple built
> To chastity and sweetness, let her know
> I'll follow him to hell, but I will find him,
> And there live a fourth Fury to torment him.
> Then, for this cursed hand and arm that guided
> The wicked steel, I'll have them, joint by joint,
> With burning irons sear'd off, which I will eat,
> I being a vulture fit to taste such carrion. (121–9)

Formerly nourished, as was the living Marcelia, on 'immortal viands', and hoping to extract even from her corpse a revitalising nectar, Sforza here describes the just and bloody punishment which the betrayal of his goddess has merited. In a violent and perverse reconstitution of his own metaphors of nourishment and renewal, Sforza, in hell, devours himself as a vulture devours the dead, cannibalistically obliterating his body and denying its regenerative potential. The blood of sacrifice and the blood of slaughter thereby merge in a single, powerfully nihilistic image of spiritual suicide.[54]

Because of its conceptual reliance on images of physical transformation and bodily process, especially that of the Eucharist, *The Duke of Milan* might be described as a more 'Catholic' play than *The Second Maiden's Tragedy*, that is, it resonates more strongly with rituals that emphasise the inextricability of body and soul. Sforza, the idolater, believes as a Catholic was thought to do in the viability of his idol: indeed, the materiality of Marcelia is an integral part of what makes her a goddess. Thus for Sforza, stabbing Marcelia, the 'cup' or chalice of life, is roughly analogous to desecrating a Host, and his cannibalistic self-punishment is consistent with this idea of sacrilege. In the *gestalt* of the play, however, what Sforza never recognises, despite his dying admission that 'My whole life was a frenzy' (258), is the connection between his passion and its anarchic consequences. Marcelia's bloodied corpse, the product of a murder, not a sacrifice, denies Sforza's fiction of her as sacramental phoenix. Living or dead, the idol

Marcelia is a carrier of death, her intoxicating nectar, like the wine of the drunken soldiers, an incitement to indiscriminate violence:

> We enter towns by force, and carve ourselves,
> Pleasure with pillage, and the richest wines,
> Open our shrunk-up veins, and pour into 'em
> New blood, and fervour. (3.1.18–21)

In sum, *The Duke of Milan* purports to advance two iconoclastic agendas: it renders with compelling immediacy the sensory temptations of anthropomorphic imaging; and it isolates the female body as the site of violence, or more precisely, as the bridge between sexuality and the bloody waste of war. Because both agendas depend chiefly on the representation of Marcelia, her function is markedly different from that of the Lady in *The Second Maiden's Tragedy*. As both saint *and* sex object, Marcelia collapses the roles imperfectly divided between the Lady and the Ghost, and as fully compliant partner in Sforza's idolatrous lust, rather than as spiritual adversary, she partakes directly in his sacrilege. Moreover, because Marcelia does not die until just before the final scene, she appears as lover throughout most of the action – a living version, as it were, of the Tyrant's sexual fantasy of the Lady. In Massinger's adaptation of the Herod legend, idolatry is thereby indistinguishable from lust in action.

As a consequence of this emphasis, the transvestite representation of Marcelia has a significant bearing on the play's symbolic structure. Certainly, the passionate exchanges between the lovers in the banquet scene (1.3) and the continual allusions by others to their behaviour suggest that Marcelia and Sforza did not stint in demonstrating their desire on the early modern stage.[55] If, to evoke Rainolds and his compeers once again, theatrical transvestism titillated by obfuscating the 'proper' object of desire, then the overt physicality of two male actors impersonating a heterosexual love affair throughout most of this play surely enhanced its erotic power. But in so far as such valences blurred Marcelia's fictional identity as woman, they also compromised her iconoclastic function as the symbolic site of violence. In short, because Marcelia is the *theatrical* counterpart of the concupiscent she-demons in the homily on idolatry, she does not measure up as sufficiently 'female' for a fully orthodox image.[56]

Further, in this play the ideological disruptions of shape-shifting extend well beyond the manipulations of transvestism. Interestingly, the changeable personae of Francisco, especially his mutation into diabolic magus, shift the primary onus for sacrilege away from Marcelia, and from Sforza as well, at the play's end.[57] Unlike Govianus, who hastily paints the face of the Lady's corpse with 'religious trembling', Francisco approaches his task with relish and an unseemly nastiness. Even Eugenia, the would-be murderess, recoils in horror at her brother's careless imperviousness to the perversity of his act:

> *Francisco.*   So, 'tis done.
> How do you like my workmanship?
> *Eugenia.*   I tremble;
> And thus to tyrannise upon the dead
> Is most inhuman ... (5.2.196–9)

Presumably, the primary business of the dénouement is to unveil Sforza's necrophilia, a transgression well beyond the sanctions of civilised behaviour. But ironically, Francisco's premeditated and outrageous hubris is worse:

> *All.*   Monster of men!
> *Francisco.*   Give me all attributes
> Of ill you can imagine, yet I glory
> To be the thing I was born. (220–2)
>
>   Farewell, sister.
> Now I have kept my word, torments I scorn;
> I leave the world with glory. (252–3)

The play's final judgement seems to be that cosmeticising a corpse – imposing an artificial animation, a ghastly semblance of life, on a being at the cusp of dissolution – is the ultimate desecration. The lust-driven idolatry of Sforza and Marcelia, culminating in Sforza's necrophiliac madness, is the damnable offence at the centre of the action. But Francisco would enter into an ominously uncharted space in an effort to ape an act of divine creation. By moulding a blasphemous analogue to Sforza's erotic hallucination from putrefying flesh, Francisco the 'monster' literally dips his dirty hands into the sacrosanct and terrifying liminality of the corpse.

Yet once again, as in *The Second Maiden's Tragedy*, the overdetermined staging of this atrocity delimits the theatre's potential for representing its horror. The final scene in *The Duke of Milan* thus raises a question like that of its counterpart in *The Second Maiden's Tragedy*, but in somewhat more emphatic form: was the representation of taboo a common topoi in the early modern theatre because it was likely to fall short of its potential? Or, to put it another way, did early modern performance conventions not only provide the theatrical industry with a defensive strategy against antitheatricalists, but also insulate the audience from too powerful a confrontation with the unspeakable?

Certainly, I would argue that in these two plays, performance conventions tend to obfuscate rather than enhance the dangers and attractions of the corpse. But as we have seen, this is not always the case in either play. For reasons he probably would not have recognised, Rainolds was right: the slipperiness of theatrical process was inherently subversive of categorical certainties so that even the heavy-handed representations of *The Second Maiden's Tragedy* and *The Duke of Milan* resonate beyond their ostensible boundaries. Moreover, any attempt to represent necrophilia in a reformist climate placed the theatre in a fundamentally untenable position. Since iconoclasts most feared Catholic preoccupation with liminality as a mode of animating matter, the corpse/idols of these plays called attention, however circumspectly, to an issue that reformists preferred to deny or ignore, that is, the possibility of a self-generating materiality.

On balance, then, the Middleton and Massinger plays are useful in anatomising the difficulties of staging the corpse as well as the slippages that inevitably proceed from any efforts to do so. In their own terms, of course, these plays do not 'fail'; on the contrary, their stagecraft seems in accord with their ideological emphases. But if the putrefying corpse is the very archetype of indeterminacy, and if the ostensible referent for the theatrical corpse is, as it were, a disembodied body on its way to becoming a not-body, an entity in the grips of a primordial – or, as Christianity would have it, transfigurating – process, then plays that presume to raise the spectre of *this* corpse must somehow alchemise the ingredients of theatrical representation into a headier and far more destabilising mix.

Notes

1. The *locus classicus* for this distinction is still Catherine Belsey's *Critical Practice* (London and New York: Routledge, 1980); but see also *The Subject of Tragedy: Identity and Difference in Renaissance Drama* (London and New York: Methuen, 1985), esp. Chapters 2–4, pp. 13–125. For a useful critique of conventional distinctions between realism, naturalism and ritual, see also Robert Weimann, *Shakespeare and the Popular Tradition in the Theater: Studies in the Social Dimension of Dramatic Form and Function*, ed. Robert Schwartz (Baltimore and London: Johns Hopkins University Press, 1978). For an important study of early modern concepts of inwardness and their representation in the English theatre, see Katharine Eisaman Maus, *Inwardness and Theater in the English Renaissance* (Chicago and London: University of Chicago Press, 1995). Maus argues that notwithstanding the 'shortcomings' of theatrical representation, inwardness is embedded there in 'a form of display that flaunts the limits of display' (210). My difference with Maus would be in the more positive value that I assign to meta-theatricality as a mode of representing the inexpressible.

2. In recent years, theatrical transvestism has served as a cultural crux or reference point for a broader examination of early modern gender differences and erotic practices. Among the seminal texts in this area of study are: Dympna Callaghan, *Shakespeare without Women: Representing Gender and Race on the Renaissance Stage* (London and New York: Routledge, 2000); Jean E.

Howard, 'Cross-Dressing, the Theatre, and Gender Struggle in Early Modern England', *Shakespeare Quarterly* 39: 4 (1988): 418–40; Jonathan Goldberg, *Sodometries: Renaissance Texts, Modern Sexualities* (Stanford, CA: Stanford University Press, 1992); Stephen Orgel, *Impersonations: The Performance of Gender in Shakespeare's England* (Cambridge: Cambridge University Press, 1996); Jeffrey Masten, *Textual Intercourse: Collaboration, Authorship, and Sexualities in Renaissance Drama* (Cambridge: Cambridge University Press, 1997); Valerie Traub, *Desire and Anxiety: Circulations of Sexuality in Shakespearean Drama* (London and New York: Routledge, 1992); and more recently, Traub's compendious and groundbreaking study, *The Renaissance of Lesbianism in Early Modern England* (Cambridge: Cambridge University Press, 2002).

3. See Peter Stallybrass, 'Transvestism and the "Body Beneath": Speculating on the Boy Actor', in *Erotic Politics: Desire on the Renaissance Stage*, ed. Susan Zimmerman (New York and London: Routledge, 1992), 64–83.

4. Catherine Belsey, 'Disrupting Sexual Difference: Meaning and Gender in the Comedies', in *Alternative Shakespeares*, ed. John Drakakis (London and New York: Methuen and Routledge, 1985), 166–90.

5. Rainolds, a distinguished theologian, corresponded with Gage, the leading writer of academic drama at Oxford, until 1593 when Gentili, Professor of Civil Law, took up the defence. See J. W. Binns, 'Women or transvestites on the English Stage? An Oxford controversy', *Sixteenth Century Journal*, 5:2 (1974): 95–120. Rainolds printed relevant letters from this correspondence as *Th' Overthrow of Stage-Plays* (London: 1599), ed. in facsimile reprint by J. W. Binns (New York: Johnson Reprint Corps., 1972).

6. Rainolds, *Th' Overthrow of Stage-Playes*, 34–5.

7. Elizabeth Bronfen, *Over Her Dead Body: Death, Femininity and the Aesthetic* (Manchester: Manchester University Press and New York: Routledge, 1992), 44.

8. See Stephen Greenblatt, 'Shakespeare Bewitched', in Susan Zimmerman, ed., *Shakespeare's Tragedies* (Basingstoke and London: Macmillan, 1998), 109–39.

9. For the unlikely possibility that the corpse in these scenes was a dummy, see note 35. There are, in fact, several plays, such as Chettle and Munday's *The Death of Robert Earl of Huntington* (1597–8), and John Marston's *Sophonisba* (1605), that feature corpses as idols with less pronounced or sustained necrophiliac overtones. Interestingly, Chapman's comedy *Monsieur d'Olive* (1604–5) also features a scene in which an actor/corpse is propped up in a chair to be worshipped.

10. Historically, there were three Herods who were often conflated in legend: Herod the Great, King of Judea, who met the Magi and was responsible for the Massacre of the Innocents; Herod Antipas, Tetrarch of Jerusalem (the son of Herod the Great by his fourth wife), who ordered the death of John the Baptist and conspired in the condemnation of Christ by Pontius Pilate; and Herod Agrippa, grandson of Herod the Great and his first wife Miriam, who was a persecutor of the early Church. See Maurice J. Valency, *The Tragedies of Herod and Mariamne* (New York: Columbia University Press, 1940), 33; and Barry Weller and Margaret W. Ferguson, eds., Elizabeth Cary's *The Tragedy of Miriam, The Fair Queen of Jewry* (Berkeley and Los Angeles: University of California Press, 1994), 20–2.

11. In *Of the Antiquities of the Jews*, Flavius Josephus provides the following account of Herod's death:

> This verie night the moon was ecclipsed, & *Herods* sicknesse grew more vehement. For God punished those sins which he had committed. For he was inflamed with a lent or slow fire, which to the outward sense seemed not so vehement, but inwardly searched and afflicted all his entrails ... Besides that, he had an vlcer in his bowels with a strange and furious colicke. His feet were swolne with moist and shining flegme, and his stomacke was no lesse affected also. His members rotted & were full of crawling wormes, with a filthie and no lesse troublesome Priapisme, accompanied with an intollerable stench: besides all this, he had a strong conuulsion of his nerues, and shortness of breath.

See the 1602 translation by Thomas Lodge, STC 14809, Book XVII, Chap. VIII, 448–9.

12. As a Jew who became a Roman citizen, the historian Joseph ben Matthias, or Flavius Josephus (37–100 AD), was fundamentally sympathetic to Roman rule. In these two works, his portrait of Herod details Herod's cruelty but also praises his brilliance and bravery as a politician and general. Originally written in Aramaic, Josephus's texts were among the first in the Renaissance to be printed in Greek, Latin and numerous vernaculars. For a summation of Josephus's account of Herod, see Weller and Ferguson, 19–20; Valency, 3–18.

13. In patristic commentary, Josephus's graphic description of Herod's fatal illness became the basis for increasingly elaborate versions of his death. The *Historica scholastica* of Peter Comestor, for example, following the models of Eusebius and Bede, emphasised the living putrefaction of Herod's limbs, an account which influenced the 'hideously realistic representation of Herod's death' (194) in the Benediktbeurern Christmas play. See Karl Young, 'The Christmas Play From Benediktbeurern', in *The Drama of the Medieval Church*, II (Oxford: Clarendon Press, 1933), 189–96; and Rosemary Woolf, *The English Mystery Plays* (Berkeley and Los Angeles: University of California Press, 1972), 209–10. That such exegetical additions to the legend of Herod were well known during the Reformation can be seen in the reference to Herod's death in *An Homily against Excess of Apparel*: '[God] overthrew Herod, who in his royal apparel, forgetting God, was smitten of an angel, and eaten up of worms' (*The seconde tome of homelyes*, STC 13663). See the facsimile reprint (fourth edition), of *Sermons or Homilies appointed to be read in churches in the time of Queen Elizabeth* (Oxford: Clarendon Press, 1816), 262.

14. This passage reads: 'He preserved her body in honey for seven years. Some say that he had intercourse with her, others that he did not. According to those who say that he had intercourse with her, his reason was to justify his desires. According to those who say that he did not have intercourse with her, his reason was that people might say that he had married a King's daughter' (I. Epstein, ed., *Baba Bathra I* [London: The Soncino Press, 1960], 3b). In the Talmud (but not in any of the accounts of Josephus), Mariamne kills herself after Herod's accusations of adultery. For a discussion of the influence of Jewish texts on Renaissance biblical scholarship, especially in England, see Debora Kuller Shuger, *The Renaissance Bible: Scholarship, Sacrifice, and Subjectivity* (Berkeley and Los Angeles: University of California Press, 1994), esp. 33–6.

15. In plays from the Chester, Coventry, York and Towneley cycles, Herod himself is prone to self-referential monologues praising his beauty and boasting of his power. See Woolf, 203–4.

16. For the progressive development of Herod as a farcical figure in the mystery plays, see Roscoe E. Parker, 'The Reputation of Herod in Early English Literature', *Speculum* 8 (1933): 59–67; and especially David Staines, 'To Out-Herod Herod: The Development of a Dramatic Character', in Clifford Davidson *et al.*, eds., *The Drama of the Middle Ages: Comparative and Critical Essays* (New York: AMS Press, Inc., 1982), 207–31. It is also possible that well-known iconographic features of Herod – his physical deformity, the cross-legged stance of the madman, the black face of the Saracen – were used in performances (both medieval and early modern) to undermine or demonise Herod's pre-eminence as king. See Penelope B. R. Doob, *Nebuchadnezzor's Children: Conventions of Madness in Middle English Literature* (New Haven, CT and London: Yale University Press, 1974), 109; and Valency, 28–30.

17. In her illuminating study, *Tragedies of Tyrants: Political Thought and Theater in the English Renaissance* (Ithaca, NY and London: Cornell University Press, 1990), Rebecca W. Bushnell situates 'the Vice [as] the Tyrant's double' within the tradition of 'moral ambidexterousness' characteristic of medieval drama: 'the tyrant's discontinuity implies a lack of coherence in the moral universe that his grotesque figure has come to dominate' (96–8, *passim*). Characteristically, Benjamin's commentary on the significance of the disordered Herod in the seventeenth century stresses the flamboyance of insanity as an analogue to the violence of history: 'Artists took great delight in painting the picture of him [Herod] falling into insanity, holding two babes in his hands in order to batter out their brains ... clearly what fascinated ... people [was] the seventeenth-century ruler, the summit of creation, erupting into madness like a volcano and destroying himself and his entire court' (70).

18. Although *The Second Maiden's Tragedy* has been attributed to at least six dramatists, most scholars identify Tourneur and Middleton as the most likely candidates. In her edition of the play (Manchester: Manchester University Press and Baltimore: Johns Hopkins University Press, 1978), Anne Lancashire argues that the preponderance of evidence favours Middleton (15–23), and the play is scheduled for inclusion in the forthcoming Oxford edition of Middleton's collected works. The only early modern text of the play is a manuscript (included in Lansdowne 807, ff.29–36), presumably a prompt-book for a performance by the King's Men (possibly at Blackfriars) in 1611, the date of the licence on the last page of text in the autograph of Sir George Buc, Master of the Revels from 1608 to 1622. Because, as Buc says, the manuscript 'hath no name inscribed', Buc supplied the title himself, along with at least two corrections to the text: at 5.2.167, he changes 'Your king's poisoned!' to 'I am poisoned!'; and at 3.1.61, he substitutes 'some men' for a phrase about 'great men' fearing death. Five addition slips to the manuscript are in the hand of the primary scribe: there are two or more additional correctors, including Buc and a hand that appears to be that of the playhouse reviser. The manuscript contains numerous alterations and excisions, none demonstrably authorial in origin. See Lancashire, 1–15, and Appendix A, 261–85. All references to the play are taken from Lancashire's edition.

19. The passage from Josephus reads: 'And at this time in the night season accompanied only with his most trustie friends, being verie warie that none of the people should know of it, he entred into the Sepulchre ... After the Sepulchre was thus violated, *Herods* house began to decay' (*Of the Antiquities of the*

Jews, in *The Famous & Memorable Workes of Iosephvs*, trans. Thomas Lodge [London: 1602], STC 14809, XVI.xi, p. 423; quoted in Lancashire, 295).

20. These lines are marked for excision in the manuscript by an unknown hand.

21. The subplot, which serves as an ostensible foil to the central action, features another sexual triangle in which Votarius, a friend of Anselmus, agrees to test the chastity of Anselmus' Wife, who succumbs to temptation. The adultery of Votarius and the Wife, together with the illicit affair of the Wife's waiting woman, lead to the deaths (in a single scene) of all five lovers. The 'flesh-market' (1.2.272) ambience of the subplot, its successive adulteries and betrayals, contrasts pointedly with the self-sacrifice of the chaste Lady, and functions, at least on one level, to throw her virtue into relief. Lancashire contends that the primary source of the subplot is an adaptation of the story of the Curious Impertinent in Part I of Cervantes' *Don Quixote* (1605), first printed in English in 1612, and possibly circulating in manuscript prior to that date (30–2). It is noteworthy, however, that Herod's temptation of Mariamne in similar circumstances, described by Josephus in *Antiquities* and *The Jewish War*, and appropriated by Massinger for *The Duke of Milan*, was a well-known part of the Herod legend. For an analysis of the structural relationship of the two plots, see Richard Levin, 'The Double Plot of *S.M.T.*', *Studies in English Literature*, 3 (1963): 219–31.

22. Lancashire is herself in this tradition. On the basis of a large compendium of materials, she argues that the play is heavily larded with references to saints' lives (her most persuasive case is made for Sophronia, whose literary history reaches from Eusebius to Foxe) and to the life of Christ. In Lancashire's view, the cumulative weight of these allusions suggests that the Lady functions as a Christ figure, a 'Jacobean', or 'secular' saint. For her discussion of saints' lives, see Introduction, 23–30, esp. 25–7; and '*The Second Maiden's Tragedy*: A Jacobean Saint's Life', *Review of English Studies*, n.s. 25, no. 99 (August 1974): 267–79, esp. 270–6. Although my own work on this play has led to quite different conclusions, I am greatly indebted to Lancashire for identifying the wide range of contemporary texts that may have served as sources or analogues for the play.

23. From a poststructuralist standpoint, the disjunction between allegorical framework and ambiguity of representation is implicit in the formal structure of allegory itself. That is, allegorical oppositions misrepresent the relationship of their signifiers (good/evil) as independent of each other, whereas such binaries are distinctively interdependent – each signifier can be understood only in relation to the other. Thus allegory (like language itself) would guarantee an intelligibility that its signifiers deny. Interestingly, when *The Second Maiden's Tragedy* is viewed through this theoretical lens, its allegorical absolutes seem in deliberate tension with its ambiguous representations, so that it may be said that both the conscious and the unconscious of the text challenge its structural framework.

24. The Lady, prior to her suicide in mid-play, may be viewed as a third persona. The contributions of stagecraft to the confusion of these personae are taken up later.

25. Bushnell's description of the symbiotic relationship between king and tyrant is relevant here: 'the image of the king is unimaginable without his reflection in the tyrant ... the difference between king and tyrant ... always ... threatens to collapse into identity' (22).

26. The religious controversy over the moral legitimacy of suicide as a means of forestalling rape is elided in this play. Govianus raises no moral objection to the Lady's decision to kill herself in 3.1, although he does express disapproval of the Wife's presumed suicide after the exposure of her adultery in 5.1.

27. These sentiments echo those of the Lady prior to her suicide, when she assures Govianus that her death will put her beyond the reaches of the Tyrant:

> His lust may part me from thee, but death, never;
> Thou canst not lose me there, for, dying thine,
> Thou dost enjoy me still. Kings cannot rob thee. (3.1.144–6)

28. Some references (or assumed references) to Catholicism have been excised from the manuscript, although in most instances it is difficult to know why. For example, allusions to Catholic doctrine (such as the one to Purgatory [2.1.156–7], and to the Virgin's Assumption and Coronation [5.2.195–205]) might have been viewed as unwelcome reminders of still popular beliefs, and/or as gratuitously offensive to Catholic spectators. Moreover, several of the excised passages were probably objectionable on other grounds as well: in 5.2, the crowning of the Lady's corpse by Govianus after his murder of the Tyrant had disturbing political implications quite apart from the iconography of the Virgin Mary as Queen. It is well to remember in this connection that Buc's is the only hand in the manuscript that can be confidently identified as the work of a censor, and that Buc made only two corrections (see note 18). None the less, the preponderance of manuscript cuts does suggest (as do Buc's) an effort to remove passages that might be construed as critical of the Jacobean court. For a classification of manuscript alterations by topic, see Lancashire, Appendix A, esp. 280.

29. My term is a paraphrase of Bushnell's description of Seneca's tyrant (34). Bushnell's analysis of Plato's tyrant, 'a man who gives free rein to desire' (13) also seems relevant to Middleton's protagonist (see 9–29), as do certain passages from *The Republic* itself, such as the following: 'There is a dangerous, wild, and lawless form of desire in everyone … It doesn't shrink from trying to have sex with a mother, as it supposes, or with anyone else at all, whether man, god, or beast' (*Plato/Republic*, trans. G. M. A. Grube, rev. C. D. C. Reeve [Indianapolis: Hackett Publishing Co., Inc., 1992], ix, 572b, 571d, 78).

30. Even the Lady herself is metonymically described as an eye: 'for where she goes / Her eye removes the court' (1.1.147–8).

31. In the tomb scenes (4.2 and 4.3) as well as elsewhere in the play, Middleton interpolates comedy at moments of great dramatic tension (as do the medieval Herod plays). Here, the Tyrant's despoliation of the tomb takes place amid the bawdy protests of his incredulous soldiers, which partially neutralise the Tyrant's necrophiliac threat:

> *Tyr.* Take up her body.
> *1 Sol.*   How, my lord!
> *Tyr.*   Her body!
> *1 Sol.* She's dead, my lord!
> *Tyr.*   True, if she were alive,
> Such slaves as you should not come near to touch her.
> Do't, and with all best reverence; place her here.
> *1 Sol.* Not only, sir, with reverence, but with fear.
> You shall have more than your own asking once.

> I am afraid of nothing but she'll rise
> At the first jog, and save us all a labour.
> *2 Sol.* Then we were best take her up and never touch her!
> *1 Sol.* Life, how can that be? Does fear make thee mad?
> I've took up many a woman in my days,
> But never with less pleasure, I protest! (4.3.68–79)

In general, the Tyrant's imagery in opening the tomb exploits the sexual implications of forcible violation ('Pierce the jaws / Of this cold, ponderous creature' [25–6]), language which the soldiers echo irreverently ('This is ten thousand times worse than ent'ring upon a breach, / 'Tis the first stone that ever I took off / From any lady' [56–8]). The Tyrant's erratic behaviour may also have elicited laughter at certain points, as when he proclaims 'The monument woos me; I must run and kiss it' (9) shortly after entering the tomb. Other comic, or quasi-comic, interpolations in the play include the scurrilous asides of Sophronius, a noble at the court, on the Tyrant's behaviour (1.1.35–54, 120–1); and the ineptitude of Govianus who (in 2.1) almost kills the Lady's father (acting as pander for the Tyrant), and then faints in his effort to obey the Lady's command that he kill her.

32. Prior to this critical juncture, the Tyrant's erotic ministrations have gradually become more resolute, as has his apotheosis of the Lady's body:

> Madam! 'Tis I, sweet lady. Prithee speak!
> 'Tis thy love calls on thee – thy king, thy servant.
> No? Not a word? All prisoners to pale silence?
> I'll prove a kiss. (4.3.86–89)

> > Since thy life has left me,
> I'll clasp the body for the spirit that dwelt in't,
> And love the house still for the mistress' sake.
> Thou art mine now, spite of destruction
> > And Govianus, and I will possess thee. (110–14)

33. For an insightful analysis of early modern poisonous cosmetics as signifiers of 'the inseparability of external from internal, of material from immaterial', see Tanya Pollard, 'Beauty's Poisonous Properties', *Shakespeare Studies* XXVII (1999): 188, 187–210.

34. The notation 'ENTER LADY/RICH ROBINSON' appears alongside the stage direction for the apparition scene (4.4). Lancashire (following the suggestion of W. W. Greg) contends that only actors of minor or doubled parts were customarily cited by name in promptbooks. In this instance, the manuscript notation for 'Lady' at the first appearance of the ghost 'make[s] clear that the actor who played the Lady was also to play her spirit' (see note to S.D. 42.2–3, 222–3). Lancashire suggests further that Robinson may have played the Wife, but this is unlikely since it would have required an interlude between the end of Act 3, when the Lady is still on stage, and the beginning of Act 4, when the Wife enters.

35. The stage directions do not make clear who (or what) represented the corpse. Although, as we shall see, the staging of a similar scene in *The Duke of Milan* allowed for the same actor who played the living woman to represent her corpse, thereby providing continuity of image, this option would seem less likely here because of Robinson's dual role as Lady and ghost, and the presence of both ghost and corpse on stage at the end of the play. However, I think it

possible, even likely, that in 5.2 Robinson appeared as corpse rather than as ghost. It seems curious that the ghost has only one and a half lines (163–4), after which the actor presumably exited (there is no stage direction) and did not reappear '*to go out with the body*' (S.D. 205.1–2) until immediately before the end of the play. The corpse, on the other hand, and especially the face of the corpse, was the centre of attention throughout the scene. If the body in the chair was Robinson's, then presumably he also represented the corpse in 4.3, the tomb scene with the Tyrant preceding the first apparition of the Lady as ghost in 4.4. It is also possible (although I think much less likely) that in both scenes the corpse was a dummy, an alternative which would have altered the erotic *frisson* of the Tyrant's love-making while emphasising (albeit from another direction) the artifice of theatrical performance.

36. Massinger's play was first entered into the Stationers' Register on 20 January 1623, licensed by Sir John Ashley and assigned to Edward Blackmore and George Norton. In a second SR entry on 5 May 1623, Norton assigned his rights to Blackmore. The play was published in the same year; the title-page states that it 'hath been often acted by his Maiesties seruants, at the blacke Friers'. There are minor corrections in the hand of the author in the Harbord copy of Q1 at the Folger Shakespeare Library. See Philip Edwards and Colin Gibson, eds., *The Plays and Poems of Philip Massinger,* Vol. I (Oxford: Clarendon Press, 1978), 199–211, esp. 199–200, 204–9. All references to the play in this essay are taken from the Edwards-Gibson edition.

37. Josephus gives these incidents far more extensive treatment in *Antiquities* than in *Of the Warres of the Jewes.* In *Antiquities,* Herod twice leaves secret orders that Mariamne be killed in the event of his own death at the hands of his Roman superiors, Mark Antony and Julius Caesar, respectively. During his first absence, Herod swears his uncle Joseph to secrecy, and in the second instance Sohemus the Iturian. Both Joseph and Sohemus reveal Herod's intentions to Mariamne and are summarily executed after Herod learns of their betrayals. Mariamne, angered at Herod's scheme, is herself under suspicion of adultery with her informers, but her life is spared until Salome, Herod's sister, succeeds in a ruse that convinces Herod of Mariamne's desire to kill him. Mariamne is then brought up for a mock trial and executed. In *Warres,* Herod leaves secret orders only once, with (another) Joseph, the husband of his sister Salome, prior to his meeting with Mark Antony. This time, after learning of Joseph's betrayal and (again with prompting from Salome) his presumed adultery with Mariamne, Herod orders both adulterers to be summarily executed. See STC 14809, Thomas Lodge, trans., *Of the Antiquities of the Jews,* Book XV, Chap. iiii, 387–8; Chap. xi, 396–9; and *Warres,* Book I, Chap. xvii, 589–90. Massinger, working from Lodge's translations, makes several notable changes. He features only one meeting, between Sforza and Charles V; greatly elaborates the Joseph/Sohemus figures in Francisco, a revenger (Sforza was formerly his sister's lover), and would-be seducer of Marcelia; provides equally strong roles for Sforza's scheming sister, Mariana (the Salome figure), and for Sforza's mother, Isabella; and has Sforza stab and kill Marcelia directly.

38. The passage in Josephus reads:

> Oftentimes he did inuocate her name, and more often vndecently lamented her ... And in such sort was he ouerwhelmed with griefe, that oftentimes he commaunded his ministers to call his wife *Mariamme,* as if as yet she had beene alive ... he at last hid

himselfe in a solitarie wildernesse, vnder pretext of hunting; where afflicting himself incessantly, at last he fell into a most grieuous sicknes. This disease of his was an inflammation or paine in the necke: he seemed also in some sort to raue and waxe mad; neither could any remedies relieue him of his agony ...' (*Antiquities*, Book XV, Chap. xi, 399)

39. Edwards and Gibson speculate that Massinger may have contemporised his play because of the recent success of Markham and Sampson's *Herod and Antipater* (STC 17401), set primarily in Jerusalem (201). This episodic history of Herod which, according to the title-page of the 1622 quarto, was 'divers times publiquely Acted (with great Applause) at the Red Bull, by the Company of His Maiesties Revels', has several notable features: Josephus as Prologue and interpreter of dumb-shows; Mariamne (like the Lady in *The Second Maiden's Tragedy*) first as saint and later as ghost; and in its last scene, the sensational double-deaths of Herod and Antipater, Herod's villainous son by his first wife Doris, whom Herod divorced in order to marry Mariamne. See Valency, 216–23.

40. Massinger drew most of his Italian material from Geoffrey Fenton's translation of Guicciardini's *Historia d'Italia*, first printed in 1579, with later editions in 1599 and 1618. Massinger freely adapted his source, conflating the exploits of Ludovico Sforza with those of his son Francesco. See Edwards and Gibson, 203.

41. Although Josephus is clear in his summary judgement of Herod as a man of virtually unprecedented barbarity, he none the less portrayed him as a skilled administrator and politician. In 3.1, Sforza's defence to Charles V of his alliance with the defeated King of France seems closely modelled after that of Herod before Caesar after the defeat of Mark Antony (see *Antiquities*, Book XV, Chap. x, 395–6; and *Warres*, Book I, Chap. xv, 585–6). But see also Edwards and Gibson (203), who cite Fenton as a source for this scene.

42. In demonstrating Mariamne's affection for Herod prior to her denunciation of him, *The Duke of Milan* and *Herod and Antipater* are in a minority of Herod and Mariamne plays. The largest single category of such plays, English and continental, portray Mariamne's hatred of her husband, taking their cue from a comment by Josephus in *Warres*: 'For *Mariamne* hated him as much as he loved her' (Book I, Chap. xvii, 589). For discussions of the Herod dramatic tradition (including Elizabeth Cary's *The Tragedy of Miriam, The Fair Queen of Jewry*, 1613) see Valency, 68–137, 174–212; and Weller and Ferguson, 23–6.

43. Although Josephus criticises Mariamne for intemperance, he none the less judges her positively:

> For being entertained by him [Herod] who intirely loued her, and from whom she receiued nothing that might discontent her, she presumed vpon a great and intemperate libertie in her discourse ... Thus died *Mariamne,* hauing beene a woman that excelled both in continence and courage: notwithstanding that she defaulted somewhat in affability and impatience of nature: for the rest of her parts, she was of an admirable and pleasing beautie, and of such a cariage in those companies wherein she was intertained, that it was impossible to expresse the same, in that she surpassed all those of her time ... (*Antiquities*, Book XV, Chap. xi, 399).

44. Francisco the revenger utters this line to Sforza with feigned sincerity. Francisco continually manipulates Sforza through his ironic use of the Duke's own rhetoric of idolatry, for example, 'She's indeed / The wonder of all times' (3.1.28–9).

45. Marcelia's insistence on a show of deference is most evident in her enraged response to attacks on her chastity by Mariana and Isabella:

> [I am] us'd with more contempt, than if I were
> A peasant's daughter; baited, and hooted at
> Like to a common strumpet: with loud noises
> Forc'd from my prayers ...(2.1.217–20)

This enmity between Marcelia and Sforza's family parallels an emphasis in Josephus:

> But *Mariamne* vpbraided and publikely reproched both the kings mother and sister, telling them that they were but abiectly and basely borne, whereupon there grew a great enmitie and vnrecouerable hatred betweene the Ladies ... (*Antiquities*, Book XV, Chap. xi, 398)

46. See *The Compact Edition of the Oxford English Dictionary*, I (Oxford: Oxford University Press, 1971): 789–90. Examples of the use of 'dotage' and its derivatives in the play include:

> *Mariana.* ... since dotage makes you / Wilfully blind ... (4.3.114–15)

> *Eugenia.* It is impossible he could be wrought
> To look on her but with the eyes of dotage,
> And so to serve her. (5.1.15–17)

> *Francisco.* [to Marcelia] ... nay, [he] dotes on you
> As there were something in you more than woman; (2.1.340–1)

> His dotage like an ague keeps its course, (4.1.78)

> [to Sforza] Your love and extreme dotage as a cloak
> Should cover our embraces ... (4.3.213–14)

47. In one instance he complains to Francisco: 'There is no heaven without her; nor a hell / Where she resides' (1.3.356–7), and in another to Pescara, his friend and confidant: 'Alas, / live not here; my wife, my wife, Pescara, / Being absent, I am dead' (3.1.261–2).

48. The influence of Shakespeare's *Antony and Cleopatra* on Massinger's play is apparent not only in the competition between love and duty but also in the borrowing of images. One of the most notable parallels is in 3.1, the scene which introduces Sforza and Marcelia. Although interrupted twice by messengers bringing him unwelcome news of the war, Sforza idealises their love in the fashion of Antony:

> Out of my sight!
> And all thoughts that may strangle mirth forsake me.
> Fall what can fall, I dare the worst of fate.
> Though the foundation of the earth should shrink,
> The glorious eye of heaven lose his splendour,
> Supported thus, I'll stand upon the ruins,
> And seek for new life here. (122–8)

49. Marcelia is so incensed when Sforza calls her 'whore' that she brings on her own death by seeming to confirm his suspicions. Like Desdemona, to whom she is sometimes compared, Marcelia had earlier promised a supposedly repentant Francisco that she would shield him from Sforza's wrath:

> Be undaunted.
> For now, as of a creature that is mine,

> I rise up your protectress. All the grace
> I hitherto have done you, was bestow'd
> With a shut hand. It shall be now more free,
> Open, and liberal (4.2.55–60).

Ironically, Marcelia's own version of 'fair madonna' is grounded in the same attitude of superiority as that described by the soldiers.

50. As mentioned earlier, Herod does not kill Marimane directly in either account of her death by Josephus.

51. Earlier in the play, Tiberio, a critic of Marcelia, compared her to Poppaea, Nero's mistress, and to Cleopatra (2.1.37–8). Shortly before he turns on his wife, Sforza himself alludes to Messaline, nymphomaniacal wife of the Emperor Claudius:

> Were I match'd to another Messaline,
> While I found merit in myself to please her
> I should believe her chaste, and would not seek
> To find out my own torment. But alas,
> Enjoying one that but to me's a Dian
> I am too secure. (4.3.102–7)

52. Sforza and Marcelia frequently betray their moral deviance by subscribing to beliefs and practices condemned by Christianity as pagan. For example, Sforza tells Francisco that the Hindu practice of suttee should serve as model for Marcelia's grief in the event of his death:

> The slavish Indian princes, when they die,
> Are cheerfully attended to the fire
> By the wife, and slave, that living they lov'd best,
> To do them service in another world;
> Nor will I be the less honour'd, that love more. (1.3.360–5)

Earlier in the same scene, Marcelia herself declares the right to commit suicide as a heavenly 'blessing', although hardly in the context imagined by Sforza:

> the only blessing that
> Heaven hath bestow'd on us, more than on beasts,
> Is, that 'tis in our pleasure when to die. (209–11)

53. In the same scene, Stephano describes Sforza's corpse infatuation with another ironic reference to a 'miracle':

> But that melancholy
> Though ending in distraction, should work
> So far upon a man as to compel him
> To court a thing that has nor sense, nor being,
> Is unto me a miracle. (7–11)

54. Sforza's image of self-degradation as a metamorphosis in which he embraces the flesh of the dead is similar to Ferdinand's lycanthropy in *The Duchess of Malfi*. See Chapter 4, pp. 155–7.

55. That this was indeed the case is also implicit in the contrast drawn between the love-making at the banquet and Marcelia's refusal to embrace Sforza after she has learned of his injunctions (3.3):

> *Sforza.*   I have stood
> Silent thus long, Marcelia, expecting
> When with more than a greedy haste thou wouldst
> Have flown into my arms, and on my lips

Have printed a deep welcome ...
Marcelia.   Sir, I am most happy
To look upon you safe, and would express
My love and duty in a modest fashion ...
                         ... not like a wanton
Fir'd with hot appetite ...
Sforza.   How! Why, can there be
A mean in your affections to Sforza?
                    ... Do not move me;
My passions to you are in extremes,
And know no bounds. Come, kiss me!
Marcelia.   I obey you.
Sforza. By all the joys of love, she does salute me
As if I were her grandfather! What witch
With cursed spells hath quench'd the amorous heat
That liv'd upon these lips? (91–5, 100–2, 105–6, 107–8, 111–17)

56. The play also takes advantage (if rarely) of the comic possibilities of trans-vestism, further discrediting Marcelia's credibility as woman. In 2.1, for example, Mariana and Isabella lure Marcelia (who appears on a balcony above them) into a public brawl by first ridiculing her pretensions to holiness (131–4). Enraged, Marcelia trades insults with Mariana (like Helena and Hermia in *A Midsummer Night's Dream*) about their respective sizes until the two come to blows, while attendants make bets as to the victor, as at a cockfight (156–82). The indignity of Marcelia's literal and figurative descent to Mariana's level is visually reinforced by the uncommon disparity in their heights, summed up in Mariana's claim that Marcelia is a 'monster ... three feet / Too high for a woman' (188–9). Throughout this exchange, the tongue-in-cheek allusions by the 'women' to markers for femininity – cosmetics, perfume, delicacy of appearance – are of course self-referential in comically ironic ways. There is no woman on the stage, but the actor playing Mariana in effect critiques Marcelia's impersonator because this actor has the conventional stature of a male. The comic effects of such meta-theatrical by-play suggest, if only briefly, that Marcelia as sex goddess is a travesty.

57. Marcelia, who dies at the end of 4.3, seems less culpable than Sforza because she forgives him with her dying breath and she is, after all, guiltless of adultery. However, prior to her death Marcelia gives no indication that she has renounced her status as idol.

Chapter 4

Invading the Grave: Shadow Lives in *The Revenger's Tragedy* and *The Duchess of Malfi*

The Second Maid's Tragedy and *The Duke of Milan* portray idolatry as a monomaniacal obsession that appropriates the language of the sacred to reify erotic love – for the dead as well as the living – as the ultimate form of transcendence. But for all their sensationalism, neither of the Herod plays takes full advantage of the theatrical potential implicit in the taboo against necrophilia. The chief reasons for this delimiting of theatrical power are the flatness in the portrayals of the key figures, who for the most part have no semblance of interiority, and the related absence in these plays of a sense of the mysterious, the unseen. In contrast, the tragedies under analysis in this chapter – Middleton's (?) *The Revenger's Tragedy*[1] and Webster's *The Duchess of Malfi* – are steeped in a far more unsettling kind of graveyard ambience that (at least in the case of *The Duchess*) instantiates a powerful psychological dimension.

In accordance with Benjamin's prescriptions for the *Trauerspiel*, these are indeed plays that mourn. Marked to be sure with an 'obsessive physicality' (Benjamin, 17), an almost palpable sense of corruption and decay, they would expose disease in the human mind as well as in the body politic, eschewing the transfiguration of nature for 'the artificial light of apotheosis' (180). Replete with 'extravagant pomp' (177) and melodramatic excess, they are suffused with the death-obsessed imaginings of *intrigants* who pursue 'the illusion of freedom – in the exploration of what is forbidden' (230).

The distinctive gruesomeness of each play is in large part a function of these imaginings. In *The Revenger's Tragedy*, Vindice (who fuses the roles of protagonist and *intrigant*) expresses his morbidity, in Benjamin's terms, through a sinister merriment, a 'bitingly provocative scorn'. Notwithstanding his bitter ruminations on sexuality and death, Vindice takes a capriciously sadistic pleasure in manipulating his adversaries, much like Marlowe's Barabas, Shakespeare's Richard III or Shakespeare's Aaron, a penchant that provides numerous instances of grotesquely outrageous humour.[2] However, *The Revenger's Tragedy* is neither as bizarre as Webster's play nor nearly as complex. In triangulating the sex-charged antagonisms of Ferdinand, the Duchess and Bosola, Webster manages to provide scenes of extraordinary barbarism while simultaneously creating an illusion of interiority in each of his major figures. A powerful tour de force, *The Duchess of Malfi* is an outstanding exemplar of the theatrical adaptation of sensationalist conventions for subtle psychological effects.

It will be the argument of this chapter that what I call the 'graveyard ambience' of these plays proceeds in part from their appropriation of popular notions of the corpse, particularly the long tradition of its mysterious, semi-animate status. In Middleton's play the shifting symbolic values of Gloriana's skull serve to activate, as it were, the latent power of her original corpse; and the newly dead and eroticised body of Antonio's wife evokes the preoccupation in Renaissance iconography with the sexual/ reproductive power of the female corpse, seen in phenomena as disparate as the *danse macabre* and the illustrations of anatomical treatises. Even more strikingly, Ferdinand's lycanthropy in *The Duchess of Malfi* ostentatiously foregrounds a dangerously liminal state in which death and sexuality are savagely joined.

The deeply entrenched 'superstition' about the indeterminacy of the corpse was, of course, precisely what the anti-materialist agenda of the Reformation was set against. But the idea of a kind of smothered sentience in dead bodies did not die easily, as witnessed by the difficulties encountered by Tudor authorities in attempting to scale down or eradicate corpse-related practices that would either protect against or exploit the corpse's latent power.[3] In addition, the controversy over anatomical dissection suggests that many individuals, both within the English intelligentsia and without, viewed this practice as a startling new mode of illicitly trafficking with the dead. Thus despite the best efforts of the new religion and the new science, fearsome images of the corpse were still prevalent in the popular imagination – images that permeate, overtly and implicitly, these Jacobean tragedies of the *Trauerspiel*.

1. Disposing of the dead in early modern England

Katherine Park's extensive study of the practices of embalming, post-mortem examination and anatomical dissection in early modern Europe suggests some of the reasons for the English frame of mind. According to Park, corpses were handled with considerably more trepidation in England and the northern countries than in Italy.[4] Both the private, diagnostic postmortem and the public, illustrative dissection met little resistance in late medieval Italy, presumably because of the Italian belief in 'a quick and radical separation of body and soul' at death: as a shell or memorial to the living person, the body could be put to practical or scientific use without violating the 'personhood' of the deceased.[5] In the north, on the other hand, death was envisaged 'as an extended and gradual process', more or less concomitant with putrefaction. It could take up to a year or more for the corpse to decompose, to become a skeleton, during which time it was perceived as 'active, sensitive, or semianimate, [and] possessed of a gradually fading life' or 'personhood'. In this interim, the corpse had the power to pollute and also to torment the living (as did vampires, for example), but the 'vital spirits' of the recently dead could also produce an elixir for life, the so-called *mummia* (116).[6] The corpse was, then, an object of fear and reverence in northern Europe, and it inspired what Phillipe Ariès calls 'an iconography of the macabre' (110) in the late medieval period.

This iconography of the north demonstrates a preoccupation with putrefaction, very possibly exacerbated by outbreaks of the plague and the accompanying proliferation of rotting corpses.[7] It is readily apparent in the graphic imagery of the popular sermon and in other religious literature, but is perhaps most dramatically manifested in the bizarre sculptures of the transi tombs, and in the disturbing eroticism of the *danse macabre*. The transi sculptures, which date from the late fourteenth century and first appear in England in 1425, represent decaying corpses with protruding intestines in the process of being consumed by snakes, worms, lizards and frogs (these were thought to generate spontaneously from the body's 'manure').[8] In order to emphasise the inextricability of life and death, the sculptor often provided two figures situated above and below the coffin, one depicting the decomposing body of the deceased and the other his or her fully clothed figure; alternatively, a single sculpture was sometimes divided so that the putrefying half was juxtaposed to the intact and living form, or was shown as a rear view of a frontally clothed figure.[9]

The violent and voyeuristic imagery of the transi tombs, particularly the horrific detailing of vermiculation,[10] had a ghoulish counterpart in the 'grim coupling', the 'shaking of the sheets' of the *danse macabre* (Neill, 75). The erotic iconography of the Basel *Totentanz*, for example, depicts the skeleton-lover Death as a series of 'prancing cadavers' (74), including one that is partly fleshed, which seek to copulate with victims of both genders. Death's 'absent genitalia' are rendered variously – 'chastely' concealed, or revealed as 'stripped' by 'worms of corruption', and in one instance Death's loins are adorned with the 'obscene simulacra ... [of] shin-bone and skull' (76). As 'a revel of monstrous uncreation', a copulation that generates food for worms, the death-dance, like the vermiculation of the transi tombs, graphically identified 'the vicious place of begetting as the fountainhead of death' (77).[11]

This iconographic blurring of the boundaries between putrefaction and reproduction underscores Park's contention that the corpse in northern Europe was not viewed as wholly dead: to be rendered fleshless, beyond the process of consumption and generation, took time. Accordingly, the preparation of the corpse for burial functioned as a containment: 'in the north ... the dead body was tightly sewed into a cloth shroud ... and, increasingly, beginning in the fourteenth century, shut up in a wooden coffin' (Park, 'The Life of the Corpse', 118), as opposed to its sometimes sumptuous display in Italy. Ironically, embalming, which was limited to persons of importance, was an effort to prolong the physical integrity of the deceased (usually for practical reasons, as, for example, a state funeral),[12] but in effect, the temporary staunching of the process of putrefaction succeeded only in extending the liminal power of the corpse (Park, 'The Criminal and Saintly Body', 6). In general, northern European burial customs, especially those deriving from popular tradition, were designed to immobilise and demystify the corpse and prevent its remigration. Thus it was common practice to ring bells and make other kinds of noise; to stop clocks and cover mirrors;[13] to tie the feet of the shroud and sprinkle the corpse with salt to prevent it from walking; and to assume the sins of the deceased through the ritual of 'sin-eating' – that is, the consumption (usually by a poor person) of bread and beer that had been in direct contact with corpse or coffin (Gittings, 135–56; Cressy, 421–5).[14]

This wrapping up and shutting down of the corpse was complicated, however, both literally and metaphorically, by the difficulty of containing its great quantity of fluids, especially its blood. The foul liquids produced by mouldering bodies (partly absorbed through sawdust and bran in the case of coffined corpses [Litten, 92]), were composed in part of 'dead' blood, but the oxymoronic concept of blood divested of its vivifying power was difficult to grasp, at least by the popular imagination. Thus the beliefs in *mummia* and in the notion of the corpse as contagious – that is, able to transmit death – and the expectation that the corpse of a murder victim would start to bleed if the murderer touched it.[15] Such notions were at least indirectly reinforced by Galenic medical theory, which privileged blood as the primary bodily concoction resulting from the transmutation of food and drink, a concoction that not only stimulated the production of other life-sustaining bodily fluids, but also enabled the body's reproductive agency.[16] Blood was, then, the primary symbol of a nourishing, generative 'nature', but the corpse served as reminder that 'nature' also figured as cannibal, converting, in a further transformative process, the 'dead' blood of the deceased into the life-sustaining fluids of other creatures.[17] Paradoxically, then, the blood of the corpse signified past and future potencies – vivifying fluid as it was and as it would be, mysteriously shifting between temporal states of being.

Certainly, funerary practices in early modern England, both liturgical and secular, attempted to 'de-animate' the corpse during its period of putrefaction, to disempower its fetishistic presence in the cultural consciousness. But the fear of the corpse's indefinable influence, especially the fear of its indeterminate yet material blood, was not easily displaced, and it is probable that the social practices I have outlined here, which aimed at defusing this fear, served equally to reinforce it. In any event, it would seem that the pre-Reformation culture of the dead in early modern England is relevant to the theatrical representation of post-Reformation corpses because of the tenacity with which popular beliefs about the dead resisted erasure.

None the less, hegemonic pressures for change, as we have seen, were formidable. On the one hand, Protestant reformers attacked the idolatrous worship of painted images and relics through state-sanctioned homilies, issued new regulations for the decorations of churches, homes and tombstones, and attempted to overhaul 'superstitious' attitudes towards the corpse as manifested in Catholic burial and funerary practices. Concurrently, English practitioners of the new anatomy were following the model of Andreas Vesalius, whose *De Humani Corporis Fabrica,* 1543 (published in England in 1545), was hugely influential. These new men of medicine were dissecting corpses in order to demonstrate anatomical and physiological principles to medical students and other onlookers.[18] Presumably, anatomy's precision instruments, its ordered and sequential methodology, its names and categories, were directed at harnessing the gruesomeness associated with dismembering a body. Nevertheless, resistance to anatomical dissection in England was far stronger and more sustained than that in southern Europe.

According to Park, the difference between English and Italian responses to Vesalius and his methods can once again be attributed to the northern European belief in the corpse's liminality. In both countries, the public display of an anatomised body was viewed as a violation of personal identity, but in England 'the complete or near-complete disaggregation of the body including the face' ('The Criminal and Saintly Body', 8) also violated the invisible, liminal principle that was still believed to animate the corpse.[19] Thus public execution of traitors in England by means of drawing and quartering was deliberately punitive: dismembering the body was meant to symbolise the complete disintegration – both physical and spiritual – of the criminal.[20] But the practice of anatomy, even when restricted to the bodies of criminals (which, of course, was rarely feasible), presupposed that the materiality of any corpse was open to empirical investigation because all corpses were devoid of animation. This objectification of the 'specimen' helped anatomists to justify (at least to themselves) such scandalous practices as procuring bodies by means of grave-robbing, or ghoulishly monitoring the deaths of gibbeted felons, which in the public imagination had a decidedly sacrilegious resonance.[21]

To be sure, the iconography of the frontispiece of the *Fabrica* and of other illustrations of anatomical theatres attempted to confer a magisterial dignity onto the new profession, presumably as part of a larger effort to contravene public scepticism. Thus the anatomist, invariably situated in these illustrations at or near the central axis of a circular, basilica-like structure, suggested a kind of physician/sovereign/priest – privileged to 'open to our gaze ... the principle of life' concealed within the corpse, and to explore the principles of 'divine craftsmanship' (Park, 'The Criminal and Saintly Body', 70, 16; see also Sawday, 68–78). This inscription of the new science as a quest for mysteries of the body that 'were not merely physiological, but moral-ontological' (Neill, 123) was, in fact, largely promoted by members of the seventeenth-century English intelligentsia, writing in genres ranging from *belles lettres* to pseudo-scientific treatises, and including such notable figures as Phineas Fletcher, Helkiah Crooke and Sir Thomas Browne. The defensive stratagems of these men represent a somewhat awkward effort to accommodate empirical method while simultaneously insisting on 'occluded meanings' that lay 'deep within the fabric of the body' (125).

As physicians with strong religious convictions, Crooke and Browne attempted to justify, even sanctify, the bodily fragmentation of anatomy as a mode of understanding the divine principle of the body/soul unity. As Crooke puts it,

> Seeing then that Man is a Litle world, and contains in him selfe the seeds of all those things which are contained in the most spacious and ample bosom of this whole Vniuerse, Starres, Meteors, Mettals, Minerals, Vegetables, Animals, and Spirits; whosoeuer dooth well know him selfe, knoweth all things, seeing in himselfe he hath the resemblances and representations of all things ... But this same knowledge of a mans selfe, as it is a very glorious thing, so it is also very hard and difficult. And yet by the dissection of the body, and by Anatomy, we shall easily attaine vnto this knowledge. For seeing the soule of man being cast into this prison of the body, cannot discharge her offices and functions without a corporeall Organ or instrument of the body; whosoeuer will attaine vnto the knowledge of the soule, it is necessarie that hee know the frame and composition of the body.[22]

Stated thus abstractly, anatomy becomes, in a recurrent metaphor of both writers, a spiritual voyage of discovery. But in each work there is a tension between lofty philosophical aim and the realities of the dissection table, especially as envisaged, as these proselytisers knew well, by the popular imagination. On occasion, Browne tackles this issue directly:

> Not that I am insensible of the dread and horrour thereof, or by raking into the bowels of the deceased, continuall sight of Anatomies, Skeletons, or Cadaverous reliques, like Vespilloes, or Grave-makers, I am become stupid, or have forgot the apprehension of mortality, but that marshalling of the horrours, and contemplating the extremities thereof, I find not any therein able to daunt the courage of a man much less a resolved Christian ...[23]

For the most part, however, Browne is engaged, as is Crooke, with justifying a paradox: because the soul cannot be found anywhere in the body (even in the brain),[24] it cannot be harmed by dissection; none the less, it is only by anatomising the body that man 'attaine[s] vnto the knowledge of the soule'.[25]

Such measured, if qualified, assessments of anatomical practice by influential thinkers would seem to have little in common with popular outrage over the medical violation of the corpse. But the insistence in these writings on the body's occluded meanings – meanings not visible to the ocular investigative techniques of the new science, but secret, hidden, mystifyingly intangible – had, on the contrary, much in common with the popular notion of the semi-animate corpse, and even with the popular fear of the corpse's power. The antithetical relationship between 'occluded' and 'ocular' suggests that there is perhaps much that should not be seen, that is deliberately proscribed from view, that will, in fact, destroy the viewer.[26] One of the mythological formulations for this taboo is, of course, the story of Medusa, the female Gorgon who turned to stone anyone who dared look on her, and Sawday invokes this myth to identify the early modern concept of petrifying vision as the view of the 'interiority' of the corpse – that is, the body in dissolution, its status indeterminate (6–15). From this perspective, the frontispiece of Vesalius's *Fabrica*, showcasing the author as 'sovereign priest' as he opens the interior of a female corpse to full frontal view, was profoundly significant.[27]

2. *The Revenger's Tragedy* and *The Duchess of Malfi*

The Revenger's Tragedy and *The Duchess of Malfi* are tragedies imbued with the power of death – not only its inevitability, but more particularly, its insidious permeation of life. In the view of Vindice, and of Ferdinand/ Bosola, the symbiotically linked transgressors of *The Duchess of Malfi*, beauty, whether that of nature or of human artifice, masks a terrible underside, a corrosive chaos that is encapsulated in the disintegrating corpse. For these *intrigants*, 'evil' in its multiple manifestations becomes the symptom, the stalking-horse, of this desperate vision: as moral arbiters, malcontents and doomsayers, they presume both to decry and judge the corruption of the physis. Unsurprisingly, they find in the sexual and reproductive potencies of the female body a correlative for moral and physical 'rot', a fixating focus for their obsession with death.

However, as we have seen, 'dirt' represents only one extreme of a patriarchal fantasy in which woman also appears as an unspotted 'lapidary form' (Douglas, 162),[28] and such idealisations in *The Revenger's Tragedy* and *The Duchess of Malfi* focus ironically on the *corpses* of women, such as that of the Duchess in Webster's play and Antonio's wife in Middleton's. In her compelling analysis of the representation of female corpses in eighteenth-century visual art, Elizabeth Bronfen argues that by rendering the dead woman as still, timeless, cut off from organic process, the male artist would enact 'a triumph over disseverment and facticity' (11), would, in effect, disempower female corruption. Inevitably, however, because 'the urge for order [is] inhabited by a fascination with disruption and split', no such image can fully repress the viewer's consciousness of fragmentation in the imaged corpse. On the contrary, the artist's pretence, his attempt to fix an ideal of woman in a time- and putrefaction-free dimension, succeeds only in calling attention to the unsignifiability of the corpse's petrifying interior, to the hidden and insistent mystery of Medusa.

Early modern stage images were, of course, very differently configured from eighteenth-century painterly ones, but on one level these differences serve to reinforce the relevance of Bronfen's insights to Middleton's and Webster's corpses. As Philippa Berry usefully puts it, theatrical transvestism constructed bodies not as female but as feminised (7). Thus early modern principles of male ascendancy were compromised directly in staged representations of the female corpse; and – to extrapolate once again from Benjamin – the ghoulishly violent ambience of death-centred tragedies of blood hyperbolised this paradox. From this perspective, the irony at the core of both plays is that in proportion to the vehemence with which Vindice, Bosola, and Ferdinand defy the power of Medusa, the corpse-Gorgon, they wreak havoc on the presumed autonomy of their own sovereign status.

The Revenger's Tragedy

In *The Revenger's Tragedy*[29] two violated female bodies serve as dual emblems of material dissolution and of transcendent wholeness: the corpse of the raped wife of Antonio, who has killed herself; and the skull of the poisoned virgin Gloriana, grotesquely 'at-tired' in the scene of the Duke's murder (3.5). These corpse/skeletons signify interdependently in the play.

On one level Antonio's wife, as a suicide in the tradition of Lucrece, and Gloriana, as blanched bones, function respectively as symbols of the radically cleansed and transcendently pure. Yet they also represent horrific states of marginality. The fully fleshed corpse of Antonio's wife, centrepiece of her own wake, remains erotically powerful in its showcased state. Far more perversely enticing is the 'fleshed out' figure of Gloriana, the corpse-in-disguise that arouses the Duke's lust and poisons him with a kiss. Symbolically mediating between these two ambiguous emblems of death is the living Duchess, a depraved and emphatically feminised force of nature.

As dual emblems of purity and putrefaction, skull and corpse figure the oppositional extremes in the patriarchal symbolisation of woman. Bataille argues that the decomposing human corpse, the flesh as food for worms, serves as an anguishing reminder of 'the sickening primary condition of life', whereas 'whitened bones' close the disgusting connection with decomposition, 'draw the first veil of decency and solemnity over death' (56). The newly dead are 'held in the clutch of violence ... part and parcel of [their] own disorder', 'contagious'; only bones 'put an end to close connections between decomposition, the source of an abundant surge of life, and death' (47, 56). Addressing the same phenomenon psycho-analytically, Bronfen contends that the bones/flesh binary is often gendered, that women are frequently associated culturally with 'decomposition, with first burial (they ... wash and guard the corpse)' (199). Bones and tombs, on the other hand, the secondary, unpolluted symbols of death, are appropriated by males. Thus in the bones of a female corpse, the female is reborn as masculine sign.

Within this theoretical framework, the clean, hard surface, the 'very ragged bone' (1.1.18) of Vindice's 'bony lady' (16) fixes Gloriana in a defleshed, degendered and uncontaminated state, a purity reinforced by her former virginity. For Vindice, the skull is a metonymic, benign stand-in for his betrothed – Gloriana converted to masculine sign. But as Susan Stewart has demonstrated, relics as *memento mori*, 'the mere material remains of what had possessed human significance', are actually an anti-souvenir:

> *Memento mori* mark the horrible transformation of meaning into materiality more than they mark, as other souvenirs do, the transformation of materiality into meaning. If the function of the souvenir proper is to create a continuous and personal narrative of the past, the function of such souvenirs of death is to disrupt and disclaim that continuity. (140)

Vindice's insistence on Gloriana's skull as a material reminder of her former inviolate virtue is a sham: he appropriates the skull as a fetishistic tool in the service of his own morally ambiguous purposes.

From the outset of the play, the juxtapositions in Vindice's imagery betray his inability effectively to separate skull and corpse, to isolate Gloriana's emblematic remains from the corruption, primarily sexual, that he finds virtually everywhere. Repelled most strongly by the spectacle of lust in the old Duke, who remains 'hot and vicious' (2.1.37) as he 'mould[s] away' (71), Vindice imagines him as a kind of skeleton with an obscene sexual appetite:

> Oh that marrowless age
> Would stuff the hollow bones with damned desires,
> And 'stead of heat kindle infernal fires
> Within the spendthrift veins of a dry duke,
> A parched and juiceless luxur. (1.1.5–9)

Significantly, in the same speech, he introduces the Duke's opposite, the 'ragged imperfections' of Gloriana's skull, another 'shell of death', but one in whose 'unsightly rings' were once set 'heaven-pointed diamonds' (15, 20, 19). Clearly, the apotheosised Gloriana represents the counterforce to the Duke's lust, and in the larger context of Vindice's lust-ridden world, the one hard, moral certainty.

But the jewel/eye imagery takes a curious turn with the introduction of the Duchess (1.2), Gloriana's female opposite. Because as woman she serves as both stimulus and partner in the act of lust, her carnal appetites are at least as threatening to Gloriana's ideal virtue as those of the Duke. In the incestuous seduction scene between the Duchess and her bastard stepson Spurio, for example, the 'rings' of Gloriana's eye sockets are transformed into the collet or setting for a now debased diamond (Spurio), and also for the withered body of her hated husband:

> *Duchess* (to Spurio)
> Let it stand firm both in thought and mind
> That the duke was thy father: as no doubt then
> He bid fair for't, thy injury is the more;
> For had he cut thee a right diamond,
> Thou had'st been next set in the dukedom's ring,
> When his worn self like Age's easy slave
> Had dropped out of the collet into the grave. (145–51)

Later in the play (3.5), when Vindice finally enacts his vengeance through the medium of the poisoned kiss, the debasement of Gloriana's skull is complete: Vindice's language conflates the 'sparkling eye' (33) of the dressed-up skull with the Duke's death-head. The Duke's eyes, soon to be glistening with blood, 'start into' the sockets that once held diamonds:

> Place the torch here that his affrighted eyeballs
> May start into those hollows. (3.5.146–7)

> Let our two hands tear up his lids
> And make his eyes, like comets, shine through blood. (198)[30]

This pattern of imagery unfolds throughout the play along the same trajectory as Vindice's growing complicity in the moral miasma he would externalise. Ironically, in his role of the malcontented *intrigant*, Vindice assumes that his own marred vision is the equivalent of that 'eternal eye / That sees through flesh and all' (1.3.68–9). When Vindice focuses his supposedly prescient eye at the 'three-piled flesh' of 'fat folks' (1.1.46, 45), he envisages an interior corroded by sin, as if physical nutrients have spontaneously morphed into parasites that eat from within:

> Oh think upon the pleasure of the palace,
> Securèd ease and state: the stirring meats,
> Ready to move out of the dishes
> That even now quicken when they're eaten … (2.1.195–8)

Similar images pervade the speeches of others as well: the obsequious courtiers who follow Lussurioso are, in Hippolito's view, like 'flesh-flies that will buzz against supper time' (5.1.12–13), that is, insects that will lay their eggs in putrefying flesh; and Lussurioso himself describes Vindice's blandishments as 'bone-setter', or bawd, as 'rubb[ing] hell o'er with honey' (1.3.43, 2.1.22). But Vindice in particular identifies the symptoms of moral carnality in the decomposition that for him lurks beneath every 'artificial shine', every 'silk and silver' surface (1.1.21, 52), and that pushes against the wall of the flesh itself.

Notwithstanding this obsessive vision, Vindice strives to maintain a clear distinction between artifice and substance, the putrefying and the pure.[31] Thus, on the one hand, he demonises the hyperbolised figure of the Duchess, invariably linking her transgressiveness to female sexual and reproductive potencies. The Duchess, for her own part, amply justifies his point of view. She sees no cause for censure when Antonio's wife is raped by her 'youngest dearest son' (1.2.103), and persuades Spurio that incest is no worse a sin than 'to live a bastard, / The curse o' the womb' (158–9). Transgression of the primary taboos is power: 'Who but an eunuch would not sin?' (165). In responding to her amoral dynamism, Spurio associates his lust for the Duchess with his own reckless conception; his images echo Vindice's, and curiously implicate Spurio himself in the 'swell' of gestation:

> *Spurio*
> Faith if the truth were known I was begot
> After some gluttonous dinner – some stirring dish
> Was my first father, when deep healths went round
> And ladies cheeks were painted red with wine,
> Their tongues as short and nimble as their heels,
> Uttering words sweet and thick …
>   … oh damnation met
> The sins of feast, drunken adultery.

I feel it swell me; my revenge is just,
I was begot in impudent wine and lust. (178–83, 187–90)

Although the maternal seducer is not mentioned in Vindice's castigation of incest, the Duchess's lascivious conduct with Spurio, as manifested in their repeated kissing, for example, gives visible shape to it:

> *Vindice.*   O Dutch lust! Fulsome lust!
> Drunken procreation, which begets so many drunkards;
> Some father dreads not, gone to bed in wine,
> To slide from the mother, and cling the daughter-in-law;
> Some uncles are adulterous with their nieces,
> Brothers with brothers' wives. – O hour of incest!
> Any kin now next to the rim o' the sister
> Is man's meat in these days … (1.3.59–66)

The mother-lover who provokes her bastard stepson, her 'love's true-begot' (1.2.110) to 'double' and 'heap', who publicly flouts her violation of taboo, represents the threat of female sexuality fully unleashed. For Vindice, the Duchess is what any woman is capable of becoming – unless, of course, her potencies are cut off, her power neutralised, her body itself converted to male sign.

The scene of the wake for Antonio's wife (1.4) partly exposes the contradictions in Vindice's polarising approach to woman and prepares for his unmasking in the murder scene (3.5). Although Vindice (here disguised as Piato) would join Antonio and his colleagues in idealising the wife's corpse ('The virtuous lady!', 'Precedent for wives!', 'As cold in lust as she is now in death' [1.4.6, 36]), the sexual attractiveness of the beautiful and fully fleshed body is not easily obscured. Displayed with a Latin prayer-book pointing to a maxim on deathless honour, the corpse would be inscribed by its male observers with a timeless stability that denies the violence of the rape: Vindice insists that the lady 'Merits a tomb of pearl' (71). Nevertheless, it is Antonio's graphic description of the crime itself that dominates the scene while the still and prostrate body, 'discovered' to the onlookers, perversely invites the imaginative re-enactment of its public rape:

>   some courtiers in the masque
> Putting on better faces than their own,
> Being full of fraud and flattery, amongst whom
> The duchess' youngest son – that moth to honour –
> Filled up a room; and with long lust to eat
> Into my wearing, amongst all the ladies
> Singled out that dear form …
> And therefore in the height of all the revels,
> When music was heard loudest, courtiers busiest,
> And ladies great with laughter …

He harried her amidst a throng of pandars
That live upon damnation of both kinds
And fed the ravenous vulture of his lust. (29–35, 38–40, 43–5)

In this speech, sexual violence, rendered once again in images of destructive consumption, disrupts the apotheosis of the corpse: the scene ends with a solemn pact among the courtiers to dip 'the ruins of so fair a monument / ... in the defacer's blood' (68–9).[32]

But although Vindice would cast himself in the role of honourable avenger, his murder of the Duke makes it clear that he is himself a defacer, and to an extreme that surpasses even the sacrilege of Francisco in *The Duke of Milan*. If as skull Gloriana represents the supposed 'truth' of the uncorrupted male subject, Vindice's dressing up or 'fleshing' of the 'bony lady' stages sensationally the fatal potency that the sanitised, masculine sign would mask.[33] In this outrageous reconstruction of Gloriana's living body, erotic appeal and implicit putrefaction are fused: Vindice's own artifact serves as material metaphor for his consuming obsession.[34]

The death of the Duke is fully sensational. He mistakes the cosmeticised skull for the 'bright face' (1.1.16), the draped form for the 'life and beauty' (17) of a maid like the original Gloriana. Prior to the Duke's arrival, Vindice has boasted to Hippolito of his artistry in shaping a simulacrum of Gloriana from a skull, and in a speech reminiscent of his introduction of the *memento mori* in 1.1, he extols this painted version of her 'face' as a powerful emblem of putrefaction:

Does every proud and self-affecting dame
Camphor her face for this ... all for this?
Here might a scornful and ambitious woman
Look through and through herself; see, ladies, with false forms
You deceive men but cannot deceive worms. (3.5.83–4, 95–7)

'Pure' and 'impure' female beauty are, finally, indistinguishable. Both are subject to corruption but, more dangerously, are themselves corrupting, death-dealing to men. The ideal Gloriana to whom Vindice is supposedly devoted is no longer separable from the 'quaint piece of beauty' (53) that he serves up to the Duke. When Hippolito asks, 'Is this the form, that, living, shone so bright?' (66), Vindice replies, 'The very same. / And now methinks I could e'en chide myself / For doting on her beauty' (67–9).[35]

In the scene's climactic metamorphosis, the Duke's own head is transformed into a spontaneously putrefying piece of flesh, an incipient skull. Shortly after he kisses Gloriana's poisoned lips, the Duke's teeth 'are eaten out' (159), his tongue starts to rot and his eyes take on a ghastly shine. The 'quaintness of [Vindice's] malice' (108), as Hippolito puts it, satisfies Vindice's notion of justice in several ways: by replicating the Duke's attempted seduction of Gloriana; by killing the Duke with poison, the means of Gloriana's own death; and by rendering the Duke as a hideous counterfoil to Vindice's instrument of revenge. But such satisfaction comes at a price: in crafting this bizarre scenario and taking intimate pleasure in its unfolding, Vindice forfeits his own presumed inviolability from the moral corruption he has condemned so relentlessly.

Vindice's shift from voyeur to defiler not only exposes the tenuous façade of his moral rightousness, it also collapses the underlying rationale that has propped it up. The emblematic tableau of Gloriana and the Duke in mirror images of dissolution, with Vindice as sacrilegious puppeteer effecting their union, represents the collapse of gender-based defences against putrefaction itself. Gloriana's skull no longer has the fetishistic power of displacement that is suitably invested in a 'lapidary form'; and in deconstructing his own binary, Vindice has made clear the artificiality of his original apotheosis. Emptied, finally, of transcendent value, the Gloriana that murders the Duke is, after all, Vindice's creation.

But although the contamination of Gloriana's skull unequivocally exposes Vindice as fraud, prior appearances in the play of other 'females' – the women *manqué* of the Jacobean stage – have already compromised the misogyny he represents. The body beneath the corpse of Antonio's wife, for example, displayed so as to act as sexual stimulant, is that of a male actor, and Antonio's graphic reconstruction of 'her' rape serves to heighten the ambiguity of the figure's erotic appeal. Similarly, the repeated embraces of the Duchess and Spurio, together with the depiction of the Duchess/boy actor through images of wombs, conception and reproductive power, demonise the Duchess's sexuality while calling attention to it as an artificial construct. In one noteworthy instance, Middleton subverts the fiction of the Duchess's gender through comic means. The most meta-theatrical moment in her portrayal, a kind of early modern travesty of the 'primal scene', occurs when Lussurioso bursts into his father's bedchamber mistakenly expecting to find the Duchess in bed with Spurio (2.3).

But the scene (2.1) in which Vindice attempts to seduce his sister on behalf of Lussurioso, and to conjure his mother to join in his pandering, creates perhaps the most complicated aggregation of incestuously erotic tensions in the play.[36] In order to enlist his mother's services, Vindice incites her greed through a perversely erotic *blazon* in which he describes Castiza's body parts as properties to which his mother has a lover's claim. Developing this fantasy with his customary relish, Vindice includes in it a cross-gendered version of himself, through which he may identify simultaneously with the roles he has assigned to his mother and his sister's lover:

Would I be poor, dejected, scorned of greatness …
No, I would raise my state upon her [Castiza's] breast
And call her eyes my tenants; I would count
My yearly maintenance upon her cheeks,
Take coach upon her lip, and all her parts
Should keep men after men and I would ride
In pleasure upon pleasure. (2.1.90, 94–9)

Throughout the play, Vindice's many disguises serve to unfix his putative 'self', and his descriptions of himself as Piato are revealing in this connection. Shortly after presenting an idealised image of the skull of Gloriana at the outset of the play, Vindice conjures Piato in similar terms: 'Strike thou my forehead into dauntless marble, / Mine eyes to steady sapphires' (1.3.8–9), the sapphire eyes evoking Gloriana's diamond ones, as well as the incorruptible pearl of Antonio's wife's tomb. But by the end of the play, after Vindice has contaminated the whitened bones, that is, sexualised them in the service of death, he renounces his Piato-self, and in terms usually reserved for women: ''Tis well he died, he was a witch!' (5.3.121).

Thus in *The Revenger's Tragedy*, the threatening interstitiality of the female body is symbolically inscribed in men as well, and in a double sense. From a psychoanalytical perspective, the mutually dependent terms of any binary necessarily collapse into each other, so that woman as death-carrier and as incorruptible absolute represent an untenable, patriarchal bifurcation of the human subject's repressed fears and desires. But in the context of the unconscious, repression is precisely the point: the death drive is what *lies behind* the process of desire, the categories of 'male' and 'female' working to occlude the repressed connections between sexuality and death. Interestingly, and in contradistinction to these mechanisms, early modern theatricality seems deliberately to have 'played' with the very liminalities that such gender categories would deny, and in so doing to implicate man overtly in his self-serving constructions of woman. Indeed, it might be argued (again, in accordance with Benjamin) that the more extreme a symbolic demonisation appears to be, the more radically dual its signification. Vindice presents himself as misogynist, but reveals himself as witch.

The Duchess of Malfi

In *The Duchess of Malfi*,[37] the misogynist distortions of *The Revenger's Tragedy* are shaped into what we might anachronistically call a representation of sexual pathology. Albeit fully sensational, the play is very tightly crafted so as to concentrate its power on the creation of an aberrant, psychic underworld. Whereas the ingenuity of Vindice's 'devilish glee' counters, to some degree, the ambience of death in *The Revenger's Tragedy*, Webster's play is saturated with the humourless and often nightmarish imaginings of its *intrigants*. Like *Macbeth*, Shakespeare's tragedy of the netherworld, *The Duchess of Malfi* is replete with unsettling, slippery images of the interstitial, the in-between: images of dung, poison and blood; of wolf-men, wax figures, witches and lunatics; of mandrakes, hyenas and basilisks; of echoes, shadows and evanescent stains in snow. The pervasive sense of dislocation evoked by these images culminates in the Duchess's death-chamber – taboo sphere of Ferdinand's incestuous desire, nexus of sexuality and death.

Both the Duchess and Bosola eventually become suspended in the strange half-life created by Ferdinand's melancholic obsession with his sister. In psychoanalytical terms, melancholia itself is a dislocation, pointing back to an originary displacement, and in her study of the myth of Narcissus as a central trope in early modern writing, Lynn Enterline positions Webster's reference to this myth in a Lacanian framework. Narcissus, who cannot distinguish between himself and his reflection, dies as a result of unrequited desire, from an inability to separate an idea of 'self' from his mirrored image. Enterline (citing Kristeva) identifies the markers for such melancholia and its representation in Webster's play:

> melancholic affect accompanies the distinction between semiotic and symbolic functioning, for it marks 'separation and the beginnings of the dimension of the symbol'... As a *literary effect* [my emphasis], the representation of melancholia marks ... the ever present possibility of 'symbolic breakdown' ... in Webster's *The Duchess of Malfi* ... a vanishing distinction of sign from referent or an impasse in our ability to determine whether or not something is a sign defines the play's representation of 'melancholia' as a confusion between life and death, human and thing. (10, 6)[38]

As we shall see, Ferdinand's lycanthropy, a self-induced bestiality that immediately precedes his death, makes sense in early modern terms as one of the possible fates of the melancholic, marking the final stage of his progressive affliction. But it is also a wholly appropriate psychoanalytical emblem for Ferdinand's estrangement from the symbolic order. As Enterline demonstrates cogently, for the melancholic the mirroring likeness, like that of Narcissus, can turn 'unexpectedly deadly' (15):

> the melancholic subject's relentless search for its own origin – which is figured, in the [Lacanian] mirror, as a place from which the self may see and know itself – constantly puts the possibility of knowing such origin in doubt.(16)[39]

In Webster's play, 'the mirrored relation unto death' is 'between a brother and his twin sister ... in the mirror of his twin sister's desire, and of her maternal body, the melancholic Ferdinand finds himself reflected and estranged at once' (242). His inability to forfeit his fantasy of identification and his fury at its impossibility preclude his integration into the social order as represented in the play: Ferdinand's lycanthropy emblematises a psychic estrangement or exile from the ordinary structures of human life.

Although in an important sense the Duchess seems to direct the action in Webster's tragedy, I would argue that she functions primarily as Ferdinand's self-distorting mirror, the 'glass-house' (2.2.6) onto which he, and also Bosola, project their most extreme fantasies and fears.[40] Webster's triangulation of these figures is, in fact, so intimate that the death of the Duchess is not, as her persecutors hope, the end of their attachments. On the contrary, Ferdinand and Bosola find an inescapable oppression, an even worse torment, in the after-life of her corpse: because the death of the Duchess erases nothing, Ferdinand and Bosola would follow her to her grave.

As the ideological touchstone of the play, the Duchess appears in three avatars: as lover, mother and corpse.[41] These transformations not only mark her progress in the plot, they also define her changing relationships with Ferdinand and Bosola, as well as her self-appraisal. In describing her personal priorities, the Duchess, aware of the power of lineage, none the less values most highly those satisfactions that derive from her roles as lover and mother. The private world of the Duchess, as Susan Wells has argued, is given shape through an array of domestic details: 'She is the "sprawling'st bedfellow" … she eats apricots greedily; she calls out in childbirth; her hair turns grey';[42] she playfully teases and kisses her husband, and in her final moments she worries about cough syrup for her children. The curious insensitivity of the Duchess during much of the play to the precariousness of her position underscores the enormous gap between her sense of entitlement to marriage and maternity and Ferdinand's unrelenting prohibition: 'Why should only I, / Of all the other princes of the world, / Be cas'd up, like a holy relic? I have youth, / And a little beauty' (3.2.137–40).

The descent of the Duchess into nightmare, nobly borne, is none the less precipitous: 'I stand / As if a mine, beneath my feet, were ready / To be blown up' (3.2.155–7). This sense of alarming dislocation surfaces in her farewell to Antonio, in which she recounts a 'very strange dream' (3.5.12) of her own disempowerment[43] and begins to speak in metaphors of death – of withered laurel, of Charon's boat on the 'dismal lake', and of kisses as cold as 'a dead man's skull' (90). The fable she tells Bosola of the dogfish and the salmon, ostensibly a defence of Antonio's integrity, has a terrible subtext: equality is the gift of a ruthlessly indifferent nature, understood by the rival fish only when they are at the point of extinction:

Our value never can be truly known,
Till in the Fisher's basket we be shown;
I' th' Market then my price may be the higher,
Even when I am nearest to the Cook, and fire. (135–8)

Although the Duchess's exemplum alludes to Christ's promise as 'fisher of men' to establish man's 'value' according to a heavenly measure, its marketplace imagery suggests instead a reckoning of mankind's fate in terms of commerce and consumption.

The unvarnished starkness of this metaphor anticipates the courageous honesty that the Duchess will show in her decline, but also contrasts tellingly with the domestic commonplaces of her earlier conversation. In light of what awaits her, there is an affecting poignancy in the differences between the fish fable and the simple, beneficent nature that she invokes almost nostalgically in parting from Antonio:

The birds, that live i' th' field
On the wild benefit of nature, live
Happier than we; for they may choose their mates,
And carol their sweet pleasures to the spring. (17–20)[44]

Notwithstanding her assertiveness in challenging her brothers,[45] the Duchess seems content to remain in what she considers to be an unexceptional private sphere that fulfils her sexual and maternal needs.

The ordinariness of this perspective is, however, beyond the mental reach of her tormenters, for whom the Duchess exemplifies a sexuality so rooted in corruption that it literally poisons the bloodlines that underwrite the patriarchal order. Although markedly different in temperament, Ferdinand and Bosola are united in the impulse to displace their spiritual bankruptcy onto the unsuspecting Duchess, to construct an image of her as a mode of defining and defending themselves. In this sense they function as *alter egos*, or more precisely, as uncanny doubles, refracting each other's image; and this fragmentation of identity is repeated, albeit in a different key, in their individual relationships with the Duchess. Ferdinand, her twin, is unable to imagine a self apart from that of his contaminated sister; Bosola, Ferdinand's intelligencer, is himself indistinguishable from the multiple personae that he adopts in his employment. In contrast to the Duchess, both men seem unmoored from any stabilising centre, whereas she stands, as it were, in relief – the wife, the mother who finds nothing amiss in the natural order, whose own identity is secure.

But, of course, the figure of the Duchess on the early modern stage was itself unsecured, and the deliberate emphasis in Webster's fiction on her pregnancy, the delivery of her first child with Antonio and her subsequent fertility foreground a body that was itself 'split' or double, a body that complicates the emblematic status of the Duchess as a sexual benchmark in the play. These complications are especially apparent in 2.1, which represents, in highly unusual detail, a woman/boy actor in the last stages of pregnancy. Here, the condition of the Duchess, inadequately disguised by what Bosola calls a 'bawd farthingale' (153), is confirmed first by her greedy consumption of the apricots Bosola offers (a favourite food of expectant mothers), and later by the 'extreme cold sweat' (160) that marks the onset of her labour. This spectacle of the pregnant Duchess follows soon after her protracted courtship of Antonio (1.2): taken together, these scenes establish the symbolic centrality of the Duchess's erotic and reproductive functions. But their elaborate meta-theatricality sets up yet another screen, or mirror, in which the idea of gender identity slips between the gender of the image that is seen (the body of the actor as Duchess) and the imagined body that is obscured (that beneath the prosthesis of the costume).[46]

In a play that would probe the disruptive imbrication of sexuality in disease, corruption and death, such slippages dislocate and realign viewer perceptions so as to match those of the protagonists. Ferdinand and Bosola continually speak of the *inside* of the female body – its contaminating blood, its deteriorating flesh: they do not so much apprehend the bodily surfaces that confront them as the corruption (moral and physical) that these surfaces seem to mask. Since their misogynistic fantasies fix primarily on the Duchess, her body becomes in turn the visual focus of the viewer, who in another kind of split vision occasioned by transvestism, sees the Duchess as doubly gendered. Thus the dynamic of the play, its tenor and tonality, reside in the shifts among these inside/outside perspectives: in the process of witnessing (and identifying with) the fragmenting effects of sexual fixation, the spectator's own gaze is itself fragmented.

As the play's protagonists/fantasists, Ferdinand and Bosola are symbiotically linked, on the one hand, by a self-hating destructiveness, and, on the other, by an erotic *frisson* proceeding from their absorption in, and competition for, the Duchess. Their approaches to her subjugation, however, are characteristically different. Ferdinand, the fiery 'salamander' (3.3.49),[47] explosive and monomaniacal, seeks to exercise a near-absolute authority over her, and the eruptions of his imagination 'grown mad' (2.5.2) are, as Antonio puts it, 'perverse and turbulent' (1.2.94). Bosola, the 'impudent snake' (2.3.38), would control the Duchess by means of an intellectual gamesmanship, exploiting his acute instinct for human vulnerability in an intricate match of wits. Whereas Ferdinand is invested in an intensely personal fantasy of female corruption, Bosola's despairing vision is more comprehensive.

For Bosola, appearances are always deceptive, a form of 'candying' over the 'sin' (1.2.200) or 'swinish' disease (2.1.58) that invariably lies beneath. He speaks continually in images of rot – of disease and of dung and other animal by-products. His contemptuous castigation of the 'face physic' of the 'Old Lady' (2.1) suggests that, for him, the 'deep ruts and foul sloughs' (that is, layers of dead tissue) that lie beneath her cosmetics anticipate the corruption of the corpse:

> What thing is in this outward form of man
> To be belov'd? ...
> Though we are eaten up of lice, and worms,
> And though continually we bear about us
> A rotten and dead body, we delight
> To hide it in rich tissue; all our fear –
> Nay, all our terror – is lest our physician
> Should put us in the ground, to be made sweet. (45–6, 55–60)

In Bosola's inside/outside vision, the 'candy' of false appearances collapses into the sweetness of putrefaction. Just as on the physical level his metaphor obliterates the corporeal body that would lie between surface and interior, so too does its extended meaning deny the possibility of goodness.

For the most part, Bosola's tirades single out women as the consummate maskers whose 'witchcraft' finds the makings for artificial beauty in 'the fat of serpents; spawn of snakes, Jews' spittle, and their young children's ordure' (40–1). Significantly, his two meetings with the Old Lady, during which he expresses an unrestrained disgust for female degeneracy, frame the scene with the pregnant Duchess. In manipulating the Duchess, Bosola masks his scorn for sexual duplicity through the ploy of the apricots: after she has eaten them 'most vulturous[ly]' (2.2.2) as he puts it, he mentions in mock apology that the gardener 'did ripen them in horse-dung' (2.1.144). Although Bosola's abuse of the high-ranking Duchess is necessarily indirect, he envisages her transgression as endemic to her gender: 'I do wonder,' he queries of the Old Lady, 'you do not loathe yourselves' (47–8).

It is, however, already apparent at this point in the play that Bosola chiefly loathes *himself*, and that the image of dung is what he habitually associates with his erotically inflected role as Ferdinand's intelligencer. In the first of their contretemps, Ferdinand secures Bosola's service by offering what Bosola most wants: a place at court, an identifying status. But even as he capitulates, Bosola knows that this devil's bargain precludes both honour and autonomy: ' – what's my place? / The provisorship o' th' horse? say then my corruption / Grew out of horse dung: I am your creature' (1.1.285–7). Earlier, in a curiously self-abnegating attack on the syco-phancy of others, Bosola had scorned the courtiers who 'feed' on Ferdinand and his brother the Cardinal like 'crows, pies, and caterpillars' do on carrion: 'could I be one of their flattering panders, I would hang on their ears like a horse-leech till I were full, and then drop off' (52–4). But in recognising that his new position as intelligencer is tantamount to becoming

Ferdinand's 'familiar', that is, 'a very quaint invisible devil, in flesh' (260), a demon that sucks blood from the teat of a witch, Bosola confesses to a monstrous, yet intimate 'feeding' on Ferdinand that will indeed 'grow' his own corruption. In Bosola's curious case, however, this feeding or sucking of an animating body fluid (blood, semen) is simultaneously a savage regression to infantile dependency.

Even in his arrogant manipulation of the Duchess, Bosola's language is frequently laced with self-contemptuous images of disease: 'There's no more credit to be given to th' face / Than to a sick man's urine', Bosola informs Ferdinand (236–7), but later, in pretending to chastise the Duchess for her criticism of Antonio, he uses a similar image to indirectly castigate himself:

> I would sooner swim to the Bermudas on
> Two politicians' rotten bladders,
> Tied together with an intelligencer's heart-string,
> Than depend on so changeable a prince's favour. (3.2.266–9)[48]

Bosola's *double entendres* betray his sense of himself as a 'political monster',[49] a masquerader whose faces are as inscrutable as 'a sick man's urine'. 'Thou dost blanch mischief, / Wouldst make it white' (3.5.24–5) the Duchess tells him later, recognising the hypocrisy of his blandishments and unwittingly evoking the leper image ('the whiter, the fouler' [3.3.64]) – that Ferdinand uses to condemn the Duchess herself. Her remark is astute, but she does not yet fathom the degree to which Bosola's moral 'rot' is leprously whitewashed, or masked: when he promises to wear her secret (that of Antonio's identity) 'on th' inside of my heart' (3.2.302), the effect is chilling.

Bosola's strategic triumph in discovering Antonio's identity precipitates a crisis in which he, as well as the Duchess, is caught up in the otherworldly ambience of Ferdinand's waking nightmare. In this destabilising domain, the *pas de deux* between the Duchess and Bosola is no longer under Bosola's control: on the contrary, the Duchess's resolve in submitting to her tortures leaves him powerless to persuade or deceive her: 'I will save you', he promises at one point, perhaps sincerely, but Bosola's obligation to murder her instead is the inevitable outcome of his sinister pact with Ferdinand. As he moves inexorably towards this moment, Bosola's personae for once seem to shift involuntarily, alternating between cruelty and distress: the terrible intimacy of killing her seems virtually identical to that of preparing her for death.

Ironically, after the Duchess confronts the bizarre spectacle of Antonio and her children as wax figures, 'appearing as it they were dead' (4.1.55.2 S.D.), she gains the ascendancy in her power struggle with Bosola. Here acting as impresario of Ferdinand's elaborate subterfuge, Bosola seems unprepared for the Duchess's response:

There is not between heaven and earth one wish
I stay for after this: it wastes me more
Than were 't my picture, fashion'd out of wax,
Stuck with a magical needle and then buried
In some foul dunghill ... (61–5)[50]

In this strange adaptation of Bosola's own imagery of corruption, the Duchess describes her horror at what she sees in terms of a palpable wasting, the eating away of her insides magically corresponding to the deterioration of her imaged body in 'some foul dunghill'.[51] 'I am full of daggers' (90), she goes on to say, the daggers and the needle describing her personal pain, but also the process of decay that these instruments initiate, as well as her victimisation through a demonic "magic"'.[52] Paradoxically, by passionately insisting on an even worse fate for herself, the Duchess spurns the perversity of Ferdinand's tableau: defiant in an ostensible 'submission' to her tormenters, she appropriates the very devices by which they would subjugate her.

Ferdinand's sadistic spectacle may have been as unsettling for the early modern viewer as for the Duchess, in large part because of Webster's skill in disseminating his visual images through multiple screens. At first sight the audience, like the Duchess, is 'fooled' because Ferdinand has not yet identified the motionless figures as 'artificial': thus whereas in the fiction the Duchess understands these figures to be dead, the viewer would presumably understand them as representations of the dead. If the actors on Webster's stage were pretending to be wax impressions of themselves (and this seems highly likely), the usual double perspective would be in place (actor 'playing', living actor playing dead). But once Ferdinand announces that these are not 'true substantial bodies' (4.1.115), the spectator's perception is jolted by yet another layer of artifice: what is made to look dead might be, in Bosola's oxymoronic image, 'feign'd statues' (4.2.351). The effect is one of uncanny dislocation in Freud's sense of the term: for the viewer, the wax images do not seem to inhabit any familiar category of representation or being.[53] Presumably, there would also be a retroactive shock in realising that in the fiction the Duchess, unaware of the artifice of the tableau, has imagined the instrument of her own death as a wax image, eerily and magically animated to kill, as would a corpse, by wasting.

The alienating ambience of the wax figures is compounded by the unseemly elements of Bosola's charade of death: the 'dismal music', disjointed speeches and antic dance of the madmen; Bosola himself disguised as tombmaker and as bellmen; the executioners with 'a coffin, cords, and a bell' (4.2.165.1 S.D.).[54] Strangely, however, although Bosola is an active agent in persecuting the Duchess, he appears unable to detach himself from the nightmare to which he subjects her. Surprised by the Duchess's self-assurance in the face of death, he would find a new footing, as it were, for their relationship. But in their final struggle Bosola, who has vowed, ironically, never again to appear before the Duchess 'in my own shape' (4.1.124), cannot seem fully to inhabit his masks either. After the cruelty of the wax apparition, in a moment of self-disgust, he tells Ferdinand 'when you send me next, / The business shall be comfort' (136–7), but Ferdinand's response pointedly ridicules Bosola's claim to empathy: 'Very likely – / Thy pity is nothing of kin to thee' (137–8). Trapped in his unique no man's land, Bosola the comforting killer becomes a reluctant companion to the Duchess as she recedes into an otherworldly 'charnel' (165), a gloomy and menacing interstitial space.

'My trade is to flatter the dead, not the living – I am a tomb-maker' (147–8) Bosola tells his quarry, and in the hour of her death the Duchess indeed seems suspended in a half-life between the two. Regretting that she cannot 'hold but two days' conference with the dead' (22), the Duchess thinks 'of nothing' (15), 'sleeps' with open eyes;[55] to Cariola, she resembles her 'picture in the gallery, / A deal of life in show, but none in practice' (30–1). When the Duchess asks of Bosola, 'Who am I?' (123), he answers that she is a 'green mummy', that is, a living corpse, one that is not yet 'ripe' enough to produce the revivifying medicine, or *mummia*, that was extracted from the dead:[56]

> Thou are a box of worm-seed, at best, but a salvatory of green mummy: – what's this flesh? A little crudded milk, fantastical puff-paste; our bodies are weaker than those paper prisons boys use to keep flies in; more contemptible, since ours is to preserve earth-worms. (124–8)

For Bosola all bodies, not only that of the Duchess, are 'in show', like the picture in the gallery and the wax figures: *animation* is the sham. The 'real' purpose of the body is to become a corpse: to 'seed' a new generation of worms while producing a 'medicine' that ironically prolongs the 'contemptible' half-life of other bodies destined for consumption.

Bosola's reduction of human life to fundament or worm food indirectly connects his fate to the Duchess's, as does his perversely intimate conflation of funerary and bridal imagery in the ritual he stage directs for her death.[57] These stratagems seem directed at neutralising the difference between himself as murderer and the Duchess as victim, of exploiting her desperation in order to force her assent to his view of her fate. But once again the Duchess pre-empts Bosola's offensive by appropriating his weaponry – in this case, the idea of her corpse as 'worm-seed'.

With her customary gift for ironic inversion, the Duchess acknowledges that her body has already served as food for Bosola's gruesome feast, and recommends in particular its consumption by her brothers:

> In my last will I have not much to give;
> A many hungry guests have fed upon me. (199–200)

> I have so much obedience in my blood,
> I wish it in their [her brothers'] veins. (169–70)[58]

Given Ferdinand and the Cardinal's uncompromising repudiation of her blood as contaminated, her 'obedience' represents the afterlife of the Duchess's defiance, inescapably coursing through her brothers' veins. Her final command to Bosola – 'Go tell my brothers, when I am laid out, / They then may feed in quiet' (237) – is again double-edged, at once an acquiescence to her death and a condemnation of her brothers as blood-suckers: worms, certainly, the favoured image in Bosola's lexicon, but also perhaps, vampires.

The Duchess's transformation of her degradation, her refusal to submit to Bosola's nihilistic vision ('I am the Duchess of Malfi still'), finally usurps the power of this vision in Bosola himself. Alternating confusedly in the aftermath of her death between powerful, unanticipated emotions and his customary self-loathing, Bosola strikes out at Ferdinand, the 'cruel tyrant' (372):

> Your brother and yourself are worthy men;
> You have a pair of hearts are hollow graves,
> Rotten, and rotting others ... (318–20)

But Bosola's own heart, however momentarily refashioned, is hardly any less 'rotten' than that of his collaborator,[59] and his impulse to revive the Duchess after she stirs – 'Upon thy pale lips I will melt my *heart* / To store them with fresh colour' (344–5, my italics) – is from this point of view an obscenity. Heaven may seem 'to ope' (348) momentarily with the Duchess's eyes, but Bosola still finds 'writ' upon the 'black register' of his conscience 'a perspective / That shows [him] hell' (357–9).

None the less, the death of the Duchess makes a difference in the quality of this hell by challenging the premises of Bosola's misogynistic vision. Obsessed with what Benjamin would call the corruption of the physis, nature's mindless cycle of death and regeneration, Bosola would project the human manifestations of this corruption onto the female gender. He recognises the organic process he so despises in reproduction, in the Duchess's pregnant body: worse, he views women, whose reproductive bodies are especially mutable, as committed to an elaborate hypocrisy to mask the symptoms of organic decay. Despite the mobility of his own shape-shifting, itself an analogue to what he condemns in the cosmeticising of women; and despite the sexual ambiguities in the triangulation of his relationship with the Duchess through Ferdinand,[60] Bosola would none the less isolate himself from a physical and moral corruption that he identifies as distinctively female.

However, after the Duchess has established her moral ascendancy with unequivocal clarity, Bosola's system, always tenuous, is no longer workable. This loss of ideological purchase is immediately evident after the necrophiliac kiss when, bearing the Duchess's corpse in his arms, he is surprised to find himself weeping:

> This is manly sorrow:
> These tears, I am very certain, never grew
> In my mother's milk. My estate is sunk
> Below the degree of fear: where were
> These penitent fountains while she was living?
> O, they were frozen up! Here is a sight
> As direful to my soul as is the sword
> Unto a wretch hath slain his father. (361–8)

In this curious passage, Bosola, confused by his emotion, attempts to recoup his masculinity: by promoting, as it were, the Duchess's corpse to the status of a dead father, a patriarchal authority figure, he, the parricide, can locate the origin of his tears somewhere other than in 'my mother's milk'. But by the time of his own death, Bosola's turmoil has become a terrible detachment, unlike his earlier game-playing and beyond the defences of gender. Meta-theatrically describing the stance of his life as that of an 'an actor in the main of all' (5.5.85), he mourns the 'womanish' fear that inhabits the 'shadow' of human existence. And, in a final, haunting metaphor of his own impending 'voyage', Bosola exiles himself from those 'worthy minds' (including, of course, the Duchess) who despite everything suffer for justice:

> *Mal[ateste]*: How came Antonio by his death?
> *Bos[ola]*: In a mist: I know not how –
> Such a mistake as I have often seen
> In a play ...
> We are only like dead walls, or vaulted graves,
> That ruin'd, yields no echo: – Fare you well –
> ... O, this gloomy world!
> In what a shadow, or deep pit of darkness,
> Doth womanish and fearful mankind live!
> Let worthy minds ne'er stagger in distrust
> To suffer death, or shame for what is just –
> Mine is another voyage. (94–8, 100–5)

Bosola's ultimate fate as Cain-like human exile, cut off not only from salvation but also from any attachment to his fellow man, is replicated in that of Ferdinand. Because of his obsession with the Duchess ('My sister! O! my sister! there's the cause on 't' [5.5.71]), Ferdinand too ends up suspended in a marginal half-life, but sensationally so, by imagining himself to be a wolf-man or lycanthrope. This radical form of self-punishment reflects Ferdinand's inability to escape his obsession even after he has re-moved its object. That is, throughout the play Ferdinand's unacknowledged desire for his sister prompts him to require that she occupy one of the two emblematic positions prescribed by the symbolic order: that of chaste ideal (Douglas's unchanging lapidary state), wherein her sexual desires are wholly forbidden; or of 'notorious stumpet' (5.1.4), diseased in both body and spirit, and deserving of her brother's repudiation.[61] But because in Ferdinand's imagination his fate is 'twinned' to that of the Duchess, he is trapped by the impossibility of the choice he has constructed for her.

By delineating this conflict through a sequence of contrasting but interlocking images, Webster renders a brilliantly detailed portrait of the imbrication of death in sexual obsession. Ferdinand's language is rife with images of blood and fire, elements that are themselves unfixed, trans-formative. 'I could kill her now, / In you, or in myself, for I do think / It is some sin in us, heaven doth revenge / By her' Ferdinand says to his brother the Cardinal (2.5.63–6), acknowledging the blood lineage that connects them all, while coming perilously close to admitting a self-destructive complicity in his sister's supposed vice. This same complicity is implicit in the ambiguity of his fire images: on the one hand, fire represents self-consumption, that of both his own rage and of the Duchess's lust; and on the other, a purifying immolation.

It is, of course, the Duchess's failure to sustain Ferdinand's ideal of her that he blames for polluting the Calabrian bloodline: whereas once this blood – Ferdinand's own – 'ran pure' (4.1.122) in the Duchess's body, her promiscuity has rendered it rank, even demonic ('The witchcraft lies in her rank blood' [3.1.78]). The beauty of the Duchess may appear unblemished to others, but to Ferdinand the corrosive that now runs in her veins is like a self-consuming disease: 'methinks her fault and beauty / Blended together, show like leprosy / The whiter, the fouler' (3.3.62–4). In imagining the Duchess in terms of such extreme forms of defilement as leprosy and witchcraft, Ferdinand inadvertently reveals the power her beauty holds for him, as well as the counterweight he must construct to oppose it. No sexual or reproductive function that the Duchess considers 'natural' escapes this demonising scheme: Ferdinand transforms even her maternal milk into the blood of the witch/leper, perversely nursing a demon familiar at her witch's teat:

> For they whose faces do belie their hearts
> Are witches, ere they arrive at twenty years –
> Ay: and give the devil suck. (1.1.309–11)

Cleansing the Calabrian bloodline of such thoroughgoing contamination requires 'desperate physic', a kind of immolating exorcism:

> We must not now use balsamum, but fire,
> The smarting cupping-glass, for that's the mean
> To purge infected blood, such blood as hers: – (23–6)

Caught in an impossible dilemma of his own making, Ferdinand insists that his consuming anger – the 'wildfire rages' that erupt, in Pescara's phrase, 'like a deadly cannon' (3.3.54) – can be extinguished only when the polluted body of the Duchess is reduced to ashes. Short of this irrevocable repudiation of his sister, every other instance of violence (such as Antonio's murder) serves but to 'feed a fire, as great as my revenge' (4.2.140–1). Ironically, however, in describing the Duchess's lust as another kind of 'unquenchable wild-fire' (3.2.115), Ferdinand once again implicates his passion in hers. And in fantasising the incineration of the Duchess and Antonio at the moment that they are coupled sexually, he conflates his rage, the incestuous desire that compels his rage, and the sexual desire of the lovers in a single, brutal image:

> I would have their bodies
> Burnt in a coal-pit, with the ventage stopp'd,
> That their curs'd smoke might not ascend to heaven:
> Or dip the sheets they lie in, in pitch or sulphur,
> Wrap them in't, and then light them like a match ... (2.5.66–70)[62]

In Ferdinand's violent metaphor, the immolation of the Duchess is in-distinguishable from a vicarious fantasy of sex: paradoxically, his exorcism takes the form of an erotic investment. But Ferdinand also envisages an even more intimate way of killing his sister, which would purge her infected blood while asserting the priority of his sexual claim to her: that is, he would 'bleed' the Duchess with his father's dagger:

> You are my sister –
> This was my father's poniard: do you see?
> I'd be loth to see 't look rusty, 'cause 'twas his: – (1.1.330–2)

Later, immediately prior to threatening Antonio with death,[63] Ferdinand orders her to thrust the poniard into herself ('Die then, quickly!' [71]). Her refusal to 'die' in either the literal or sexual meaning of the term symbolically denies the precedence of their blood bond over her marriage bond, as well as Ferdinand's sexual ascendancy over Antonio.[64] It also marks Ferdinand's last attempt to urge the Duchess to acquiesce to his demands: the horrors that ensue recall his earlier resolve to spill her blood himself:

> here's the cursed day
> To prompt my memory, and here 't shall stick
> Till of her bleeding heart I make a sponge
> To wipe it out. (2.5.13–15)[65]

Go to, mistress!
'Tis not your whore's milk that shall quench my wild-fire,
But your whore's blood. (46–8)

Notwithstanding his threats, however, Ferdinand does not kill the Duchess directly and his sequence of sadistic tortures may be seen as a final, confused effort to force her into some kind of union with him. 'Why do you do this?' asks Bosola, and Ferdinand replies, 'To bring her to despair' (4.1.116) – that is, to wrench her from her domestic securities and make her an accomplice, albeit an unwilling one, to his own despair. The madmen, the wax tableau, the severed hand proffered in greeting, collectively create a transgressive, interstitial space in which the symbolic order is suspended and the line between reality and hallucination blurred. Because of the chiastic nature of his obsession, Ferdinand already inhabits this space: the indeterminate emblems of the death scene are, in a sense, extensions of his earlier fixations with blood and fire.

But Ferdinand's twin is 'the Duchess of Malfi still' – resistant to his domination, unassimilated to his desire – even when trapped in the murky netherworld of taboo. Worse, her murder fails to 'fix her in a general eclipse' (2.5.79), as Ferdinand hoped it would: on the contrary, the corpse of the Duchess exerts a powerful influence of its own over Ferdinand that sustains his obsession while reversing its direction. The serene beauty of the dead Duchess confuses him ('Cover her face: mine eyes dazzle: she died young' [4.2.264]), giving the lie to his notion of her living body as a conduit for the pestilent infection of 'whore's milk' and 'whore's blood' (2.5.46–8). Indeed, for Ferdinand the bright, clear corpse represents the Duchess as he would have her, the ideal before its ruination at his own hands: beautiful but self-possessed, whole and incorruptible. Caught up in a crisis of remorse, he rails at an uncomprehending Bosola for failing to intervene 'Between her innocence and my revenge' (4.2.278).

The curious circumspection of Ferdinand's question, 'Who doomed her to non-being?' encapsulates his reluctance to call the Duchess *dead* and to admit responsibility for her 'doom', even though he recognises she is no longer a 'being'. His lycanthropy thereby functions as a parallel state that dooms *him* to 'non-being' of a peculiar sort and that simultaneously allows him to violate the graveyard that she will soon inhabit.[66] He tells Bosola 'I'll go hunt the badger, by owl-light: / 'Tis a deed of darkness' (4.2.334–5), and later the Doctor describes other such deeds:

In those that are possess'd with [lycanthropy] there o'erflows
Such melancholy humour, they imagine
Themselves to be transformed into wolves,
Steal forth to churchyards in the dead of night,
And dig dead bodies up: as two nights since

> One met the duke, 'bout midnight in a lane
> Behind Saint Mark's church, with the leg of a man
> Upon his shoulder; and he howl'd fearfully;
> Said he was a wolf, only the difference
> Was, a wolf's skin was hairy on the outside,
> His on the inside; bade them take their swords,
>   Rip up his flesh ... (5.2.8–19)[67]

As lycanthrope, or werewolf, Ferdinand imagines himself to be a beast, but unlike the conventional image of the wolf-man, his carnivorous violence is turned back against himself:

> O, I'll tell thee
> The wolf shall find her grave, and scrape it up;
> Not to devour the corpse, but to discover
> The horrid murder. (4.2.308–11)

'To discover the horrid murder' is, of course, to discover not only the falsity of his former grounds for vilifying the Duchess but also the desire that prompted his fabrication. But because this desire is – literally – unspeakable, Ferdinand's lycanthropy functions more as a final, outrageous dodge than as a mode of exploring the causes of his affliction. Thus his resolve to invert the renowned cannibalism of the werewolf is, in a sense, consistent with the contradiction that inheres in his relationship with the Duchess: still striving in this pathetic new avatar to join his now dead sister, Ferdinand would, at the same time, devour her murderer, 'rip up' his own (twinned) flesh.

In the Greek myth of Lycaon, the namesake of Ferdinand's disease, cannibalism also figures as both transgression and punishment: because he offered Zeus human flesh to eat, Lycaon is himself transformed into a carnivorous wolf-man. This core metaphor – the turning against one's own flesh, both in the sense of one's humanity and one's own body – is figured in many early modern accounts of the lycanthrope's gruesome targeting of children, including his or her own. Stubbe Peter, for example, was said to have devoured thirteen children (after ripping some from the wombs of their mothers), before murdering his own son and taking particular pleasure in eating his brains.[68] With Ferdinand, Webster characteristically transforms the crassness of legend so as to represent the intricacies of aberration. When Ferdinand orders that the Duchess's children be strangled, presumably to cleanse the world of her memory, he calls them 'cubs' (4.1.33). But the flesh of the Duchess thus dehumanised is also Ferdinand's, and his dismissive remark to Bosola after the killings points ominously towards his own future: 'The death / Of young wolves is never to be pitied' (4.2.258–9).[69]

Ferdinand's fate as wolf-man is also implicit in his identifications with mutants or freaks of nature, such as mandrakes and basilisks: 'I have this night digg'd up a mandrake … And I am grown mad with't' (2.5.1–2), he cries after learning of the Duchess's 'bastard', referring to a plant resembling the lower half of the human form that supposedly fed on blood from a gallows; when uprooted, its shriek was thought to cause madness.[70] This simulacrum of man, nourished, as is a vampire, by human blood, is what Ferdinand has himself 'digg'd up', the metaphoric substitute for his madness. On other occasions, Ferdinand invokes the cockatrice or basilisk, a fabled reptile whose eye could kill and whose eggs – hatched by snakes, toads or wicked men – were equally poisonous when eaten. First imagining himself as 'changing eyes' with a basilisk in order to kill Antonio, he later turns the poison inward, hoping that the cockatrice 'remedy' used by the Doctor to treat his 'cruel, sore eyes' is that of a 'new-laid' (that is, deadly), egg (5.2.63–5).[71]

According to Mary Douglas, the dangerous influence of mutant creatures lies precisely in their status as hybrids, at once a part of the natural world yet outside its ordinary boundaries: because of this ambiguous relationship to the categories that structure nature, they function as powerful totems in the rituals of early societies.[72] But interestingly, in Webster's play it is the metamorphosed and freakish Ferdinand who castigates the Doctor/anatomist, together with his fragmented corpses, as unnatural:

> I will stamp him [the Doctor] into a cullis, flay off his skin, to cover one of the anatomies this rogue hath set i'th'cold yonder, in Barber-Chirurgeons' Hall. Hence, hence, you are all of you like beasts for the sacrifice; there's nothing left of you, but tongue, and belly, flattery, and lechery. (5.2.77–82)

Ferdinand's mixed metaphor of flaying and feeding, stripping down and breaking apart, evokes, in turn, a disease known as the 'ulcerous wolf' once referenced by Bosola. Like Ferdinand's lycanthropy, the ostensible 'wolf' in this disease is *in*side:

> There is a disease called a Wolf, because it consumeth and eateth up the flesh in the body next the sore, and must every day be fed with fresh meat, as Lambs, Pigeons, and such other things wherein is bloud, or else it consumeth all the flesh of the body, leaving not so much as the skin to cover the bones. (Topsell, Vol. 1, 577)

It is as if the body is flaying itself from within, leaving nothing, as an anatomist would, to 'preserve'.

There is, finally, no way for Ferdinand to exorcise his wolfish interior short of his own death; the murder of the Duchess is irrevocable, but it does not foreclose the interstitial world of his private nightmare. Still, Ferdinand's flirtation with death is hardly new. In both demonising and idealising the Duchess, his imaginings have never strayed far from the tomb: prior to her death it represents the murderous antidote to the fires of his rage and her lust; afterwards, it entices him as the hallowed site of her corpse, a place he will approach only as a beast. '[H]er marriage! – / That drew a stream of gall, quite through my heart' (4.2.286–7) he tells Bosola, transfixed by the sight of the dead Duchess, and it is indeed this unstaunchable wound to the heart that throughout the play drives him inexorably to his death.

'Make not your heart so dead a piece of flesh / To fear, more than to love me' the Duchess commands Antonio before taking him as husband: 'This is flesh, and blood, sir; / 'Tis not the figure cut in alabaster / Kneels at my husband's tomb' (1.1.451–5). From the outset, what the Duchess insists that she is not is, of course, what Ferdinand would have her: a stone image of sensate life, an immobilised corollary to her first husband's corpse. But the 'stream of gall' through Ferdinand's own heart deadens him instead, leaving in its wake a despair that feels like her husband's coffining:

> Thou art undone
> And thou hast ta'en that massy sheet of lead
> That hid thy husband's bones, and folded it
> About my heart. (3.2.111–14)[73]

As substitute corpse and substitute husband, Ferdinand's proprietary claim to the Duchess is absolute, but only in the realm of the dead, where their double deaths will 'twin' them forever.

Ferdinand comes close to expressing this wish directly when his horrible handiwork is finished and he finds himself 'dazzled' by the face of his sister's corpse: 'She and I were twins: / And should I die this instant, I had liv'd / Her time to a minute' (4.2.267–9). His response to the beautiful clarity of the Duchess in death evokes Antonio's earlier encomium which ironically encapsulates the idealisations of both 'husbands': 'All her particular worth grows to this sum: / She stains [eclipses] the time past, lights the time to come' [1.1.208–9].[74] At the moment of his death, Ferdinand seems to lament his desecration of this ideal. None the less, in suggesting the mutuality of their 'dust', as he once did their blood, he again claims his sister as origin of, and partner in, his destiny:

> My sister! O! my sister! there's the cause on 't:
> Whether we fall by ambition, blood, or lust,
> Like diamonds, we are cut with our own dust. (5.5.71–3)

The extraordinary psychological affect of *The Duchess of Malfi* may seem remarkable in light of its no-holds-barred approach to sensationalism, but I would again invoke Benjamin's thesis concerning the interdependence of 'interiority' and excess in the *Trauerspiel*. Benjamin has argued that no playwright matches Shakespeare in this transformative skill, but it is noteworthy that only Webster made a woman/boy actor the ethical and structural centrepiece of a tragedy about sexual obsession.[75] If, as I have suggested, the play explores misrecognised and taboo desire, then the foregrounded, transvestite and larger-than-life figure of the Duchess – and especially the figure of the Duchess's corpse – incite the viewer's apprehension of structures that have become unfixed[76] while providing an aptly ambiguous focus for the symbiotic obsessions of Ferdinand and Bosola. In the end, it is as difficult for the spectator to evade the death-obsessed imagination of the play as it is for the lycanthropic Ferdinand, in the fullness of his distraction, to obliterate his own shadow.

Notes

1. For a brief review of the controversy surrounding the authorship of this play, see Bryan Loughrey and Neil Taylor, eds., *Five Plays: Thomas Middleton* (London: Penguin, 1988), xxv–xxix. Most scholars now accept Middleton's authorship; the play will be included in the forthcoming edition of Middleton's works to be published by Oxford University Press.

2. The most incisive treatment of the parodic tonalities of Middleton's play is Jonathan Dollimore's '*The Revenger's Tragedy*: Providence, Parody, and Black Camp', which argues that 'In *The Revenger's Tragedy* a vital irony and a deep pessimism exist in disjunction' (117). See *Radical Tragedy: Religion, Ideology and Power in the Drama of Shakespeare and his Contemporaries* (Chicago: The University of Chicago Press, 1984); reprinted in Stevie Simkin, ed., *Revenge Tragedy* (Basingstoke: Palgrave and New York: St Martin's Press, 2001), 107–19. Two recent editors of the play have also usefully addressed this issue. Brian Gibbons discusses the play's affinities with classical satire as well as with the 'precarious, sardonic comedy' (xvii) of Marlowe and Marston; and Lars Engle nicely integrates the 'funny, satiric, and parodic' tone of much of the action with other features of the revenge tragedy genre. See Brian Gibbons, ed., *The Revenger's Tragedy*, 2nd edition (London: A & C Black and New York: Norton, 1997); and Lars Engle, Introduction to *The Revenger's Tragedy*, in David Bevington *et al.*, eds., *English Renaissance Drama* (New York and London: W. W. Norton, 2002), 1297–1302. Instances of extravagant humour in Middleton's play include Lussurioso's misguided intrusion into his father's bedchamber; the mistaken execution of the Younger Son; and in a decidedly more complex vein, the murder of the Duke (see below).

3. According to Clare Gittings' account of English funerary practices from 1580 to 1660, 'religious and doctrinal changes [had] little actual effect' on attitudes towards death and burial. See *Death, Burial, and the Individual in Early Modern England* (London and Sydney: Croom Helm, 1984), 59: 38–9. In a similar vein, David Cressy acknowledges that rituals of birth, marriage, and death customarily undergo gradual rather than radical transformation, however thoroughly the official prescriptions for such rituals may be reformulated. See *Birth, Marriage, and Death: Ritual, Religion, and the Life-Cycle in Tudor and Stuart England* (New York: Oxford University Press, 1997), 396–411. The most extensive demonstration of the gradations of change is Peter Marshall's

study of the Reformation dead. Marshall concludes that 'the Protestant Reformation ... represented in practice a complex and protracted process of cultural exchange in which the teachings of the reformers were adapted and internalized in sometimes unforeseen ways, and in which the concerns of the people helped to shape and direct the priorities of reformers ...' See *Beliefs and the Dead in Reformation England* (Oxford: Oxford University Press, 2002), 311.

4. For a thoroughgoing study of the development of European medicine from classical times to the early modern period, including medical training in fifteenth-century Italian and French universities, see Nancy G. Siraisi, *Medieval and Early Renaissance Medicine: An Introduction to Knowledge and Practice* (Chicago and London: University of Chicago Press, 1990).

5. Park states that 'the first unambiguous record of an Italian autopsy dates from 1286', and that by the fourteenth century, postmortems and anatomical dissections were being performed in Italy; however, 'there are few known references to autopsies and only one to a dissection in Germany, England, or France before the late fifteenth century'. There was, none the less, serious resistance in Italy to the northern practice of dividing the body in order to bury its parts in different places (expressly forbidden in 1299 by Pope Boniface VIII in his bull *Detestande feritatis*). In this connection, Park contends that 'Italians treated the body as an object of memory and commemoration', whereas believers in the 'liminal' corpse assumed that this liminality 'could inhere in its scattered parts as easily as in the whole'. See 'The Life of the Corpse: Division and Dissection in Later Medieval Europe', *Journal of the History of Medicine and Allied Sciences* 50: 1 (1994), 111–32, esp. 113, 114, 119. For a further development of these distinctions, see Park, 'The Criminal and the Saintly Body: Autopsy and Dissection in Renaissance Italy', *Renaissance Quarterly* 47: 1 (1994), 1–33; and Elizabeth A. R. Brown, 'Death and the Human Body in the Later Middle Ages: The Legislation of Boniface VIII on the Division of the Corpse', *Viator* 12 (1981), 226–41.

6. Other fluids from the corpse were efficacious as well. Phillipe Ariès cites a belief that 'the perspiration of corpses is good for haemorrhoids and tumours, and the hand of a cadaver applied to a diseased area can heal, as in the case of a woman suffering from dropsy who rubbed her abdomen with the still-warm hand of a corpse'. See *The Hour of Our Death*, trans. Helen Weaver (New York: Alfred A. Knopf, 1981), 357.

7. For an authoritative account of the plague in England during the reign of James I, see Leeds Barroll, *Politics, Plague, and Shakespeare's Theater: The Stuart Years* (Ithaca, NY: Cornell University Press, 1991). For an estimate of population reductions in England as a result of plague (from 4–6 million people in 1348 to 2.25–2.75 in the 1520s, rising to 4 million only in the 1590s), see Ralph Houlbrooke, *Death, Religion and the Family in England 1480–1750* (Oxford: Oxford University Press, 1998), 5. For comments on the influence of the plague on the developing taste for the macabre in northern Europe, see Cohen, 27–9; and Michael Neill, *Issues of Death: Mortality and Identity in English Renaissance Tragedy* (Oxford: Charendon Press, 1997), 19–22. In his study of plague in England from *c.* 1347 to 1700, Colin Platt puts the case strongly:

> Incontestably, neither the shroud brass nor the cadaver effigy was known before the pestilence. And whereas painted renderings of *The Three Living and the Three Dead* [a popular motif in which three courtiers encounter their skeletons] were relatively

common before the plague, it was in its later post-plague treatments that the legend lost its levity, to become at once more realistic and more socially aware, in the same spirit as the contemporary *Dance of Death*.

See *King Death: The Black Death and its Aftermath in Late-Medieval England* (Toronto and Buffalo: University of Toronto Press, 1996), 183–4.

8. This was a common belief, cited in a variety of medieval and early modern texts. See, for example, Question X of *The Malleus Maleficarum*, 1486–7; and Henri Bouguet, *Discours des Sorciers*, 1590, repr. in *The Lycanthropy Reader: Werewolves in Western Culture*, ed. Charlotte Otten (Syracuse, NY: Syracuse University Press, 1986), 106–14, esp. 111, and 77–90, esp. 84, respectively.

9. Representative tombs in England include those of the Duchess of Suffolk at Ewelme in 1475, and of John Wakeman at Tewkesbury in 1569. Suffolk's tomb positions an effigy with folded hands above and a decomposing corpse beneath; the corpse is 'carved with infinite detail' and includes long hair falling backwards from the skull. Wakeman's tomb depicts snakes, snails (a symbol of the resurrection) and a mouse preying on his corpse. See T. S. R. Boase, *Death in the Middle Ages: Mortality, Judgment, and Remembrance* (London: Thames and Hudson, 1972), esp. 82; and Kathleen Cohen, *Metamorphosis of a Death Symbol: The Transi Tomb in the Late Middle Ages and the Renaissance* (Berkeley and London: University of California Press, 1973), esp. 37–47. Paul Binski (134–52) analyses the transis as a manifestation of the late medieval concept of the double as seen also in the iconography of The Three Living and the Three Dead, and in the *Disputacione Betwyx the Body and Wormes* (see n. 10). See *Medieval Death: Ritual and Representation* (Ithaca, NY: Cornell University Press, 1996). In *Vampires, Burial, and Death: Folklore and Reality* (New Haven, CT and London: Yale University Press, 1988), Paul Barber points out that transi motifs may owe something to direct observation: 'sometimes a corpse can appear to be intact on the top, yet be disintegrated underneath, owing to the presence there of maggots, which require darkness and moisture' (163 n.).

10. Such detailing is also apparent in late medieval literature, for example, the anonymous thirty-one-stanza poem entitled *Disputacione Betwyx the Body and Wormes*, 1435–40 (London, BL, Add. ms. 37049, fols. 33ff.). The poem stages a debate between the corpse of a Lady and the worms that are preparing to eat her; the Lady ultimately submits to her own ravishment/consumption. See Cohen, 29–30.

11. With respect to late medieval depictions of the *danse macabre*, Barber contends that 'contrary to popular belief, many are not skeletons at all but decomposing bodies. Commonly they appear to be disemboweled, and sometimes worms or snakes emerge from the body cavity. Often the figures are shown emerging from charnel houses ... and it is clear that they are intended to represent bodies in a state of decay' (90).

12. The embalming of Henry VIII (which involved surgeons, apothecaries and wax chandlers) may be taken as representative of the process at its most elaborate, and involved spurging, or the washing and spicing of the body; cleansing, or the emptying of the bowels and the plugging of the rectum; bowelling, or the removal of the soft organs by means of a cut from the bottom of the rib cage to the pelvis; searing, or the cauterising of, the blood vessels after bowelling; embalming, or the purification of the inner cavity; dressing, or the application

of balms and oils on the outer body; and furnishing, or the positioning of the sudarium, or linen square covering the face, and the wrapping of the corpse in cere cloth and waxed twine. See Julian Litten, *The English Way of Death: The Common Funeral Since 1450* (London: Robert Hale, 1991), 39–40. As Park points out, techniques of embalming and autopsy were very similar ('The Criminal and Saintly Body', esp. 4–8).

13. Barber cites a folkloric superstition claiming that death can be caught by a living person by seeing the reflection of a corpse in a mirror. Vampires, the deadly revenants, are also associated with mirrors: they avoid them 'because they fear that someone may notice that they cast no reflection' (33).

14. See also Ruth Richardson, *Death, Dissection, and the Destitute* (Chicago: University of Chicago Press, 2000), 26–7; Clare Gittings, 'Sacred and Secular: 1558–1660', in *Death in England: An Illustrated History,* ed. Peter C. Jupp and Claire Gittings (New Bruswick, NJ: Rutgers University Press, 2000), 147–73, esp. 158–9; and Peter Marshall, *Beliefs and the Dead in Reformation England,* 134–9, 161–8, 292.

15. See Gittings (1984), 108–90; and Barber, 121. See also Kenneth Muir, ed., the Arden *Macbeth* (Cambridge, MA: Harvard University Press, 1957), 100–1, n. 125. Muir quotes James I's *Daemonologie* (1616): 'for as in a secret murther, if the dead carkasse bee at any time thereafter handled by the murtherer, it will gush out of bloud, as if the bloud were crying to the heauen for revenge of the murtherer'.

16. See Thomas W. Laqueur, *Making Sex: Body and Gender from the Greeks to Freud* (Cambridge, MA: Harvard University Press, 1990), 38–42, *passim*; and Gail Kern Paster, *The Body Embarrassed: Drama and the Disciplines of Shame in Early Modern England* (Ithaca, NY and New York: Cornell University Press, 1993), 68–84, *passim*.

17. Alchemical transmutation was viewed analogously. In alchemical theory, matter contains a 'spiritual' principle that perfects it through 'repeated reversions to the state of prime matter', a 'process at once self-devouring and self-generating' (Berry, *Shakespeare's Feminine Endings*, 18). Cohen quotes this principle as stated in the *Margarita Pretiosa* of Petrus Bonus of Ferrara (1330): 'When the stone decomposes to a powder like a man in his grave, then is that substance strengthened and improved, as after the resurrection man becomes stronger and younger than he was before.' See *Bibliotheca chemica curiosa*, ed. I. Magnetus (Geneva, 1702), Vol. VIII; Cohen, 97.

18. In England, as elsewhere, the practice of anatomical dissection had preceded its public demonstration in amphitheatres. For a description of dissections in the mid-sixteenth century by practitioners at Oxford and Cambridge, by members of the Companies of Barbers and Surgeons (united by the Act of 1540) and by the College of Physicians in London, see Sawday (1995: 4, 56–7); see also Neill, 102–40, esp. 115–17, n. 21.

19. Park notes that 'the continuing and widespread popular resistance' to the practice of anatomical dissection in England and other northern European countries 'culminated in the Tyburn riots of the mid-eighteenth century, in which Londoners protested violently at the gallows to deny surgeons access to the bodies of the hanged' ('The Life of the Corpse', 130). See also Peter Linebaugh, 'The Tyburn Riot against the Surgeons', in Douglas Hay, Peter Linebaugh, John Rule and E. P. Thompson, eds., *Albion's Fatal Tree: Crime and*

Society in Eighteenth-Century England (Harmondsworth: Penguin, 1975), 65–117.

20. In Christian hagiography, on the other hand, the death of the martyr by some mutilating means, such as being torn by animals, was considered a sign of special holiness. Park discusses the often contradictory linkages between the martyr, the criminal and the anatomist's corpse in 'The Criminal and Saintly Body', esp. 23–9.

21. Many reports of such practices in Italy and elsewhere originated with Vesalius himself, who, in the first edition of the *Fabrica*, 'recounts with evident relish and amusement' the illegal lengths to which he and his students were willing to go to obtain cadavers (and if necessary to obscure their identities by flaying). Not surprisingly, fear of vivisection was also common among opponents of anatomical dissection. See Park, 'The Criminal and Saintly Body', 18–20.

22. Helkiah Crooke, MIKPOKO MO PA IA. [Mikcrocosmagraphia] *A Description of the Body of Man*, 1615, STC 6062.2; B4v (12). Trained in Leiden, and a well-known follower of Vesalius in England, Crooke's inclusion of the Vesalian illustrations in his anatomical treatise evoked a protest from the English religious authorities, directed especially against 'vernacular discussion of the mechanism of generation' (Sawday, 226). In quoting from this and all other early modern texts, I have silently altered long ſ to 's'.

23. Thomas Browne, *Religio Medici*, 1642, STC B5166; E4v, E5 (72, 73).

24. 'In our study of Anatomy there is a masse of mysterious Philosophy ... [yet] I find not any proper Organ or instrument for the rationall soule; for in the Brain, which we terme the seate of Reason, there is not any thing of moment more then I can discover in the crany of a beast' (E3v, [70]).

25. Unlike the prose expositions of Crooke and Browne, Fletcher's *The Purple Island, or The Isle of Man* (1633), STC 11082, is an extravagant allegorical poem that represents the body as the map or design for Christian salvation. In a presumed imitation of classical models of annotation, Fletcher divides his poetic text (an allegory of the 'body' of England dismantled, reborn and redeemed) from his marginalia (notes on anatomical learning), a stratagem which, in this case, mystifies the relationship between the religious and the scientific. Fletcher's metaphor for the 'membrane or skinne' that covers the flesh of the body, for example, is curiously erotic:

> As when a virgin her snow-circled breast
> Displaying hides, and hiding sweet displaies,
> The greater segments cover'd, and the rest
> The vail transparent willingly betraies;
> Thus takes and gives, thus lends and borrows light:
> Lest eyes should surfet with too greedy sight,
> Transparent lawns withhold, more to increase delight. (C1v, [18])

For a useful analysis of Fletcher's anomalous position within the 'culture of dissection' (177), see Sawday, 170–82. For discussion of Browne, see Neill, 125–6; of Crooke, Neill, 130–3, and Sawday, 167–9; of Fletcher, Sawday, 170–82, and Neill, 130–3.

26. In her seminal essay on *Othello* and *Hamlet*, Patricia Parker explores the tension between images of discovery, of opening up, and images of the secret and frequently monstrous, especially as they delineate concepts of the female. See *Shakespeare from the Margins: Language, Culture, Context* (Chicago and

London: University of Chicago Press, 1996), 229–72.

27. In an analysis of *The Revenger's Tragedy*, Karin S. Coddon cites several gendered illustrations of dissection, including a woodcut from Jacob Rueff's *De conceptu et generationis hominus* (1554) that 'shows a (presumably) living, naked woman with her abdomen – from her vaginal lips to just below her breasts – completely opened up, her reproductive organs once again directly facing the reader's eye'. Coddon points out that 'illustrations of the dissection of male corpses typically present the body laid in horizontal (that is left to right) position; even Rembrandt's *Anatomy of Dr. Joan Deyman*, in which the male body is facing the spectator of the painting, depicts the corpse with his groin area discreetly covered' (126). See '"For Show or Useless Property": Necrophilia and *The Revenger's Tragedy*', in Stevie Simkin, ed., *Revenge Tragedy* (Basingstoke: Palgrave and New York: St Martin's Press, 2001), 121–41.

28. Kristeva argues that there are only two modes of identification with the symbolic order open to women: as virgin, the sadistic model, in which she identifies with the father, renouncing *jouissance* and the mother; and as mother, the masochistic model, in which she engages in 'an endless struggle between the orgasmic maternal body and the symbolic prohibition' (147). Both models mediate the needs of the male community. See 'About Chinese Women', in *The Kristeva Reader*, ed. Toril Moi (New York: Columbia University Press, 1986), 138–59. Kristeva's position is indebted to Lacan's essay on the symbolic construction of 'woman' in relation to superseding male categories, as encapsulated in his controversial statement, 'The woman does not exist' (144). See 'God and the *Jouissance* of The Woman. A Love Letter', in *Feminine Sexuality: Jacques Lacan and the École Freudienne*, eds. Juliet Mitchell and Jacqueline Rose (New York: Norton, 1985), 138–48.

29. The play was entered in the Stationers' Register on 7 October 1607 (along with *A Trick to Catch the Old One*) with no ascription of authorship, and printed in the same year by George Eld; estimated date of composition is 1606–7. References to the text in this essay are taken from Gibbons' 1997 Norton edition (see n. 2, p. 159).

30. Jewels also function as the currency of lust. In 1.2, the jewel that 'quivers' (114) in Spurio's ear is a gift from the Duchess, his stepmother and future mistress; Lussurioso sends 'jewels that were able to ravish' (1.3.96) to Castiza, Vindice's virtuous sister; and Vindice, posing as Lussurioso's pander, assures his sister that as mistress to the Duke's son her forehead will 'Dazzle the world with jewels' (2.1.188).

31. In 'Reading the Body and the Jacobean Theater of Consumption: *The Revenger's Tragedy* (1606)', Peter Stallybrass examines 'the symbolic burden that women are forced to bear … when they are conceptualized as mapping both an ideal enclosure and its impossibility, both the negation of and the figures for eating/being eaten, corrupter/corrupted' (218). Images of eating and kissing, which foreground the mouth, also figure prominently in the representation of the Duchess, and of Gloriana as agent of death. See *Staging the Renaissance: Reinterpretations of Elizabethan and Jacobean Drama*, eds. David Scott Kastan and Peter Stallybrasss (New York and London: Routledge, 1991), 210–20.

32. Dollimore and Coddon also comment on the patriarchal appropriation of the wife's corpse. Dollimore argues that 'A language of artificial grandeur reeking

of affected grief tells us that what is being celebrated is not her innate virtue but her dutiful suicide, her obedience to male-imposed terms of sexual honour' (110); and Codden that 'The paeans to the woman's corpse ... seem to imply that the emblematic desirable female body is a dead one, spectacularly displayed to appraising, evaluating male gazes' (132).

33. Vindice's rendering the skull as corpse resonates with the contrast between intact and putrefying bodies in the transi tombs (although here, of course, Vindice is reversing the process); and with the eroticised enlivening of skeletons as agents of death in the *danse macabre*.

34. Interestingly, Coddon finds the necrophiliac eroticism of this scene reminiscent of the simultaneous attraction and revulsion felt by some anatomists (including Leonardo) towards the horrors of dissection (125, 128).

35. Coddon points out that in presenting the skull to Antonio, Vindice 'pictures [its] presence at "revels, forgetful feasts and unclean brothels" (3.5.89 [90–1 in Gibbons]), a peculiar imagined situation of the virtuous lady's skull in the very spaces of lechery' (135). Vindice's imagery here also evokes Spurio's description of his conception 'in impudent wine and lust' (1.2.187–90).

36. For further commentary on Vindice's relationships with his mother and sister, see Stallybrass, 210 and *passim*.

37. John Webster's name appears on the title-page of the first publication of the play, printed by Nicholas Okes 'As it was Presented priuatly, at the Black-/Friers; and publiquely at the Globe, By the/Kings Maiesties Seruants'. A list of actors' names prefixed to the first edition helps to date these performances at *c*.1613–14, with the date of composition likely to be 1612–13. See John Russell Brown, ed., 'Introduction' to the Revels edition (Manchester and New York: Manchester University Press, 1974), xvii–xxiv.

38. See *The Tears of Narcissus: Melancholia and Masculinity in Early Modern Writing* (Stanford, CA: Stanford University Press, 1995), 7. In the course of developing her argument, Enterline makes a compelling case for the relevance of psychoanalytical theory itself to literary analysis. At the outset of her book, she addresses this issue briefly in personal terms that apply equally to my own study of the indeterminate corpse:

> I have nonetheless found that psychoanalytic work on the constitution of the subject in language, if read with a certain lively feminist suspicion, is crucial for asking how, and with what effects, melancholia disrupts the smoothly working relationship between the sign, the subject, and sexuality in these texts. It is in short, precisely psychoanalysis's speculation about the production and dissolution of the subject in language that helped me to understand why melancholia became such a persuasive literary (and not just a psychological) category. (7)

39. In this connection, Enterline analyses Freud's metaphor that in melancholia the 'shadow of the object' has 'fallen back on the ego' as a way of describing the role of introjection in ego formation. According to Enterline, Freud argued in *Mourning and Melancholia* (1917) that

> self-hatred in fact disguises anger directed against another who has already become internalised and about whom the lamenting subject remains deeply ambivalent ... [But] in *The Ego and the Id* (1923), [Freud] returns to melancholia as a process that illuminates *the very mechanisms by which an ego is constituted* ... Freud solders identification, melancholia's chief mechanism, together with those negotiations with loss that establish the subject per se. (21, 22, my italics)

Lacan's mirror stage of development, in which a fantasy of union inaugurates a fissure, is one such negotiation on a pre-discursive level, as is Kristeva's pre-imaginary 'primal repression' (see Chapter 1, nn. 7 and 8, pp. 19–20, and *passim*).

40. The glass-house, or factory, is one of Bosola's sardonic sexual images:

    > There was a young waiting-woman, had a monstrous desire to see the glass-house ... And it was only to know what strange instrument it was, should swell up a glass to the fashion of a woman's belly. (2.2.5, 6, 3–10)

    During the Duchess's death scene, the second Madman describes the glass factory as hell, and the glass-blower as the devil: 'Hell is a mere glass-house, where the devils are continually blowing up women's souls, on hollow irons, and the fire never goes out' (4.2.77–9). In this context, a 'soul' is 'probably imagined ... as a naked body, as in pictorial representations of hell' (see Revels edition, note, p. 120).

41. In 'The Theme of the Three Caskets', Freud discusses the function of ancient female deities as dual symbols of love and death, and in this context examines the interdependence of the 'three inevitable relations that a man has with a woman': his relation to 'the woman who bears him, the woman who is his mate and the woman who destroys him', namely, Mother Earth (522). See *The Freud Reader*, ed. Peter Gay, trans. James Strachey (New York and London: Norton, 1989), 514–22. In a fascinating essay on *The Merchant of Venice*, John Drakakis adapts Freud's paradigm to a reading of Portia, but especially of Jessica, as transformed 'goddesses of death', taking into account the uses of cross-dressing in the play's manipulation of gender roles. Drakakis points out that whereas Portia's mode of self-assertion remains within the patriarchal boundaries of her father's will, Jessica's transgression against Shylock is not inscribed in the law, but 'is the metaphorical equivalent of death itself'. Like Derrida's pharmakon, Jessica acts as both 'poison' and 'cure', 'is not anything in herself, but rather an effect of the structures in which she is variously inscribed'. See 'Jessica', in *The Merchant of Venice: New Critical Essays*, ed. John W. Mahon and Ellen MacLeod Mahon (New York and London: Routledge, 2002), 145–63, esp. 148, 154.

42. See Susan Wells, *The Dialectics of Representation* (Baltimore: Johns Hopkins University Press, 1985), 66.

43. 'Methought I wore my coronet of state, / And on a sudden all the diamonds / Were changed to pearls' (3.5.12–14).

44. Bird imagery is used throughout the play in connection with the Duchess. In 3.2, for example, after Ferdinand has surprised her in her bedchamber, she rebuffs him with a pragmatic declaration that woefully misjudges her brother: 'I am married ... Happily, not to your liking: but for that / Alas: your shears do come untimely now / To clip the bird's wings, that's already flown' (84–87). Once she is in prison, her references are to caged birds – the robin redbreast, nightingale and lark (4.2.13–14), the latter image picked up and elaborated by Bosola to express the human condition itself: 'Didst thou ever see a lark in a cage? such is the soul in the body: the world is like her little turf of grass, and the heaven o'er our heads like her looking-glass, only gives us a miserable knowledge of the small compass of our prison' (128–33).

45. The Duchess's fearless iconoclasm – 'Shall this move me? / If all my royal kindred / Lay in my way unto this marriage / I'd make them my low foot-steps'

(1.1.333–5) – is ruefully acknowledged in the farewell scene:

> Must I like to a slave-born Russian
> Account it praise to suffer tyranny?
> And yet, oh heaven, thy heavy hand is in't.
> I have seen my little boy oft scourge his top
> And compared myself to 'it: naught made me e'er
> Go right but heaven's scourge-stick. (3.5.74–9)

The Duchess also reveals her impatience with constraints at less critical points in the play, such as when she urges Antonio to remove his hat in defiance of court convention (2.1).

46. As Stallybrass points out ('Transvestism and the "Body Beneath"'), this imagined body (in any early modern play) need not be that of a male.
47. The salamander, a kind of lizard, was 'emblematic of passion, destruction, or torment' because it lived in fire (see the Revels edition, note p. 94). After the Duchess's death and Ferdinand's imagined metamorphosis, the doctor who would treat his lycanthropy offers him the skin of the salamander as an atropaic device: 'I have brought your grace a salamander's skin to keep you from sun-burning' (5.2.62–3).
48. Bosola refers disparagingly to intelligencers at another time in this scene, also in the context of a betrayal of trust:

> these [Antonio's followers] are rogues ...
> Would have prostituted their daughters to his lust;
> Made their first-born intelligencers ...
> ... and do these lice drop off now? (228, 32–3, 35)

49. The phrase is Antonio's, used in a conversation with Delio to describe the followers of the Cardinal: 'he strews in his way flatterers, panders, intelligencers, atheists, and a thousand such political monsters' (1.1.161–3).
50. Dekker also refers to this tradition in *The Whore of Babylon* (1605–7):

> This virgin waxe
> Bury I will in slimy putrid ground,
> Where it may piecemeal rot: As this consumes,
> So shall shee pine, and after languor die.
> These pins shall stick like daggers to her heart,
> And eating through her breast, turn there to gripings,
> Cramp-like convulsions, shrinking up her nerves,
> As into this they eat. (2.2.207–14)
>
> *3 King*   Where wilt thou bury it?
> *Conjurer*   On this dunghill. (219–20)

See *The Whore of Babylon: A Critical Edition*, ed. Marianne Gateson Riely (New York and London: Garland Publishing, Inc., 1980).
51. In Henri Bouguet's account of lycanthropes, or werewolves, he describes a common association of female hair and dung: 'Also we observe that if a woman's hair be hidden in dung, it is changed to a serpent, as also is a rotten rod or wand' (83). See Otten, 77–90.
52. There is also a clear association here with Ferdinand's poniard, which will be discussed shortly.
53. For a commentary on the uncanny, see Chapter 1, note 10, p. 20.
54. The fourth act of *The Duchess of Malfi* is one of the clearest early modern English examples of Benjamin's *Trauerspiel* in that its full-blown sensationalism

none the less works to intensify the viewer's identification with the Duchess.

55. *Duch.* When I muse thus, I sleep.
   Cari. Like a madman, with your eyes open? (16–17)

56. See Revels edition, note, p. 123; and p. 130 of this chapter.

57. Call upon our dame, aloud,
   And bid her quickly don her shroud ...
   Strew your hair with powders sweet,
   Don clean linen, bathe your feet ... (180–1, 189–90)

   During Bosola's dirge, he may well have sounded his bell (see Revels edition, note, p. 126). Bosola's ceremony fulfills Ferdinand's prophetic threat to the Duchess when denying her right to remarry: 'Such weddings may more properly be said / To be executed, than celebrated' (1.1.322–3).

58. Enterline points out that 'read in light of the play's fascination with [the Duchess'] maternity, such "feeding" pictures a gruesomely incestuous meal' (247).

59. Bosola's extreme cruelty in executing Cariola, and his order to 'strangle the children', were enacted just moments before this accusation.

60. Here again Webster's use of the transvestite convention underscores the artificiality of gender and its supposed relationship to 'identity' as Bosola would construct it: the erotic valences in the Ferdinand/Bosola/Duchess dynamic are not always object-specific.

61. Ferdinand's construction of woman is, of course, similar to that of Vindice and also of Bosola, but in focusing on his sister's failure to achieve an ideal, Ferdinand shifts the emphasis of Bosola's misogyny. Moreover, I would argue that Ferdinand's explosive violence is a function of frustrated desire, whereas Bosola's calculated cruelty represents a resistance to the experience of desire.

62. Ferdinand's graphic sexual imagination is apparent at other times as well. In 5.2, for example, he would restrain himself from mentally visualising the Duchess in the act of sex because to do so incites him to violence:
   Ferd. Methinks I see her laughing –
   Excellent hyena! – talk to me somewhat, quickly,
   Or my imagination will carry me
   To see her, in the shameful act of sin.
   Card. With whom?
   Ferd. Happily [haply] with some strong thigh'd bargeman;
   Or one o' th' wood-yard, that can quoit the sledge,
   Or toss the bar, or else some lovely squire
   That carries coals up to her privy lodgings.
   Card. You fly beyond your reason. (38–46)

63.   ... for thine own sake
   Let me not know thee:
   ...
   It would beget such violent effects
   As would damn us both (3.2.91–2, 94–5)

64. Ferdinand's command that the Duchess 'die' is part of a series of parallel images that underscores the sexual rivalry of Ferdinand and Antonio. Ferdinand's poniard is matched by the 'naked sword' that the Duchess would lay between her and Antonio (1.1.501); the ring that Antonio wins at tilting becomes the wedding ring that binds him to the Duchess, and later the 'love-token' on the hand that Ferdinand proffers as Antonio's, but the Duchess initially mistakes

for Ferdinand's own (4.1.47); the 'keys' that Antonio holds to the Duchess's heart are invoked by her at the moment (3.2.62) that Ferdinand enters 'into her bed-chamber' by means of a 'false key' (3.1.81, 80) and is first perceived by the Duchess in her mirror: 'You have cause to love me', she says to Antonio immediately before seeing Ferdinand; 'I enter'd you into my heart / Before you would vouchsafe to call for the keys' (3.1.61–2). Webster makes clear the structural parallel between the courtship / wedding and execution scenes (1.1, 3.5) through Ferdinand's reference to 'executed' marriages (1.1.323) and through the Duchess's playful pretence with Antonio that she has summoned him to make her will:

> *Ant.*   I'd have you first provide for a good husband,
>   Give him all.
> *Duch.*   All?
> *Ant.*   Yes, your excellent self.
> *Duch.*   In a winding sheet?
> *Ant.*   In a couple. (1.1.387–9)

Ferdinand's own 'marriage' to the Duchess is finally effected through the noose with which she is strangled, described in reference to Cariola's similar death as a 'wedding ring' (4.2.249).

65. Again, Ferdinand's metaphor foregrounds an unacknowledged irony in the notion that contaminated blood could serve as a cleansing agent. A few lines later, his image of his own tear-stained handkerchief as a dressing for the Duchess's wounds suggests the same paradox in a different register:

> *Ferd.*   There is a kind of pity in mine eye,
>   I'll give it to my handkercher; and now 'tis here,
>   I'll bequeath this to her bastard.
> *Card.*   What to do?
> *Ferd.*   Why, to make soft lint for his mother's wounds,
>   When I have hew'd her to pieces. (27–32)

66. There was considerable controversy during the early modern period over whether the metamorphosis of the human body actually occurred as a function of witchcraft or demonic influence, or was imagined (as is Ferdinand's) as a function of delusion or madness. Fundamentally, the issue is implicated in that of the Incarnation, as the medieval cleric Giraldus Cambrensis recognised:

> It cannot be disputed, but must be believed with the most assured faith, that the divine nature assumed human nature for the salvation of the world, while in the present case, by no less a miracle, we find that at God's bidding, to exhibit his power and righteous judgment, human nature assumed that of a wolf. (59)

See *Topographia Hibernica* (1187), trans. Thomas Forester in *The Historical Works of Giraldus Cambrenis*, ed. Thomas Wright (London: Bell, 1913), 79–84; repr. Otten, 57–61. Possibly seeing the danger of debating the core issue, Reginald Scot stressed the absurdity of human metamorphosis as well as its impossibility as a manifestation of demonic agency (see *The discouerie of witchcraft*, 1584, STC 21864, 5 Booke, Cap. 1–6 (Hv–J3v [89–102]). But for most the issue was not so clear. For example, Henri Boguet, a prominent French judge, Robert Burton and King James I all concluded with Scot that lycanthropy was a form of madness or melancholy, but they provided more measured opinions. In *The Anatomy of Melancholy* (1621), STC 4159, Burton classified it as a 'Disease of the Minde':

> *Lycanthropia*, which *Avicenna* calles *Cucubuth*, others *Lupinam insaniam*, or Woolfe madnesse, when men runne howling about graues and fields in the night, and will not be perswaded but that they are Wolues, or some such beasts. *Aetius* and *Paulus* call it a kinde of *Melancholy*, but I should rather referre it to *Madnesse*, as most doe. (I.i.i.A7 [13])

See also James VI and I, *Daemonologie*, Edinburgh, 1597, STC 14364, 60–2; and Henri Boguet, Otten, 77–90. The verdict of trial records, on the other hand, was often far less ambiguous: for example, the 1589 record of the trial of the Dutchman Stubbe Peter (probably the most notorious lycanthrope of the period) insists that numerous witnesses to a metamorphosis establish its material existence. See f. E. Venge, *A True Discourse Declaring the Damnable Life and Death of One Stubbe Peter*, 1590, STC 23375. In a useful analysis of the historical complexity of the issue, Stuart Clark stresses that the modern distinction between science and the occult distorts the ambiguities of early modern hermeneutics, in which it was virtually impossible to distinguish between the miraculous and the magical, the supernatural and the '*unusual*', that is, phenomena that were thought to have natural causes not yet discovered or understood. See 'The Scientific Status of Demonology', in *Occult and Scientific Mentalities in the Renaissance*, ed. Brian Vickers (Cambridge: Cambridge University Press, 1984), 351–73; repr. in Otten, 168–94.

67. The doctor's description is a adaptation of a passage (386–92) in I. Goulart's *Admirable and Memorable Histories*, translated from the French by Ed. Grimeston in 1607 and published in London; repr., Otten, 41–4. In re-assembling details from Goulart, Webster substitutes, significantly I think, the more personalised 'inside/outside' of ll.17–18 for Goulart's phrase 'Wolves were commonlie hayrie without, and hee was betwixt the skinne and the flesh' (42). Enterline comments tellingly on this change:

> With his body's envelope inverted, the hair on the skin's outside folding back into the skin's inside, Ferdinand loses the boundary that marked the difference between inside and outside the self ... As this double-crossing takes place – inner and outer worlds, psychic and somatic experience – Ferdinand seems, strangely, neither absent nor present (275–6).

68. See Otten, 69–72. In *History of Four-footed Beasts and Serpents*, 1607, STC 24123, Edward Topsell includes child sacrifice in his description of the Lycaon myth:

> this disease some call *Lycaon*, and men oppressed therewith *Lycaones*, because that there was one *Lycaon* as it is feigned by the Poets, who for his wickedness or *sacrificing of a childe*, was by *Jupiter* turned into a Wolf, being utterly distracted of humane understanding ... And this is most strange, that men thus diseased should desire the graves of the dead. (Vol. I, 578, my italics).

Reginald Scot scornfully singles out child-eating as a link made by the credulous between lycanthropy and witchcraft:

> Item, Bodin saith, that the reason whie witches are most commonly turned into wooloues, is; because they vsuallie eate children, as wooloues eate cattell. (5.1. H5v [92])

69. There is also a connection between the lycanthrope's torture of children and Ferdinand's reference to a 'cullis' in his exchange with the Doctor. Earlier, Ferdinand had threatened 'to boil the [Duchess'] bastard to a cullis, / And give't his lecherous father, to renew / The sin of his back' (2.5.71–3). Otten points out that Continental Renaissance physicians refer to a ointment rendered from 'the

boiled, congealed fat of the dead body of an unbaptised infant'; when applied
to the body of a man, this salve effects his transformation into a wolf (27).

70. See Revels edition, note, p. 63.

71. Enterline contends that the basilisk imagery is reversed when Ferdinand's eyes
'dazzle' after viewing the Duchess's corpse: 'The Duchess's body … is not a
passive or inert object … [it] challenges visual mastery. Her body becomes a
spectacle that even in surrendering to the possessive power of viewing disables
the eyes that would see it' (261). Enterline also astutely suggests that
Ferdinand's description of the Duchess as 'Excellent hyena!' when he has first
learned of her sexual activity (2.5.39) evokes a mutant animal that 'since Pliny
… had also widely been understood to be hermaphroditic (*Natural History*
8.44–5 and 28.27) … Pliny writes that hyenas are a cross between a dog and a
wolf'. In this instance, Ferdinand 'obliquely underscores his resemblance to his
twin sister precisely when he suffers a "rupture" over her difference' (254–5).

72. See Mary Douglas, *Purity and Danger: An Analysis of the Concepts of
Pollution and Taboo* (London and New York: Routledge, 1988), esp. 41–57.

73. When Antonio and the Duchess bid farewell after Ferdinand has succeeded in
enveloping them in the miasma of his obsession, Antonio too feels deadened; he
describes his heart as 'turn'd to a heavy lump of lead' (3.5.91), and the Duchess
tells him that his kiss 'is colder / Than that I have seen an holy anchorite / Give
to a dead man's skull' (88–90). The anchorite image is heavily ironic in that
Ferdinand, in one of his earlier frenzies, has condemned the lovers to a
cloistered cell, to consort, suitably, with animals emblematic of lust:

> And for thee, vile woman,
> If thou do wish thy lecher may grow old
> In thy embracements, I would have thee build
> Such a room for him as our anchorites
> To holier use inhabit: let not the sun
> Shine on him, till he's dead; let dogs and monkeys
> Only converse with him, and such dumb things
> To whom nature denies use to sound his name … (99–106)

In a characteristic shift from the ideal to the depraved, Ferdinand combines in
this speech the notion of a sacred enclosure (like that of a tomb), in which the
Duchess ('cas'd up, like a holy relic' [3.2.39]) should be preserved, with that of
a habitat for 'dogs and monkeys', a kind of rutting room. The bestialising of
Antonio is, of course, a further irony in view of Ferdinand's lycanthropy.

74. The Duchess is associated with images of light throughout the play, including
that of the diamond, one of Webster's favorite metaphors. See, for example,
1.1.299 and 4.2.215–17.

75. Shakespeare also triangulates the relationships of Antony, Cleopatra and
Caesar in *Antony and Cleopatra*, but Cleopatra is not the ethical centre of
Shakespeare's tragedy, nor is her structural function in the struggle between
male protagonists analogous to that of the Duchess.

76. Enterline puts it elegantly:

> The particular turn given to transvestite practice in Webster's play is to draw attention
> to the *figural* status of this 'maternal' body. The 'truth' of maternity, hidden behind the
> veils of skin and costume, becomes the play's indispensable, yet vanishing, point of
> reference. (248)

Chapter 5

Killing the Dead: Duncan's Corpse and Hamlet's Ghost

Middleton and especially Webster developed styles of tragedy in which complex psychological concepts were successfully embedded in sensationalist dramaturgy. In an exemplary instance, as we have seen, Webster represented Ferdinand's taboo desire by means of an inferred metamorphosis, at once a literalised symbol and an aptly indirect one for a passion that Ferdinand refuses to acknowledge but never wholly repudiates. Certainly Ferdinand's lycanthropy encapsulates strikingly his defiance of the symbolic order, but it also serves partly to mitigate the transgressiveness of his illicit desire. There are moments when Ferdinand as lycanthrope is a caricature, not unlike Middleton's Tyrant in his most attenuated states.[1] This does not so much detract from Webster's representation of sexual obsession as qualify it: when symbolically displaced in the bestial hybridity of an 'other', the self-annihilating character of Ferdinand's desire is, to a degree, diminished. In contrast, *Macbeth* and *Hamlet*, while also making liberal use of hyperbolic dramatic devices, close the distance between transgressor and transgression, as well as between protagonist and spectator: Hamlet's nightmare, and even Macbeth's, become more intimately our own.

As a way of enhancing a sense of psychic dislocation in their protagonists, both plays conjure a profoundly unsettling atmosphere of existence on the margins, of half-states in which neither life nor death holds sway. This interstitial ambience derives chiefly, I would argue, from the insubstantiality of Shakespeare's corpses. The armoured ghost of Hamlet's father appears, at least initially, to be an emphatically solid apparition, yet he/it repeatedly references corrupt and corrupting bodies – its own body/corpse inhabiting the armour, as well as the 'garbage' of Claudius's body, and, by inference, of Gertrude's. Significantly, the graphic images of the ghost's bitter excoriations are virtually identical to those of Hamlet's imaginings: in so far as it is a representation of interiority, the ghost is Hamlet's. In an equally distinctive dramaturgical turn, Shakespeare constructs Duncan's corpse, especially as emblematised by his multifaceted blood, as the other-worldly presence that infects Macbeth's 'speculation', as Macbeth himself puts it, and that destabilises the categorical fixities that structure his daily life.

As haunting presences, Hamlet's ghost and Duncan's corpse serve as uncanny doubles: irresistible yet evanescent, the first disappears in the course of the play, and the second, in a remarkable *tour de force*, never actually appears on stage. The withholding of the dead Duncan from view reinforces Macduff's description of the King's body: it is a 'new Gorgon' (2.3.73),[2] a reincarnation of the female Medusa who turns to stone anyone who dares look at her, whose bodily fluids both kill and heal. In psycho-analytical terms, the prohibition of the Medusa foregrounds the danger of apprehending that which exists outside any symbolic frame of reference: the principle of death as generation, the inextricability of dissolution and becoming. To view the Medusa is to discover the indeterminacy of originary being and to lose one's 'self' as a consequence: Hamlet's fate in confronting his ghost; Macbeth's also in internalising the Gorgon that Duncan has become.

1. Macbeth

In the hallucinatory realm of Shakespeare's *Macbeth*, sex, violence and blood are inextricably meshed in a tragic mode that represents the nether-side of civilised order. If signification is structured by means of concepts that safely situate phenomena in categories – male/female, sacramental/diabolic, familiar/alien, living/dead – then Macbeth is about the tenuousness of these distinctions and the psychic and social horror that ensues when they collapse. As several scholars have noted,[3] the text is pervaded – one might say obsessed – with the *un*categorisable, the marginal, the in-between: androgynous witches who disappear into the air, 'sightless couriers' who ride the winds, nightmarish ghosts, dreams and illusions that blanket over the reassuring tangibleness of stones, sounds and corporeal life. In effect, *Macbeth* represents a realm that is worse than death because – at least in the imagination of its protagonist – nothing is totally obliterated, nothing is final.

The compact design of the play sustains the sense of an infernally enveloping darkness in which light 'thickens' and the preternatural becomes indistinguishable from ordinary life – what Garber calls 'a series of border crossings' (91). But the heart of this horror derives from the inversion of the ordinary itself in the lives of the protagonists, their recognition of the thin line that separates the reassuring structures of everyday existence from the chaos they mask. Sleep – 'Chief nourisher in life's feast' , 'that knits up the raveled sleave of care' (2.2.39, 36) – is 'murdered', revealing the hallucinatory underside of the unrelenting dream; feasting, the communal ritual with 'troops of friends' (5.3.25), becomes horrifically bound up with another kind of 'supping', with carnivorous 'magot-pies' and with bloodied ghosts. As a consequence of their sacrilege in killing Duncan, Macbeth and Lady Macbeth find themselves negotiating these alien spaces: exiled from the protective framework of human society, they are suspended in a kind of no (wo)man's land. They seek Duncan's power as King, but discover instead Duncan's power as corpse.

More than any other interstitial emblem in the play, Duncan's corpse defines the border between the licit and the taboo, and at the same time destroys this border, drowns it in 'the multitudinous seas' of his unstaunchable blood. In an ironic inversion, the play takes its metaphoric life chiefly from the blood of Duncan's dead body. The power of this blood, as Shakespeare constructs it, is its amplitude, its capacity to engross so much meaning: on the one hand, its sacramental efficacy, on the other, its elemental destructiveness.

Blood as sacramental channel and spiritual nutrient figured prominently, as we have seen, in Catholic ritual. The 'symbolic cannibalism'[4] of the Eucharist, as defined by the doctrine of transubstantiation, made it possible for the faithful to consume the sacrificed, incarnated Deity – a foretaste of immortality effected through the bodily process of ingestion.[5] Further, Christ's sacramental blood served to collapse gender distinctions. Thus in Catholic iconography the crucified body of Christ gave birth through the bloody wound in His side to the Church, a redemptive 'delivery' prefigured in the cutting and bleeding of His foreskin at the circumcision, and anticipating the perpetuation of Christ's self-sacrifice in the Eucharist. Such symbolic linkages imbued Christ's blood with a double efficacy: not only did it blur the boundaries between the material and the spiritual, but also between male and female. Blood as nurture (emphasised in depictions of Jesus as Mother) and blood as power (the blood of the cut foreskin) were inextricable in the iconology of the incarnated Christ.[6]

Duncan's blood bears the full weight of these associations in Shakespeare's play. Macduff's description of the King's bloodied corpse as 'the new Gorgon' – the Medusa head that petrifies the viewer – establishes its sacramental dimension: Duncan's hacked body, unthinkable and unviewable, is hypostatised as sacred.[7] The Eucharistic imagery that precedes the murder conflates the murder of Duncan as 'the Lord's anointed temple' (2.3.69) with the sacrifice of Christ (both Duncan and Jesus have 'almost supped'; Jesus tells his betrayer, 'That thou doest, doe quickly'; Macbeth refers to 'our poison'd chalice' [1.7.11; see also John, XIII.27, as cited in

Muir's edition n. 2, p. 37]). Later in the play, a second inversion of the Eucharistic feast invests Banquo's ghost with a similar sacramental significance. As Garber has pointed out, Banquo's Medusa-like 'gory locks' replicate Duncan's Gorgon (108–90, 115–16), so that the terrible sacrilege of Duncan's murder bleeds afresh, as it were, in the 'twenty mortal murthers' of the 'blood-bolter'd Banquo' (3.4.80, 4.1.123).

Flowing from multiple wounds, like stigmata, Duncan's blood is endowed by Macbeth and the Scots with a fearsome, animating power that redeems but also destroys. Macbeth's hope that 'the spring, the head, the fountain of [Duncan's] blood / Is stopp'd; the very source of it is stopp'd' (2.3.98–9) proves hopelessly wrong. After the murder of Banquo, Macbeth alludes to 'the time has been, / That, when the brains were out, the man would die, / And there an end' (3.4.77–9), but he has already recognised that *his* times are saturated in a blood so potent it can 'incarnadine' 'the multitudinous seas' (2.2.61). To the Scotsmen who hope to reclaim their country, Duncan's blood is holy, generative; it will mingle with 'Each drop of us' (5.2.29) in 'our country's purge' (28), 'Or so much as it needs / To dew the sovereign flower, and drown the weeds' (29–30). But to Macbeth and Lady Macbeth, the murderers, Duncan's blood is a deadly contagion; like the knife in Duncan's wound, it sticks deep, an unexpungable mark of death.

Prior to the murder the Macbeths do not, of course, anticipate the 'uncanny retaliatory power'[8] of Duncan's corpse. On the contrary, they construct individual fantasies of regicide in which the appropriation of Duncan's sovereign power depends on their own superior strength: thus the double action of hyperbolising their potency in overtly sexual terms and of diminishing Duncan's. Lady Macbeth's scenario would reduce Duncan to the status of an old man, sleeping, unguarded, not unlike the image of her own nursing babe, dashed to death at a moment of intimate trust;[9] Macbeth, as Tarquin, would descend upon his unsuspecting victim 'with ravishing strides' (2.1.55). Significantly, both fantasies depend upon the confusion of gender identities in the Macbeths themselves, but also in Duncan. By infantalising and feminising Duncan, the Macbeths rob him (at least for the duration of the murder) of the patriarchal power they seek to procure; by denying their own procreant, nurturing qualities (the very qualities so admired in the 'gracious' Duncan) they idealise a delusional notion of masculinity. The dreadful consequences of these sexually inflected fantasies of power are inscribed in the play's representation of the bi-gendered agency of Duncan's blood – its excessive, generative flow, and its power to kill.

That Lady Macbeth constructs Duncan-as-victim as disabled and therefore not to be feared is consistent with the play's representation of her mode of apprehending and categorising 'reality'. Initially, Lady Macbeth would herself be the murderer, but in her curious invocation to the furies, she seems to express opposing desires: to be unsexed, stripped of all feminising weaknesses ('Come you Spirits / ... unsex me here, / ... make thick my blood' [1.5.40–1, 43]), and yet to avoid the sight of the very act that would empower her as a kind of super-male ('Come, thick Night, / ... That my keen knife see not the wound it makes' [50, 52]). The tension in Lady Macbeth between unnatural aggression and a habit of dissociation is apparent elsewhere – for example, in her conflation of the images of sleep and death during her castigation of Macbeth's reluctance to kill Duncan ('The sleeping, and the dead, / Are but as pictures' [2.2.52–3]), and in her related insistence that pictures, painted images and air-drawn daggers, as products of the imagination, are unreal. To dare to be a man is to eschew such 'foolish thought' (21), but the success of Lady Macbeth's system for denying psychic phenomena seems to depend on keeping her distance from the act of violence itself, despite her rhetoric to the contrary. Accordingly, after Lady Macbeth is forced to dip her hands in Duncan's blood and 'gild' the grooms with it, the sensory properties of this blood – its stickiness, its smell – become ineradicable images in her mind, although, even in her madness, she instantiates this illusion as a visible stain on her hands.

Lady Macbeth's pathetic query, 'Yet who would have thought the old man to have had so much blood in him?' (5.1.38–9) resonates with her earlier excuse for failing as executioner: 'Had he not resembled / My father as he slept, I had done't' (2.2.12–13). Presumably, it is the horror of parricide that unhinges Lady Macbeth, that *un*stops 'th' access and passage to remorse' (1.5.44), and eventually prompts the obsessive re-enactment of the aftermath of the murder. But Duncan's corpse as Gorgon is more than an image of Lady Macbeth's father: as Medusa, it is unnatural, terrifying, incorporating 'both the femaleness [Lady Macbeth] sought to escape and the supermasculinity she aspired to attain' (Willis, 8). In a sense, the power of this Gorgon's blood is beyond anything Lady Macbeth dares to imagine, and her obsessive fixation suggests a final, extreme act of dissociation from the full recognition of Duncan's insensible power. Significantly, Lady Macbeth would not hesitate to confront the furies on their own turf, in 'the dunnest smoke of Hell' (1.5.52), because these monsters have a place in what might be termed her ontological universe. But the Gorgon that is Duncan's corpse does not: as a sleepwalker, Lady Macbeth fears to shut her eyes, to surrender herself to the dark; she 'has light by her continually' (5.1.21–2).

Like his wife, Macbeth also invokes a fantasy of male potency as an incitement to murder, but in Tarquin Macbeth would identify as well with a heroic persona whose warrior reputation resembles his own. As 'Bellona's bridegroom, lapp'd in proof [gore]' (1.2.55), Macbeth is famed among the Scots for his 'bloody execution' (18) on the battlefield ('he unseam'd him from the nave to th' chops' [22]). But the image of Bellona's bridegroom, 'paradoxical because the goddess of war was a fierce unyielding virgin' (Berger, 81), connects disturbingly with the surprise assault of Tarquin the rapist on another chaste woman, and also with the iconographic figure of death-as-lover in the *danse macabre*. In Macbeth's fantasy, the figure of Tarquin is overlaid with that of 'wither'd Murther' (2.1.52), so that Tarquin's 'ravishing strides' (55) are at the same time 'stealthy' (54) – he 'Moves like a ghost' (56). Thus the composite metaphor figures Tarquin/ Death/Macbeth advancing inexorably to inflict the 'deep wound' with the 'keen knife' on Duncan, the fierce and innocent Bellona/Lucrece. Macbeth vanquishes Duncan, but not, of course, in the violent throes of battle, as would befit the bridegroom of Bellona; instead, the bloody violation of Duncan's privacy and person is a shameful and secret act. The cumulative effect, then, of Macbeth's fantasy of regicide is an alienation from his own public persona. After Duncan's death, Macbeth becomes 'the *secret'st* man of blood' (3.4.125, my italics); he can never return to a battlefield on which his adversaries, however terrifying, are tangible – 'the rugged Russian bear, / The arm'd rhinoceros, or th' Hyrcanean tiger' (99–100).

The destabilising of Macbeth's familiar persona is proleptically suggested by the 'dagger of the mind' (2.1.38) that Macbeth sees but cannot grasp on his way to murder Duncan, a floating signifier that does and does not correspond to the palpable dagger in Macbeth's hand. The imagined dagger, a 'false creation', 'marshal'st me the way that I was going' (38, 42), suggesting an eerie agency that is not included in the signified of its corporeal referent. Macbeth recognises a breach between his two modes of seeing ('Mine eyes are made the fools o' th' other senses, / Or else worth all the rest' [44–5]), but his attempt to retain an empirical test for reality ('There's no such thing' [47]) ironically locates the crux of his dilemma. There is no such *thing* as the imagined dagger, but it exists none the less in some frame of vision, and to the degree that it does not correspond to the dagger 'which now I draw' (41), its signification no longer belongs to the symbolic system that orders Macbeth's world.

As Macbeth's 'horrible imaginings' worsen immediately after the murder (he is fixated on the prayers of the grooms, and on the ghostly voice that denounced him), Lady Macbeth counters with her own insistently reductive theory of perception: 'Consider it not so deeply ... The sleeping, and the dead, / Are but as pictures; 'tis the eye of childhood / That fears a painted devil' (2.2.29, 52–4). The confusions of this metaphor, as I have suggested, function for Lady Macbeth as a mode of denial, but they also suggest a larger problem in signification. The metaphor conflates the painted artifact, falsely animated, with the semi-conscious sleeper, and the de-animated dead – levelling the playing field, as it were, so that at least for Lady Macbeth Duncan's corpse is as dead as the painted image. Ironically, however, after Macbeth has seen the ghost of Banquo, Lady Macbeth invokes the same metaphor, but changes its terms so as to ascribe agency to Macbeth's insensible fear: 'This is the very painting of your fear: / This is the air-drawn dagger' (3.4.60–1). By mid-play, of course, Lady Macbeth's shaming tactics strike a hollow note, since Macbeth is already 'cabin'd, cribb'd, confin'd' (23) in a private universe in which the distinctions between painted images and horrible imaginings have all but collapsed. Thus his scornful castigation of his servant shortly before his death ('Go, prick thy face, and over-red thy fear, / Thou lily-liver'd boy ... Take thy face hence' [5.3.14–15, 19]) represents an almost comic degradation of Lady Macbeth's injunctions, as well as of Macbeth's own early efforts to objectify his fear.

Indeed, after the regicide, Macbeth's alienation from the signifying structures that once comprised 'reality' is apparent in his precipitous decline from the status of 'warrior' to that of 'hangman' and 'butcher', all of whom (together with the early modern anatomist) know how to unseam a person from the nave to the chops. 'Now does he feel / His secret murthers sticking on his hands' (5.2.16–17), observes Angus near the end of the play, referring not only to the sacrilegious stamp of Duncan's blood, but also to the plague-like pile of corpses Macbeth has left in his wake – a virtual sea of blood that Macbeth must 'wade'. For Angus and the other Scots, the gore-soaked Macbeth, 'lapp'd' in a 'proof' that befits Hecate far better than Bellona, has become a monster, no longer recognisable as a 'natural' man. In fact, by demonising Macbeth as *un*natural, the Scots are able to isolate him as sole agent of the transformation of Scotland into a nether-kingdom, an 'Acheron', rife with cannibalistic creatures of death, both in the air and under the ground (including the worms and serpents that eat the dead, as in the transi sculptures). If the 'Beauteous and swift' horses of the King, 'the minions of their race' (2.4.15), now eat each other, like the infanticidal sow in the witches' brew, it is because the butcher-fiend Macbeth, in transgressing the divide between human and inhuman, has inverted the natural order.

Macbeth himself acknowledges this transgression ('Returning were as tedious as go o'er' [3.4.137]) and is not insensible to his own transformation; his bitter irony with Banquo's murderers, for example, suggests that he, as well as they, belong in the catalogue of dogs and not of men (3.1). But Macbeth's 'fatal vision' encompasses far more than an awareness of himself as monster; it is the vision *of* the monster, in which ordinary distinctions, including the demarcation of the 'natural' from the 'unnatural', have blurred. The Scots, as 'natural' men, would appropriate Duncan's corpse so as to strengthen, not loosen, these distinctions. To them, Duncan as Gorgon bears witness to the horror of transgressing the sacred law against regicide, as does the terrible transformation of their country. In this context, the nightmarish imagery of their speech functions as a correlative to their sacramentalising of the Gorgon's blood. When appropriated as sacrifice (like the Eucharistic feast), the horrible and unholy murder of Duncan reinvigorates the Scots, refortifies the taboo against regicide and obliterates Acheron.

But for Macbeth, 'blood will have blood' (3.4.121) in a never-ending generation of death, so that the 'wild and violent sea' (4.2.21) of blood, which he cannot ford, ultimately seems to engulf both the sacred and the profane, the living and the dead. 'If charnel-houses and our graves must send / Those that we bury back' (3.4.70–1), if 'Stones have been known to move, and trees to speak' (122), then 'nothing is, but what is not' (1.3.142). 'Nature *seems* dead' (2.1.50, my italics), but so do 'the surfeited grooms' (2.2.5) before he kills them, whereas the murdered Banquo does not. Macbeth would fix Banquo among the dead ('Thy bones are marrowless, thy blood is cold; / Thou hast no speculation in those eyes / Which thou dost glare with' [3.4.93–4]), but the 'bloody business' of slaughter 'informs' Macbeth's own eyes (2.1.48), infects them, so that ultimately Macbeth's 'speculation' inhabits the hallucinatory gaps in signification. In these unfixed spaces, Macbeth's 'deep desire' is imbricated in an 'orgy of annihilation' (to invoke Bataille once again) that erases even the distinctions between the sacramental and the sacrilegious, god and devil, Duncan's blood and Macbeth's own.

At the conclusion of *Macbeth*, the Scots restore the metaphysical frame-work that they purport to represent: when Macbeth's demonic agency is destroyed, the walking dead return to their graves. In this respect, the play functions in much the same way as English rituals of the dead did, by simultaneously exploiting and defusing fear of the semi-animate agency of the corpse. But for most of the play, the dead Duncan is a fetishistic presence, foregrounded by direct and oblique references to the iconography of the netherworld, to the annihilative/generative properties of the bi-gendered blood of the corpse, and to the function of the Eucharistic feast in transforming and sacramentalising the cannibalism of nature; and the transgressive Macbeth, who sees much that he should not, evokes the popular association of hangman ('butcher') with anatomist. The play is thus saturated with an unsettling ambience of the dead that is not wholly dispelled by the recuperation of hegemonic ideology.

Significantly, it is the Medusa symbolism that intersects the transgressive and recuperative visions of the play and that strikes a particularly dis-turbing note at the end. As Garber points out, Macbeth's decapitated head is itself a Medusa image, appropriated atropaically by the Scots (as was Medusa's on the shield of Athena) to ward off future evil (114–15); for similar purposes, his image as 'rarer monster' will be 'Painted upon a pole' and displayed publicly (5.8.25, 26). On one level, the communal demonisation of Macbeth bears witness to the restoration of the natural order: for the Scots, the function of his head as trophy inverts the power of his monstrousness; and the painted image, in a return to Lady Macbeth's categorical conflations, attests to the insentience of his corpse. But the play has already dramatised the failure of Lady Macbeth's mode of apprehension, and Macbeth's Gorgon – however symbolically isolated from humankind – none the less resonates uneasily with its sacramentalised counterpart in Duncan/Banquo. In the end, the play's attempt to differentiate Gorgons seems undermined by its powerful representation of Macbeth's own deconstructive vision: such sights as none should behold cannot so easily be laid to rest.

To argue that *Macbeth* is about the representation of a deconstructive vision is to recognise that it is about the nature of representation itself, particularly as it pertains to the performative conventions of the early modern theatre. Strictly speaking, of course, there is no way to represent a vision that derives from the collapse of the discursive structures that themselves comprise signification. What *Macbeth* enacts instead is the consequences of such a collapse by extending the possibilities of a representational mode that itself functioned (like Macbeth's hallucinations) so as to destabilise distinctions.

Like the plays examined in earlier chapters, *Macbeth* is hyperbolic, over the top: the play's relentlessly sustained death-in-life ambience is itself a sensational *tour de force*.[10] But because the focal point for the play's examination of 'border crossings' is Duncan's corpse, and this corpse never appears, it cannot visibly contravene the symbolic import of its representation. What *Macbeth* does 'materialise', in a move that comes brilliantly close to representing the unrepresentable, is Duncan's blood, a substance whose *physical* properties were firmly inscribed in the cultural consciousness as fundamentally indeterminate. Thus the blood on the hands of the Macbeths has deconstructive power as both sign and substance, and this disturbing conflation serves as an ideal analogue to Macbeth's 'fatal vision', in which the relationship of signifier to referent is in jeopardy, as is the principle of differentiation in signification itself – male/female, life/death. In contrast to the torments of this 'speculation', the sexually inflected fantasies of Macbeth and his wife prior to the murder seem almost naïvely simplistic. By the end of the play, Macbeth's cosmos has been horrifically enlarged by the encompassing sea of Duncan's blood – a sea in which materiality provides no anchor, and sexuality itself is inextricably bound up with death.

By generating the possibilities of this vision, Duncan's absent corpse signifies as the play's most powerful presence.

2. Hamlet

The long-standing controversy over the kind of ghost that appears to Hamlet in the figure of his father itself suggests the ambiguity of Shakespeare's creation. Perhaps what is most surprising in this controversy is the expectation that the ghost *should* be either Catholic or Protestant, demonic or beneficent, authentic or hallucinatory.[11] It seems more reasonable to assume that the uncanny and evanescent apparition functions as an emblem for Hamlet's own deeply conflicted vision of death. More precisely, I would argue that Hamlet's vision of the *interior* of the ghost – what lies behind the warrior's armour – is a compelling but fatal apprehension of death as indeterminacy. This apprehension, because detached from categorical fixities, like Duncan's blood, is theoretically unrepresentable. None the less, the powerfully ambiguous ghost in *Hamlet* succeeds in giving a shape, as it were, to the horror of Hamlet's imaginings.

In important respects, Shakespeare's apparition bears the traces of that 'iconography of the macabre'[12] that found its fullest and most riveting expression in the corroding bodies of the transi sculptures, which depict the peeling back of the body's envelope, or as Hamlet might put it, the shuffling off of its mortal coil; and also in the 'revel of monstrous uncreation'[13] that was the *danse macabre*. Recently, Catherine Belsey has emphasised the 'extraordinary popularity of the *danse macabre* in England', citing Stowe's account of the Dance at St Paul's and other venues, and the widespread dissemination of continental woodcuts such as those by Guyot Marchant and Holbein.[14] Belsey in fact draws interesting parallels between the 'cadaverous mummies' of the Dance and the shrouded corpses of the transi sculptures, and she offers an intriguing analysis of the graveyard scene in *Hamlet* as a symbolic re-enactment of the Dance (136–47).

Early modern ghost lore shared in this *gestalt*, especially with respect to revenants. As Jean-Claude Schmitt has argued, representations of the newly dead often depicted stages of decomposition because these ghost/cadavers 'were not yet completely detached from the world of the living'.[15] For centuries, of course, the Catholic doctrine of purgatory had proved a huge stimulus to popular reportings of ghosts, so it is hardly surprising that for the most part they 'resembled men and women … looking like paler and sadder versions of their living selves' (Finucane, 81). Further, ghost stories in England, especially in the north, reflected Germanic traditions in which 'spirits had an extraordinary "corporeity"' (Schmitt, 146). One of the more interesting documents cited in this connection by Schmitt is a fifteenth-century manuscript of Yorkshire ghost stories, in which the ghosts are aggressive, terrorising:

> they came out of their graves, scattered outside the cemetery, and physically attacked the villagers. A woman was seen carrying a 'spirit' on her back; she dug 'her fingers deeply into the flesh of the spirit, as if the flesh of that same spirit were a putrid phantasm ...' These spirits were so concrete that the living could grab them and grapple with them: young Robert Foxton managed to hold a spirit at the exit of a cemetery against the door of the church. (199)[16]

Reinforcing the odd physicality of these ghosts was the fact that they were also a 'sonorous phenomenon', frequently speaking 'with the strange voices of ventriloquists' (200, 146).

At bottom, the Yorkshire ghosts, like their Germanic prototypes, implied 'a very archaic belief in the survival of the double' (148). Revenants who came out of the grave dressed in 'clothing for which they were known and which helped the living to recognise them' (202), neither fully living nor fully dead, seemed to duplicate both the corpse and the living being – a double doubling, as it were. Indeed, in some instances, 'not only did the dead person return to haunt the space of the living, but the cadaver ... was condemned not to decompose in the ground' (200). The half-life, half-death of the revenant, not so much a 'state' as a kind of suspension in the in-between, simultaneously denied material wholeness *and* decomposition.

The notion of the revenant as an indeterminate double of its living self has an intriguing analogue in that of the animated statue. The title of Kenneth Gross's remarkable study *The Dream of the Moving Statue* suggests a phantasmic longing for an impossible fusion of states of being that are ordained as necessarily opposite. The statue would freeze the image of a moving person in a form that is itself changeless, an 'idealised stone mirror'[17] in which the degeneration intrinsic to motion is stopped. But as in the case of Pygmalion, the statue fails to satisfy. Instead, it generates desire for the figured ideal as a 'redemptive gift' (9), and the dream of the *moving* statue is that of a mobile body that is also *pure*, a living body protected from its own decay and fragmentation: it is the dream of rebirth into a not-life in which desire is no longer tethered to death.

In an arresting description of this paradox, Michel Serres contends that *inside* every statue there is a corpse: the statue buries something that can never really be seen, the decaying body, the interiority of the human organism, our bondage to unhuman processes – a Gorgon that can turn the viewer to stone.[18] What the statue represents, then, is a conundrum: the subject caught between an external, idealised image of motion and a haunting awareness of the mutability that this image masks; caught, at the same time, between the desire to animate the ideal and the fear of what will be unleashed. In a psychoanalytical context, even this conflict is symptomatic of a more basic paradox, that is, the eroticism that inheres in death itself, the fantasy of fusion or imagined plenitude, which is the ultimate object of both libido and the death drive. Seen from this angle, Pygmalion's impossible union with Galatea as a moving statue is itself a stand-in for his fantasy of death – motion without mutability, fusion without fragmentation, fulfilment without annihilation.

To imagine a corpse inside a statue is to evoke a fearsome, uncanny double, and it is hardly surprising that the 'curious violence' of statues is especially apparent when they give up their ghosts, so to speak, as 'galvanised corpse[s]' (167, 10, 13). Something like this happens with the ghost of Hamlet's father, a revenant who first appears as a 'portentous figure' (1.1.112), a 'figure like the King that's dead' (44), a 'fair and warlike form' (50) that 'comes armed' (113) for battle and is encased not in stone, but in armour.[19] As a revenant, the animated 'statue' that is Hamlet's father is of course *already* a ghost ('My father's spirit – in arms!' [1.2.255]), but a peculiarly substantial ghost, a 'thing', 'nothing', 'fantasy', 'in *complete steel*' (1.1.24, 25, 26, 1.4.52, my italics). As a warrior, the ghost seems to replicate the living King Hamlet, but the very familiarity of this appearance evokes an unsettling question: who or what inhabits the armour of the dead Hamlet? Or, to put it another way: what does the impregnable-looking casing *hide*?

What lies behind the armour is, of course, a corpse: if what makes Hamlet Sr seem alive is his battle-ready fierceness – his 'martial stalk' (1.1.69), 'majestical' (48) bearing and frowning countenance – then what makes him an 'illusion' (130) is the mystery within. The singularity of this revenant is that its indeterminate status, its half-life half-death, is literally figured as a contradiction: steel exterior vs. 'no/thing', an outside enclosing and containing an unviewable inside. When Hamlet first sees the ghost, he wants to believe it is his father and is excited at the prospect: 'I'll call thee Hamlet, / King, father, royal Dane. O answer me' (1.4.44–5). The re-animation of his father's dead body – the ghost as moving statue – justifies Hamlet's *un*common mourning, his refusal to reconcile himself to the 'death of fathers' as a 'common theme' (1.2.104, 103): the figure in armour is, after all, an undeniable, imperious *presence*, uncannily like his 'noble father's person' (244).[20] In fastening on the ghost as warrior in this initial encounter, Hamlet makes his defiance and his desire manifest in a fantasy of the restoration of his father's invincible power.

But even in his frantic exhilaration, Hamlet soon becomes aware that the ghost is *his* dependant, in need of *his* assistance, that, above all else, the ghost's exhortation creates a symbiotic relationship between father and son in which the son as avenger must prove the father's invincibility. There is, then, a disturbing connection between Hamlet and the ghost which Marjorie Garber usefully connects to the concept of *prosopopeia* as described by Paul de Man:

> It is the figure of *prosopopeia*, the fiction of an apostrophe to an absent, deceased, or voiceless entity, which posits the possibility of the latter's reply, and confers upon it the power of speech.[21]

Garber contends that in addressing the 'questionable shape' (1.4.43) that is the ghost, 'Hamlet brings it to speech and therefore to a kind of life' (146), that in this sense the voice of the ghost is the ventriloquised voice of Hamlet himself, the moving statue, as it were, fully animated through the projected desire of its creator. But the reciprocal claims of Hamlet and the ghost on each other are, as Hamlet himself intuits, threatening, forbidden, unknowable: if the animated warrior-king belongs to both Hamlets, so also does the 'thing' behind the mask, the corpse within the armour.

In my view, the psychic world of the play is defined by this symbiosis, by the correlation between Hamlet's extraordinary mood swings and his growing comprehension of that which the interior of the ghost signifies. The Hamlet that 'waxes desperate with imagination' (1.4.87) and the Hamlet that ruminatively discovers Caesar in a bung-hole both confront death, but by the time of the graveyard scene the formidable warrior-ghost has found its symbolic way to the ossuary, having made a fantastical and torturous progress through the mind of the Prince. First in a sequence of doublings/ divisions, the ghost of Hamlet Sr is the ur-force that establishes fractured identity as the paradigm for the play: the ghost itself as the living and the dead King, and also as the King and his son; the double portraits, or interdependent personae of Hamlet Sr and Claudius; the overlapping symbolic identities of Pyrrhus, Priam and Hecuba in the meta-theatrical speech of the First Player; the living, mad and dead Ophelia. Throughout the play, ghosts, mirrors, and 'counterfeit presentment[s]' (55), doubles within doubles, function collectively as stand-ins for the indeterminate corpse, the inside of the martial mask that Hamlet addresses as 'Father', an inside that will eventually obliterate the mask. At the centre of Hamlet's struggle to cope with his terrible grief and rage is an apparition that is uniquely his: the invincible fantasy father corroded from within by the mindlessness of mortality.

The 'sinister reciprocity' (Garber, 147) between ghost/father and Hamlet first surfaces in the ghost's speech (1.5), which replicates the passions, preoccupations and even the language of his/its son.[22] Prior to this scene, Hamlet, the lone dissenter to his mother's marriage, has posed virtue against corruption in an unmediated opposition: at one pole, Hamlet Sr, demi-god, like Hyperion, god of the sun; at the other, Gertrude and

Claudius, demi-beasts – Claudius the 'satyr', Gertrude the creature 'that wants discourse of reason' (1.2.140, 150). For Hamlet, the split within Gertrude herself – the devotedly passionate wife of Hamlet's father, the lust-ridden companion to Claudius – is equally extreme:

> So excellent a king ... so loving to my mother
> That he might not beteem the winds of heaven
> Visit her face too roughly. Heaven and earth,
> Must I remember? Why, she would hang on him
> As if increase of appetite had grown
> By what it fed on; and yet within a month –
> ...
> She married – O most wicked speed! To post
> With such dexterity to incestuous sheets! (139, 140–5, 156–7)

According to its own hair-raising account, the ghost too is caught between life and death, 'Doom'd for a certain term to walk the night' (1.5.10), subject by day to horrors that 'Would harrow up thy soul, freeze thy young blood' (15). What the ghost requires of Hamlet is, of course, the murder of its own murderer. But in appointing Hamlet as avenger, the ghost concentrates, curiously, on *Gertrude*'s betrayal as a 'falling off', an unthinkable moral plummet from its own noble affection to the sexual inducements of the bestial Claudius:

> Ay, that incestuous, that adulterate beast,
> ...
> ... won to his shameful lust
> The will of my most seeming-virtuous queen.
> O Hamlet, what a falling off was there,
> From me, whose love was of that dignity
> That it went hand in hand even with the vow
> I made to her in marriage, and to decline
> Upon a wretch whose natural gifts were poor
> To those of mine.
> But virtue, as it never will be mov'd,
> Though lewdness court it in a shape of heaven,
> So lust, though to a radiant angel link'd,
> Will sate itself in a celestial bed
> And prey on garbage. (42, 45–57)

The ghost's derogation of Claudius by means of an unflattering contrast with itself, although not cast in mythological metaphors, is virtually identical to Hamlet's; and the contaminated 'celestial bed' in which an angel couples with 'garbage' (56–7) – an image linked a few lines later to 'the royal bed of Denmark' as 'a couch for luxury and damned incest' (82–3) – directly evokes Hamlet's revulsion at Gertrude 'post[ing] / With such dexterity to incestuous sheets'.

Although the bitterly graphic sexual imagery of the ghost's speech seems incongruent with the solemn, majestic figure described earlier by Hamlet's friends, it is altogether appropriate to Hamlet's own ghost, that is, to a spectral double whose voice bears an uncanny resemblance to Hamlet's own. Still, even in his initial identification with the ghost, Hamlet's intoxicating mix of fear and hope suggests that he already intuits the terrible duality of its 'questionable shape'. Although uncertain of the ghost's origin ('spirit of health or goblin damn'd' [1.4.40]), he is primarily struck by the contrast between the shrouded, coffined body he recently saw entombed and the ferociously vital figure before him:

> Let me not burst in ignorance, but tell
> Why thy canoniz'd bones, hearsed in death,
> Have burst their cerements, why the sepulchre
> Wherein we saw thee quietly inurn'd
> Hath op'd his ponderous and marble jaws
> To cast thee up again. What may this mean,
> That thou, dead corse, again in complete steel
> Revisits thus the glimpses of the moon,
> Making night hideous and we fools of nature
> So horridly to shake our disposition
> With thoughts beyond the reaches of our souls? (46–56)

In these exclamations, Hamlet enacts a fantasy of the ghost's explosive transmutation, the violent ejection of the 'canoniz'd bones' from their burial shroud and the 'dead corse' from the maw of the sepulchre. Unquestionably exhilarated by the preternatural power of what appears to be his reconstituted father, Hamlet is none the less aware that the ghost makes the night 'hideous'.

The ghost's account of Claudius's brutal betrayal is equally unsettling. Poisoned in the most tranquil and habitual of settings ('Sleeping within my orchard ... Upon my secure hour' [1.5.59, 61]) through the bizarre means of a 'leperous distilment' (64), Hamlet Sr awakens to the joint horror of grotesque metamorphosis and imminent death:

> swift as quicksilver it courses through
> The natural gates and alleys of the body,
> And with a sudden vigour it doth posset
> And curd, like eager droppings into milk,
> The thin and wholesome blood. So did it mine,
> And a most instant tetter bark'd about,
> Most lazar-like, with vile and loathsome crust
> All my smooth body. (66–73)[23]

The image of his father's smooth skin covered in scabs and scales in the moments just prior to death would have a special horror for Hamlet: it is Hyperion as leper, his newly 'loathsome' body preparing to putrefy. 'O horrible! O horrible! most horrible!' (1.5.80); certainly the disfiguring death of the sun-king, but also the idea of *this* 'dead corse' resurrected 'in complete steel'.

Interestingly, no one in the play alludes to the face of the ghost, visible inside the raised beaver, as crusted over or corrupted. Still, Hamlet's response to the apparition seems dictated by the tension between what he can view and what he cannot and dare not view, the corpse evoked by the ghost's own narrative. If for Hamlet the ghost's two avatars seem at once inextricable and incompatible, this is precisely the conundrum that he must solve. Hamlet's initial desire to embrace the ghost supports the hope that his father's death is not synonymous with extinction, but Hamlet's depressive ruminations circle back inexorably to the intuition that the King – demi-god *and* man – has been unceremoniously obliterated. Given these painfully ambiguous intuitions, the desperation in Hamlet's antic disposition suggests a defiant effort to maintain the apotheosis of the ghost/father against terrible odds – his own suspect investment in the command to kill, the ghost's destabilising account of the death of Hyperion and, perhaps most importantly, Gertrude's evasion of her corroborative role in Hamlet's father-fantasy.

Despite the ghost's injunction, Hamlet cannot leave Gertrude alone. As the hinge that connects him not only to his father but also to his uncle, she constitutes the emotional centre of Hamlet's idealisation, the validation of his myth-making: 'You are the Queen, your husband's brother's wife, / And, would it were not so, you are my mother' (3.4.14–15). For Hamlet, Gertrude's moral opacity, her seeming imperviousness to the implications of her betrayal, threaten the basis of his own ideological investment in Hamlet Sr. Because Gertrude's 'falling off' denies, at least for her, the transcendent value of the elder Hamlet, she endangers this value for Hamlet as well. Gertrude would leave Hamlet's father, like any other, to be forgotten in the anonymity of the grave: ''Tis common' (1.2.72). Accordingly, when after the 'Mousetrap' Hamlet visits his mother in her closet, once more wildly exhilarated (this time at the confirmation of Claudius's guilt), he demands that she recognise her husband's death as a catastrophe, one that has left an irreparable hole in their mutual universe.

In this remarkable scene, Hamlet terrifies Gertrude by invoking the bitterly violent rhetoric of the warrior-ghost. Having impulsively murdered Polonius the 'rat', Hamlet, the avenging son, confronts his mother in a kind of visionary rage. Intensely focused on wrenching her moral vision into alignment with his own, he seems oblivious to Polonius's corpse, the bloody evidence of his terrible error. Hamlet's fury and righteousness would support his father's cause, but curiously, the transformed king in the closet scene, devoid of vehemence, bears little resemblance to the over-sized, preternatural force that seemed to validate Hamlet's earlier mania. Unassumingly dressed, empathic and almost mournful, the ghost appears strangely detached from the scene of violence that Hamlet enacts in its name.[24]

This shift in the ghost's symbolic value is manifest in the contrast between the father image that Hamlet uses to prise open the 'bulwarked' conscience of Gertrude, and the unprepossessing figure that speaks briefly to Hamlet near the end of the scene. Ironically, the 'glass' that Hamlet thrusts before Gertrude so that she may see into her 'inmost part' is the 'counterfeit presentment' (3.4.18–19, 54) of Hamlet Sr and Claudius, portraits of the brothers, presumably in miniature. Hamlet insists on his own vision of these images as polar opposites, confirmed in the earlier exchange with the warrior-ghost: the king above the common race of men, fellow of Hyperion, Jove, Mars and Mercury; Claudius 'the bloat King' (184), the 'mildew'd ear' (64), the 'paddock', 'bat', 'gib' (192) and 'vice' (98). For Hamlet, the absence of a middle position (a position far more in keeping with Gertrude's temporising inclinations) is the critical point.

I would like to argue that in representing a diminution of the warrior-king, the ghost in Gertrude's closet marks Hamlet's failure to sustain his passionate investment in grief. Without Gertrude's corroboration, Hamlet's apotheosis of his father is irrelevant to anyone but himself, a solipsistic fantasy. So long as Hamlet believes that his father can defy the oblivion of body and memory, the ghost maintains its power; without Hamlet as ventriloquist, the ghost need no longer appear. Eventually, Hamlet Sr will take his place alongside Alexander and Caesar at the bunghole, part of a universal pattern of disappearance in which putrefying kings, including the most exalted of warriors, 'may go a progress through the guts of a beggar' (4.3.30–1). In my view, the disempowered ghost of the closet scene, 'steal[ing] away … out at the portal' (3.4.136, 138) after failing to spur his son's revenge, signals a brutalising shift in Hamlet, a turning away from a passion that no longer affords hope. When Hamlet attends, finally, to the corpse of Polonius, the 'foolish prating knave' (217) that was his beloved Ophelia's father, he seems singularly insensitive to the parallel between her grief and his: 'I'll lug the guts into the neighbour room' (213).

What Jacques Lacan calls Hamlet's 'paroxysm of absorption in the imaginary register, formally expressed as a mirror relationship, a mirrored reaction',[25] is chiefly manifested in Hamlet's confused identification with the shape-changing ghost of his father. But there are other uncanny doubles in the play that symbolically reinforce Hamlet's inability to hold fast to his ideal. The First Player's description of the killing and mutilation of Priam, puzzling because the bombastic metres and lurid imagery of the speech seem disturbingly incongruent with its symbolic resonances, is an important case in point.

Because Pyrrhus kills Priam as an act of revenge for the death of his father, Achilles, he is, on one level, a stand-in for Hamlet, or a surrogate caricature of Hamlet as he would presumably like to be: 'rugged' (3.2.446) and black in purpose, 'Roasted in wrath and fire' (457), 'Bak'd and impasted' (455) with the blood of battle, 'o'ersized' (458), furious and unstoppable. The connection between the two avengers seems unmistakable when, for a frozen moment, Pyrrhus is unable to act:

> For lo, his sword,
> Which was declining on the milky head
> Of reverend Priam, seem'd in'th'air to stick;
> So, as a painted tyrant, Pyrrhus stood,
> And like a neutral to his will and matter,
> Did nothing. (473–8)

But the defenceless old King, whose limbs Pyrrhus eventually minces in 'malicious sport' (509), seems an odd surrogate for Claudius, and the sympathy elicited for his 'milky head' (474) by the inconsolable Hecuba renders Pyrrhus's act barbaric. Hecuba in turn evokes Hamlet's allusion to Niobe/Gertrude at the funeral of Hamlet Sr, albeit Hecuba's grief, like the outrage that prompts it, is of catastrophic proportions. If in the reference to Hecuba the rulers of Troy and Denmark seem momentarily aligned, then Claudius in turn takes Hamlet's place as Pyrrhus, thereby deconstructing that absolute distinction between victims and victimiser – the two Hamlets vs. the tyrant uncle – which Hamlet is so keen to maintain.[26]

To complicate matters further, Pyrrhus also bears a strong resemblance to the ghost. It is, after all, Hamlet Sr who is the warrior, whose dread and oversized figure, 'Roasted in wrath and fire' (3.2.457), arises in the night with murderous intent, whose history of battle has made him no stranger to 'coagulate gore' (458), who is 'cap-à-pie' (1.2.200) in armour just as Pyrrhus is 'Head to foot ... total gules' (3.2.452–3), and who, like Pyrrhus, is 'horribly trick'd' (452) with an encompassing if (in his case) unseen disfigurement. Viewed from this angle, the identification of Hamlet the Prince with Pyrrhus works as a double mirror, Hamlet girded with the strength of his father and thereby transformed into the mythic avenger. But, of course, neither this nor any other association holds firm in the Player's narrative. What I am arguing is that, collectively, these multiple shifts dramatise Hamlet's debilitating uncertainty about where he, and everyone else, fit in the killing field that Elsinore has become.[27]

By initially attempting to anchor his identity in the warrior ghost, Hamlet reached for a categorical certainty that even he seemed to intuit the ghost could not deliver. His ensuing self-alienation resonates with the ghost's own contradiction: the deceptive substantiality of its external armour divided by the death within. Fittingly, the play's metaphoric construction of the ghost's interior expresses Hamlet's idea of horror: an awful wasting of an already disfigured body, an outrage to be shut away, masked. However, as Hamlet's tenuous identification with his father in the guise of combatant slips, he is increasingly preoccupied with that interior, with the destructive/generative agency that dissolves identity and that demands, in the end, his father's, and his own, submission to anonymity.

By the time of the graveyard scene, the ghost has disappeared and Hamlet has shifted from a passionate to a ruminative contemplation of death. As Stephen Greenblatt puts it, Hamlet perceives in the bony remains of the cemetery dead a 'drastic leveling, the collapse of order and distinction into polymorphous, endlessly recycled materiality'.[28] In this neutralising vision, Hamlet relinquishes the ghost's martial resistance for a democracy of the dead in which Hamlet Sr, Alexander, Caesar and Yorick are compeers, soon to be joined, of course, by Claudius and Hamlet himself. Given Hamlet's passion for individuation, this falling off is tormenting to be sure, but interestingly, his preoccupation with the indistinguishable skulls serves to deflect a still more horrifying recognition of their prior process of decomposition. As Bataille argues, bones are emblems of death which bear no trace of nature's cannibalism; they are the hard, clean, sanitised remnants of putrefaction. It is as if it is easier for Hamlet to focus on extinction than formlessness: there is still some comfort to be taken from contemplating the dead as determinate if anonymous material artifacts.

The arrival of Ophelia's corpse seems momentarily to break through this detachment, resuscitating the deep rage and grief with which Hamlet formerly responded to his father's murder. But Hamlet's 'tow'ring passion' (5.2.80) with Laertes, as he admits later to Horatio, is primarily prompted not by the death of Ophelia, but by 'the bravery of [Laertes'] grief' (79) – a mirror of Hamlet's *former* passion. In relying on hyperbolic self-justifications and childish dares ('Be buried quick with her, and so will I' [5.1.274]), Hamlet's chief aim is to ensure that the eloquent if melodramatic Laertes does not 'outface' (5.1.273) him publicly, that the direction of the mirror is reversed, as it were. Hamlet's outrageous query of Laertes, 'What is the reason that you use me thus? / I lov'd you ever' (284–5) exposes, almost chillingly, his seeming disconnection, despite his rage, from the emotional consequences that his acts have had for others.

Shortly, Hamlet will tell Horatio, 'There's a divinity that shapes our ends, / Rough-hew them how we will – ' (5.2.10–11), and this expectation of an intervention that will simultaneously resolve his life and his death is, finally, the only 'course of action' that seems possible. To take up arms on behalf of the warrior ghost, or on behalf of his fantasy of the warrior-ghost, is to tilt at windmills: the issues Hamlet must resolve in order to carry out his 'father's' directive are as irresolvable, as unknowable, as the leprous death in martial life that constitutes the strangely liminal apparition. For Hamlet, to give up the ghost, as it were, is to relinquish his passion, or, as Belsey puts it, to relinquish 'the desire for the closure of certainty and mastery over his own [and I would add, his father's] death: "Since no man, of aught he leaves, knows aught, what is't to leave betimes? Let be"' (5.2.218–20; Belsey, 170).

Still, there is Ophelia, the most affecting of Hamlet's doubles, whose own passion poignantly inverts Hamlet's response to his dilemma. Within the trajectory of Hamlet's struggle to come to terms with the ghost is the spectacle of Ophelia's madness. Confronted, calamitously, with a dead father who has been murdered by an alienated suitor, both of whom she loves, Ophelia is called upon to reconcile precipitous loss with divided loyalties – on the face of it, a more complex challenge than Hamlet's. Her response is to give herself over entirely to the experience of grief. Indeed, it might be said that Ophelia appropriates Hamlet's drama with the ghost, but to a very different end: enjoined to accommodate the incomprehensible, as is Hamlet, she – unlike him – submits to a self-shattering excess of emotion.

In sum, what I am suggesting here is that Hamlet's ghost, the corpse in complete steel, represents a paradox that Hamlet, at the cost of great suffering, apprehends keenly: that is, the subsumption of his father's person in an undiscriminating, obliterating deliquescence. What the armour would hide is the murderous yet generative force that forecloses all individuation, all identity. By gesturing towards this originary indeterminacy, the figure of the ghost probes the protective yet untenable boundary between consciousness and anonymity. Occluded yet compelling, the interior of Hamlet's ghost is an unsignifiable no/thing that, like the petrifying Medusa, will turn anyone who dares view it to stone – or, in the metaphor of Hamlet's tormented imagination, to dust.

Notes

1. For example, the Doctor's quasi-comic confrontation with Ferdinand in his lycanthropic fit, satirised by Pescara (5.2), is reminiscent of the Tyrant's frenzied attempt to break into the Lady's tomb, satirised by the attendant soldiers (4.3).
2. All references to the text are from Kenneth Muir, ed., *Macbeth*, The Arden Shakespeare (Cambridge, MA: Harvard University Press, 1957).
3. See especially Marjorie Garber, 'Macbeth: The Male Medusa', in *Shakespeare's Ghost Writers: Literature as Uncanny Causality* (New York and London: Methuen, 1987), 87–123; and D. Willbern, 'Phantasmagoric Macbeth', *English Literary Renaissance* 16 (1986), 520–49.

4. See Caroline Walker Bynum, *Fragmentation and Redemption: Essays on Gender and the Human Body in Medieval Religion* (New York: Zone Books, 1996), 185.
5. It is likely that the 'sin-eating' of debased forms of bread and 'wine' at early modern funerals reinforced the formalised ritual of the Eucharist. Presumably, by celebrating the process of consumption through feasting, mourners sought to disempower the fearsome feeding taking place concomitantly in the corpse. See Clare Gittings, *Death, Burial, and the Individual in Early Modern England* (London and Sydney: Croom Helm, 1984), 154–9.
6. See Caroline Walker Bynum, *Jesus as Mother: Studies in the Spirituality of the High Middle Ages* (Berkeley, Los Angeles and London: University of California Press, 1982); and Leo S. Steinberg, *The Sexuality of Christ in Renaissance Art and in Modern Oblivion* (New York: Pantheon, 1983). For a detailed treatment of these issues, see Chapter 2, esp. pp. 29–30; and n. 7, p. 68. For ways in which Galenic medical theory provided secular reinforcement for the notion of imperfectly differentiated sexes, see Chapter 2, n. 8, pp. 68–9.
7. This is not to say that Duncan merits sanctification, either as an individual or as a king. Harry Berger Jr has persuasively demonstrated Duncan's complicity in the machismo warrior ethic that has ravaged Scotland, as well as the ironies implicit in the play's seeming opposition of Duncan and Macbeth. See 'The Early Scenes of *Macbeth*: Preface to a New Interpretation', in Peter Erikson, ed., *Making Trifles of Terrors: Redistributing Complicities in Shakespeare* (Stanford, CA: Stanford University Press, 1994), 6–97. In the context of my argument, however, the social destabilisation effected by Macbeth's violation of taboo necessitates Duncan's idealisation as King and Macbeth's demonisation as Murderer.
8. See Deborah Willis, 'A New Gorgon: Engendering Horror in *Macbeth* and contemporary Film' (1994), 7. Unpublished paper submitted to seminar at the Shakespeare Association of America. Quoted with permission of the author.
9. For commentary on this image, see Willbern, 525; and Janet Adelman, 'Fantasies of Maternal Power in *Macbeth*', in Marjorie Garber, ed., *Cannibals, Witches, and Divorce: Estranging the Renaissance* (Baltimore and London: Johns Hopkins University Press, 1987), 90–121.
10. The impersonation of the 'unsexed' Lady Macbeth by a boy actor is another case in point: it exploits the ambiguities of the transvestite convention almost to the point of parody. Presumably, the violent contradictions of Lady Macbeth's 'unsexed' self would stretch the customary interpretive range of the boy actor, who in this instance was called upon to impersonate a female who herself would impersonate a super-male.
11. For an excellent summary of the often contradictory attempts of Tudor and Stuart reformers to grapple with the theological implications of ghosts, as well as their hold on the popular imagination, see Peter Marshall, *Beliefs and the Dead in Reformation England* (Oxford: Oxford University Press, 2002), 232–64. Marshall's analysis incorporates evidence from plays, but he astutely points out 'the distinctly limited utility of the Protestant demon-ghost as an embodiment of dramatic meaning. The cultural patterning of the ghost in English Renaissance theatre was a compounded one: it certainly recognised the ideas of the Reformation, and generally contained no hint (*Hamlet* is a possible exception) of Catholic notions of purgatory and intercession. None the less, as

literary ghosts seek revenge, torment the consciences of the guilty or show solicitude for loved ones, the emotive and imaginative energy of the genre is shown to be predicated on assumptions other than the doctrinally sound one that the dead had no interest in the state of affairs left behind them, or the obligations and deserts of the living' (258).

12. Philippe Ariès, *The Hour of Our Death*, trans. Helen Weaver (London: Alfred A. Knopf, 1981), 110.

13. Michael Neill, *Issues of Death: Mortality and Identity in English Renaissance Tragedy* (Oxford: Clarendon Press and New York: Oxford University Press, 1997), 77.

14. Catherine Belsey, *Shakespeare and the Loss of Eden* (Basingstoke: Macmillan, 1999), 129–74, esp. 140–50, 157. R. C. Finucane reinforces this view: 'England was partial to these displays of decomposition not only in the fifteenth century but in the sixteenth as well.' See *Ghosts: Appearances of the Dead and Cultural Transformation* (Amherst, NY: Prometheus Books, 1966), 53.

15. Jean-Claude Schmitt, *Ghosts in the Middle Ages: The Living and the Dead in Medieval Society*, trans. Teresa Lavender Fagan (Chicago and London: University of Chicago Press, 1998), 202.

16. Schmitt is quoting from Tale V in Montague Rhodes James, 'Twelve Medieval Ghost Stories', *English Historical Review* 147 (July 1922), 413–19; James's source is MS British Museum, Royal 15 A XX.

17. Kenneth Gross, *The Dream of the Moving Statue* (Ithaca, NY and London: Cornell University Press, 1992), 17.

18. See Gross, 21–5, *passim*. Gross is summarising key concepts from Serres' *Statues: Le second livre des fondations* (Paris: Éditions Francois Bourin, 1987).

19. All quotations from the play are taken from the Arden Edition, ed. Harold Jenkins (London: Methuen & Co. Ltd, 1982).

20. In an intriguing analysis of the 'materiality of memory', Ann Rosalind Jones and Peter Stallybrass discuss the ghost's armour as a 'literalized' and 'superficial' embodiment of Hamlet Sr, an 'insignia of identity' that seems to materialise the mnemonic that is the ghost. See *Renaissance Clothing and the Materials of Memory* (Cambridge: Cambridge University Press, 2001), 249–50.

21. Paul de Man, 'Autobiography as De-Facement', in *The Rhetoric of Romanticism* (New York: Columbia University Press, 1984), 75–6. Quoted in Marjorie Garber, *Shakespeare's Ghost Writers*, 137–8.

22. With few exceptions, the three texts of *Hamlet* – Q1 (1603), Q2 (1604–5) and F (1623) – refer to the ghost as 'it'. The most notable instances of 'he' or 'his' are at 1.1.46 (Q2 only), 69, 160 (all texts); 1.2.206, 228, 229, 230, 233 (all texts); 3.4.125, 138 (all texts). The S.D., 1.1.130, '*It spreads its armes*', is in Q2 only; the reference to the ghost's clothing in S.D., 3.4.103, '*Enter the ghost in his night gowne*', is in Q1 only. See *The three-text* Hamlet: *parallel texts of the first and second quartos and first folio*, eds. Bernice W. Kliman and Paul Bertram (New York: AMS Press, 2003).

23. In a private exchange, Kenneth Gross has pointed out the unsettling eroticism in the ghost's description of the act of poisoning, where Gertrude is the absent presence:

> the kind of strangely living corrupting corpse-ghost you evoke is associated not just with the body as something that dies but with a sexualised body; the word 'corruption' applies to them both, and Hamlet imagines especially his mother's sexual person like a

thing already a corpse – his fear is of its disorganised, irrational life as much as its death. Think of the amazing quickness of the poison the ghost describes rushing through his veins like some invading army through the portals and alleys of a captured city, but in that half sexual submission to the poisoner kneeling over him sleeping.

24. Jones and Stallybrass connect this demeanour directly to the ghost's garment: 'Hamlet, the old king, returns for the last time, vulnerable now, no longer the warrior hero, as if the relative impermanence of cloth prefigures his own impermanence' (266).

25. See 'Desire and the Interpretation of Desire in *Hamlet*', in Shoshana Felman, ed., *Literature and and Psychoanalysis: The Question of Reading: Otherwise* (Baltimore and London: Johns Hopkins University Press, 1992), 31. Lacan is referring here to Hamlet's relationship with Laertes. For an excellent analysis of this essay, and particularly of the ghost as Lacan's phallus/fraud, see Philip Armstrong, *Shakespeare in Psychoanalysis* (London and New York: Routledge, 2001), 52–94.

26. It might also be argued that Priam himself collapses the distinction between brothers. Priam's status as the father of fifty sons, the archetypal patriarch, suggests a sexual and generative potency that Hamlet associates emphatically with moral corruption and would foreclose: 'I say we will have no mo marriage' (3.1.149). Since Hamlet repudiates, in particular, his mother's sexual attraction to Claudius, Claudius and Priam can both be said to represent rulers whose power is linked to their sexuality. At the same time, however, the Player's description of Pyrrhus's death-dealing blow describes Priam in terms that are eerily evocative of the armoured ghost:

    And never did the Cyclops' hammers fall
    On Mar's armour, forg'd for proof eterne,
    With less remorse than Pyrrhus' bleeding sword
    Now falls on Priam. (485–8)

    I would argue that, if Pyrrhus here represents Hamlet, the fury of the blow can be linked to Hamlet's frustration at *not* being able to separate the reflections of his father and his uncle in the figure of Priam.

27. It should also be noted that later, in yet another inversion, the murderous Lucianus of Hamlet's Mousetrap will be identified with the nephew and not the brother of the King.

28. Stephen Greenblatt, *Hamlet in Purgatory* (Princeton, NJ and Oxford: Princeton University Press, 2001), 243.

Epilogue: Last Words

At the end of Chapter 1, I suggested that the methodological aim of this book was to emphasise what I see as the interdependent relationship between poststructuralist theory and historicist analysis. I would like to end my study with a further speculation on how Benjamin's *Trauerspiel* elucidates these subtle yet seminal connections.

Benjamin contends, we will recall, that unlike *Tragödie*, which appeals to the 'hidden god' in every spectator by idealising an idea of the transcendent self, *Trauerspiel* grounds itself in the idea of an unavoidable and unrelenting physis, a natural order akin to Bataille's 'orgy of annihilation'. *Trauer* is a communal, ceremonial lament for man's subjection to this physis, one that *plays out* (*spiel*) in a staged performance: it is a drama that coalesces the individual and collective histories of the spectators into a 'pageant' that is at once 'grievous' and hyperbolic. For Benjamin, there is no eschatology in the *Trauerspiel*, no redemptive escape from the physis: instead, there is an almost obsessive preoccupation with the disintegration and reintegration of materiality itself as life's greatest mystery.[1] For this reason, the 'homeland' (to use Benjamin's poignant and ironic term) of the *Trauerspiel* is the indeterminate corpse.

From my perspective as a contemporary historicist, it seems particularly interesting that Benjamin conceives of the problem of materiality as developed in the *Trauerspiel* as conjunctive with that of Christianity.[2] I have argued, particularly in Chapter 2, that the emphasis in medieval hermeneutics on the Incarnation of Christ and on Eucharistic transubstantiation established the body of Christ, and, more generally, the mystification of bodily processes, as the symbolic centre of English Catholic belief. In eschewing the pervasive anthropomorphism of Catholic iconography and ritual, the Reformation sought in its turn, to emphasise the immateriality of an antecedent and transcendent godhead. But as Benjamin demonstrates so eloquently, the conundrum of the man/God is always the centre, explicitly or implicitly, of the Christian redemptive scheme, so that the problem of materiality – that is, its relationship to immateriality – is, if anything, even more acute in a Reformation context.[3] Given this conceptual framework, the terrible indeterminacy of Duncan's blood and the occluded corpse of Hamlet's father intimate a 'grievious pageant' in which the problem of materiality is unresolved, and the lamentations of Hamlet and Macbeth become, at least in part, those of the pageant's spectators as well.

But the Christian linkages between the German *Trauerspiel* and the early modern theatre, although certainly important, do not constitute Benjamin's core concern. For me, the most original if difficult dimension of Benjamin's thought is his attempt to elucidate the counter-intuitive relationship between theatrical performance, 'baroque' sensationalism, and the unrepresentable. The problem may be stated as follows: a play in which the unrelenting physis is a pervasive presence is a play of mourning; how then might the unrepresentable corpse, the emblematic centre of the physis, be instantiated in such a play? In Benjamin's system, artifice is this nub of the issue, integral to its resolution, and I would argue that his analysis breaks open the same issue for early modern tragedies of blood, notwithstanding the many ways in which the *Trauerspiel* fails to encompass the historical particularities of Shakespeare's theatre.

On several occasions Benjamin elaborates what he means by 'artifice' through reference to the iconography of the Dance of Death, which he views, in Steiner's phrase, as the 'crowning episode of the game or play of lamentation' (18). As its name suggests, the Dance of Death is a dance that laments and a lamentation that dances: it is a 'revel of monstrous un-creation' (to cite once again Michael Neill's memorable phrase) that stages a grotesque simulacrum of both the living and the dead, or rather an eerie community of the living dead. It is grotesque in both meanings of the word – overstated and shocking, yet secret and mysterious; it is both alien and intimate; it distances and attracts. If death is what the human subject both desires and abhors, then the warring tonalities of the Dance of Death allow the spectator an ironic intimation of this ambivalence, one that is, importantly, communal, a kind of mirror imaging in which the spectator is both inside and outside the Dance.

On other occasions, Benjamin analyses artifice in terms of another kind of mirror imaging – the self-conscious manipulations of puppetry, in which he includes the convention of the play-within-a-play. Puppet theatre functions for Benjamin as a metaphor for the subject's position in the physis. If the stage is conceived of as a simulacrum of the world, then the actor's performance is like that of a puppet: he is a kind of homunculus that 'struts and frets' upon the stage in a parody of autonomy and control.[4] Just as the play-within-the-play serves, meta-theatrically, as an 'ironic or pathetic simulacrum of the main plot' (18), the performance itself – the 'main plot' – is likewise a travesty. Thus 'the power of salvation and redemption only ever lies in a paradoxical reflection of play and appearance' (82) that is counter-transcendent. Whatever 'salvation' there is resides in the play's power to mock itself: salvation is immanent in the world, in the communal recognition of the world's material dictates and in the communal response to them – a mournful play or game in which 'Prince and puppet are impelled by the same frozen violence' (18). The *Trauerspiel*, homeland of the corpse, 'has artifice as its god' (82).

Benjamin's genius for forcing new angles of vision can be divined in these suggestive connections between the Dance of Death and puppetry. Both phenomena eschew naturalism and in that sense set the spectator at a distance; but it is within the alienation of the grotesque, the overblown, the 'artificial', that intimations of the unspeakable and unviewable take imaginative shape, however paradoxically. What Benjamin's spectres and puppets help to clarify, strikingly if indirectly, is how Shakespeare was able to harness the disintegrative visions of Hamlet and Macbeth by lodging the liminal within the excesses of his own signature artifice.

My engagement with Benjamin's work, its way of resonating in my critical imagination, is not unlike my experience with other kinds of poststructuralist theory. I have concluded that although the homeland of Shakespeare's theatre must be reconstituted in terms of its own cultural determinants, there is equally compelling reason to view it from positions outside this historical framework – to multiply frames of reference, and by so doing to discover new angles of vision. Interestingly, this critical exercise is not unlike the mirroring techniques used on the early modern stage itself (and in the *Trauerspiel*) to conjure the inexpressible in a 'paradoxical reflection of play and appearance'. I have come to think that this is an apt metaphor for the elusive process by which we all shape particular bodies of knowledge – the subjects of our books – through a continual rediscovery of the permeable borders between history and theory.

Notes

1. 'The *Trauerspiel* is counter-transcendental; it celebrates the immanence of existence even where this existence is passed in torment.' See George Steiner, Introduction to *The Origin of German Tragic Drama* (London and New York: Verso, 1998), 16. This is not to imply that the early modern tragedies I have been analysing necessarily lack the suggestion of a transcendent principle. What I have tried to show is that the torment of their protagonists (for example, Ferdinand, Bosola, Hamlet, Macbeth) is, in each case, intimately tied up with an acute awareness of the disintegrative properties of the physis.
2. 'Baroque drama is inherently emblematic-allegoric, as Greek tragedy never is,

precisely because it postulates the dual presence, the twofold organizing pivot of Christ's nature – part god, part man, and overwhelmingly of this world.' See Steiner, Introduction, p. 17.

3. Benjamin points out astutely that the prohibition against graven images 'is not only a warning against idolatry. With incomparable emphasis the prohibition of the representation of the human body obviates any suggestion that the sphere in which the moral essence of man is perceptible can be reproduced.' For Benjamin, this 'sphere' is inextricably bound up with materiality: 'everything moral is bound to life [the physis] in its extreme sense, that is to say where it fulfils itself in death' (105).

4. For Benjamin's comment on the *intrigant* as puppet, see Chapter 1, n. 32.

Works Cited

Adelman, Janet (1987), 'Fantasies of Maternal Power in *Macbeth*', in Marjorie Garber (ed.), *Cannibals, Witches, and Divorce: Estranging the Renaissance*, Baltimore and London: Johns Hopkins University Press, pp. 90–121.

Ariès, Philippe (1974), *Western Attitudes toward Death from the Middle Ages to the Present*, trans. Patricia M. Ranum, London: Johns Hopkins University Press.

— (1981), *The Hour of Our Death*, trans. Helen Weaver, New York: Alfred A. Knopf.

Armstrong, Philip (2001), *Shakespeare in Psychoanalysis*, London and New York: Routledge.

The arte or craft to lyve well and to dye well (1506), London (Wynkyn de Worde), RSTC 793.

Aston, Margaret (1988), *England's Iconoclasts: Laws Against Images*, Vol. I, Oxford: Clarendon Press.

— (1993) *Earth and Fire: Popular and Unpopular Religion, 1356–1600*, London and Rio Grande: The Hambledon Press.

— and Elizabeth Ingram (1997), 'The Iconography of *Actes and Monuments*', in David Loades (ed.), *John Foxe and the English Reformation*, Aldershot: Scolar Press, pp. 66–142.

Augustine of Hippo (1988), *The City of God Against the Pagans*, trans. Philip Levine, Vol. IV, Loeb Classical Library, Cambridge, MA: Harvard University Press.

Bakhtin, Mikhail (1984), *Rabelais and His World*, trans. Helene Iswolsky, Bloomington: Indiana University Press.

Barber, Paul (1988), *Vampires, Burial, and Death: Folklore and Reality*, New Haven and London: Yale University Press.

Barker, Francis (1984), *The Tremulous Private Body: Essays on Subjection*, London and New York: Methuen.

Barroll, Leeds (1991), *Politics, Plague, and Shakespeare's Theater: The Stuart Years*, Ithaca, NY: Cornell University Press.

Bataille, Georges (1957), *Erotism: Death and Sensuality*, trans. Mary Dalwood, San Francisco: City Lights Books.

Bede, the Venerable (1990), *The Ecclesiastical History of the English People*, trans. Leo Sherley-Price, rev. R. E. Latham, London: Penguin Books.

Belsey, Catherine (1980), *Critical Practice*, London and New York: Routledge.

— (1985), *The Subject of Tragedy: Identity and Difference in Renaissance Drama*, London and New York: Methuen.

— (1990), 'Disrupting Sexual Difference: Meaning and Gender in the Comedies', in John Drakakis (ed.), *Alternative Shakespeares*, London and New York: Routledge, pp. 166–90.

— (1994), 'Desire in Theory: Freud, Lacan, Derrida', in *Desire: Love Stories in Western Culture*, Oxford: Blackwell, pp. 42–71.

— (1999), *Shakespeare and the Loss of Eden*, Basingstoke: Macmillan Press.

Benjamin, Walter (1998), *The Origin of German Tragic Drama*, trans. John Osborne, London and New York: Verso.

Berger, Harry, Jr (1987), 'Bodies and Texts', *Representations* 17, Winter, pp. 144–66.

— (1994), 'The Early Scenes of *Macbeth*: Preface to a New Interpretation', in Peter Erikson (ed.), *Making Trifles of Terrors: Redistributing Complicities in Shakespeare*, Stanford, CA: Stanford University Press, pp. 6–97.

Berry, Philippa (1999), *Shakespeare's Feminine Endings: Disfiguring Death in the Tragedies*, London and New York: Routledge.

Betteridge, Thomas (2002), 'Truth and History in Foxe's *Acts and Monuments*', in Christopher Highly and John N. King (eds), *John Foxe and his World*, Aldershot: Ashgate, pp. 145–59.

Binns, J. W. (1974), 'Women or Transvestites on the English Stage?: an Oxford Controversy', *Sixteenth-Century Journal*, 5:2, pp. 95–120.

Binski, Paul (1996), *Medieval Death: Ritual and Representation*, Ithaca, NY: Cornell University Press.

Bishops' Book (The institution of a Christen man) (1537), London, STC 5163.

Boase, T. S. R. (1972), *Death in the Middle Ages: Mortality, Judgment, and Remembrance*, London: Thames and Hudson.

Bronfen, Elizabeth (1992), *Over Her Dead Body: Death, Femininity and the Aesthetic*, Manchester: Manchester University Press; New York: Routledge.

Brown, Elizabeth A. R. (1981), 'Death and the Human Body in the Later Middle Ages: The Legislation of Boniface VIII on the Division of the Corpse', *Viator* 12, pp. 226–41.

Brown, Peter (1988), *The Body and Society: Men, Women and Sexual Renunciation in Early Christianity*, New York: Columbia University Press.

Browne, Thomas (1642), *Religio Medici*, London, STC B5166.

Burton, Robert (1621), *The anatomy of melancholy*, Oxford, STC 4159.

Bushnell, Rebecca W. (1990), *Tragedies of Tyrants: Political Thought and Theater in the English Renaissance*, Ithaca and London: Cornell University Press.

Bynum, Caroline Walker (1984), *Jesus as Mother: Studies in the Spirituality of the High Middle Ages*, Berkeley and Los Angeles: University of California Press.

— (1995), *The Resurrection of the Body in Western Christianity, 200–1336*, New York: Columbia University Press.

— (1996), *Fragmentation and Redemption: Essays on Gender and the Human Body in Medieval Religion*, New York: Zone Books.

Callaghan, Dympna (2000), *Shakespeare Without Women: Representing Gender and Race on the Renaissance Stage*, London and New York: Routledge.

Calvin, John (1599), *The Institution of Christian Religion, written in Latine by M. John Caluine, and translated into English ... by Thomas Norton*, London, STC 4423 (7th edn of STC 4415, 1560–61).

Cary, Elizabeth (1994), *The Tragedy of Miriam, The Fair Queen of Jewry*, ed. Barry Weller and Margaret W. Ferguson, Berkeley and Los Angeles: University of California Press.

Clark, Stuart (1984), 'The Scientific Status of Demonology', in Brian Vickers (ed.), *Occult and Scientific Mentalities in the Renaissance*, Cambridge: Cambridge University Press, pp. 351–73.

Coddon, Karin S. (2001), '"For Show or Useless Property": Necrophilia and *The Revenger's Tragedy*', in Stevie Simkin (ed.), *Revenge Tragedy*, Basingstoke; Palgrave; New York: St Martin's Press, pp. 121–41.

Cohen, Kathleen (1973), *Metamorphosis of a Death Symbol: The Transi Tomb in the Late Middle Ages and the Renaissance*, Berkeley and London: University of California Press.

Collinson, Patrick (1997), 'Biblical Rhetoric', in Claire McEachern and Debora Shuger (eds), *Religion and Culture in Renaissance England*, Cambridge: Cambridge University Press, pp. 15–45.

— (2002), 'John Foxe and National Consciousness', in Christopher Highly and John N. King (eds), *John Foxe and his World*, Aldershot: Ashgate, pp. 10–34.

Cressy, David (1997), *Birth, Marriage, and Death: Ritual, Religion, and the Life-Cycle in Tudor and Stuart England*, New York: Oxford University Press.

Crooke, Helkiah (1615), Μικροκοσμογραφια [Microcosmographia] A description of the body of man, London, STC 6062.2.

Dekker, Thomas (1980), *The Whore of Babylon: A Critical Edition*, ed. Marianne Gateson Riely, New York and London: Garland Publishing.

Diehl, Huston (1997), *Staging Reform, Reforming the Stage: Protestanism and Popular Theater in Early Modern England*, Ithaca, NY: Cornell University Press.

Dollimore, Jonathan (1984), *Radical Tragedy: Religion, Ideology and Power in the Drama of Shakespeare and his Contemporaries*, Chicago: The University of Chicago Press.

— (1998), *Death, Desire and Loss in Western Culture*, New York: Routledge, 1998.

Donne, John (1976), 'Death's Duel', in Martin Seymour (ed.), *The English Sermon, Vol. 1, 1550–1656*, Old Woking, Surrey: Unwin Brothers, pp. 354–90.

Doob, Penelope B. R. (1974), *Nebuchadnezzor's Children: Conventions of Madness in Middle English Literature*, New Haven and London: Yale University Press.

Douglas, Mary (1991), *Purity and Danger: An Analysis of the Concepts of Pollution and Taboo*, London: Routledge.

Drakakis, John (2002), 'Jessica', in John W. Mahon and Ellen Macleod Mahon (eds), *The Merchant of Venice: New Critical Essays*, New York and London: Routledge, pp. 145–63.

Duffy, Eamon (1992), *The Stripping of the Altars: Traditional Religion in England c.1400–c.1580*, New Haven and London: Yale University Press.

Eire, Carlos M. N. (1986), *War Against the Idols: The Reformation of Worship from Erasmus to Calvin*, Cambridge: Cambridge University Press.

Enterline, Lynn (1995), *The Tears of Narcissus: Melancholia and Masculinity in Early Modern Writing*, Stanford, CA: Stanford University Press.

Epstein, I. (ed.) (1960), *Baba Bathra I*, London: The Soncino Press.

Farmer, David (ed.) (1987), *Oxford Dictionary of Saints*, New York: Oxford University Press.

Felman, Shoshana (ed.) (1982), *Literature and Psychoanalysis: The Question of Reading: Otherwise*, Baltimore and London: Johns Hopkins University Press.

Finucane, R. C. (1966), *Ghosts: Appearances of the Dead and Cultural Transformation*, Amherst, NY: Prometheus Books.

Fletcher, Phineas (1633), *The Purple Island, or The Isle of Man*, Cambridge, STC 11082.

Foxe, John (1563) *Actes and Monuments*, London, STC 11222.

Freud, Sigmund (1968), '"The Uncanny"', in James Strachey (ed. and trans.), *The Standard Edition of the Complete Psychological Works of Sigmund Freud*, Vol. 17, London: Hogarth Press, pp. 218–56.

— (1989), 'The Theme of the Three Caskets', in Peter Gay (ed.), *The Freud Reader*, trans. James Strachey, New York and London: Norton, pp. 514–22.

Garber, Marjorie (1987), 'Macbeth: The Male Medusa', in *Shakespeare's Ghost Writers: Literature as Uncanny Causality*, New York and London: Methuen, pp. 87–123.

Geary, Patrick J. (1996), *Living with the Dead in the Middle Ages*, Ithaca and London: Cornell University Press.

Gittings, Clare (1984), *Death, Burial, and the Individual in Early Modern England*, London and Sydney: Croom Helm.

— (2000), 'Sacred and Secular: 1558–1660', in Peter C. Jupp and Clare Gittings (eds), *Death in England: An Illustrated History*, New Brunswick, NJ: Rutgers University Press, pp. 147–73.

Goldberg, Jonathan (1992), *Sodometries: Renaissance Texts, Modern Sexualities*, Stanford, CA: Stanford University Press.

Greenblatt, Stephen (1980), *Renaissance Self-Fashioning from More to Shakespeare*, Chicago: The University of Chicago Press.

— (1998), 'Shakespeare Bewitched', in Susan Zimmerman (ed.), *Shakespeare's Tragedies*, Basingstoke and London: Macmillan Press, pp. 109–39.

— (2001), *Hamlet in Purgatory*, Princeton, NJ: Princeton University Press.

Gross, Kenneth (1992), *The Dream of the Moving Statue*, Ithaca and London: Cornell University Press.

Haig, Christopher (1993), *English Reformation: Religion, Politics, and Society under the Tudors*, Oxford: Clarendon Press.

Halbertal, Moshe and Avishai Margalit (1992), *Idolatry*, trans. Naomi Goldblum, Cambridge, MA and London: Harvard University Press.

Helgerson, Richard (1992), *Forms of Nationhood: The Elizabethan Writing of England*, Chicago and London: The University of Chicago Press.

Homilies, *Certayne sermons, or homilies* (1547), London, STC 13639.

The seconde tome of homelyes (1563), London, STC 13663.

Sermons or Homilies appointed to be read in churches in the time of Queen Elizabeth (1816), 4th edn, facsimile reprint, Oxford: Clarendon Press.

Houlbrooke, Ralph (1998), *Death, Religion and the Family in England 1480–1750*, Oxford: Oxford University Press.

Howard, Jean E. (1988), 'Cross-Dressing, the Theatre, and Gender Struggle in Early Modern England', *Shakespeare Quarterly* 39:4, pp. 418–40.

James VI and I (1597), *Daemonologie*, Edinburgh, STC 14364.

Jones, Ann Rosalind and Peter Stallybrass (2001), *Renaissance Clothing and the Materials of Memory*, Cambridge: Cambridge University Press.

Josephus, Flavius (1602), *The Famous & Memorable Workes of Iosephvs*, trans. T. Lodge, London, STC 14809 (includes *Of the Antiquities of the Jews* and *Of the Warres of the Jews*).

Kastan, David Scott (1997), '"The noyse of the new Bible": Reform and Reaction in Henrician England', in Claire McEachern and Debora Shuger (eds), *Religion and Culture in Renaissance England*, Cambridge: Cambridge University Press, pp. 46–68.

— (2002), 'Little Foxes', in Christopher Highly and John N. King (eds.), *John Foxe and his World*, Aldershot: Ashgate, pp. 117–29.

King, John N. (1982), *English Reformation Literature: The Tudor Origins of the Protestant Tradition*, Princeton, NJ: Princeton University Press.

— (1997), 'Fiction and Fact in Foxe's *Book Of Martyrs*', in David Loades (ed.), *John Foxe and the English Reformation*, Aldershot: Scolar Press, pp. 12–15.

King's Book (A necessary doctrine and erudition for any Christen man, sette furthe by the Kynges maiestie) (1543), London, STC 5168.

Knox, Ronald and Shane Leslie (eds) (1923), *The Miracles of King Henry VI*, Cambridge: Cambridge University Press.

Kristeva, Julia (1982), *Powers of Horror: An Essay on Abjection*, trans. Leon S. Roudiez, New York: Columbia University Press.

— (1986), 'About Chinese Women', in Toril Moi (ed.), *The Kristeva Reader*, New York: Columbia University Press, pp. 138–59.

— (1989), *Black Sun: Depression and Melancholia*, New York: Columbia University Press.

Kruger, Steven F. (1992), *Dreaming in the Middle Ages*, Cambridge: Cambridge University Press.

Lacan, Jacques (1977), 'The Signification of the Phallus', *Écrits: A Selection*, trans. Alan Sheridan, New York and London: Norton, pp. 281–91.

— (1982), 'Desire and the Interpretation of Desire in *Hamlet*', in Shoshana Felman (ed.), *Literature and Psychoanalysis: The Question of Reading: Otherwise*, Baltimore and London: Johns Hopkins University Press, pp. 11–52.

— (1985), 'God and the *Jouissance* of The Woman. A Love Letter', in Juliet Mitchell and Jacqueline Rose (eds), *Feminine Sexuality: Jacques Lacan and the École Freudienne*, New York: Norton, pp. 138–48.

— (1992), *Seminar 7, The Ethics of Psychoanalysis, 1959–60*, trans. Dennis Porter, New York: Norton.

Lake, Peter G. (1987), 'Calvinism and the English Church 1570–1635', *Past and Present*, 114, February, pp. 32–114.

— (1988), *Anglicans and Puritans?: Presbyterianism and English Conformist Thought from Whitgift to Hooker*, London and Boston: Unwin Hyman.

— (1989), 'Anti-popery: the Structure of a Prejudice', in Richard Cust and Ann Hughes (eds), *Conflict in Early Stuart England: Studies in Religion and Politics 1603–1642*, London and New York: Longman, pp. 72–106.

Lancashire, Anne (1974), '*The Second Maiden's Tragedy*: A Jacobean Saint's Life', *Review of English Studies*, n.s. 25:99, pp. 267–79.

Laqueur, Thomas (1990), *Making Sex: Body and Gender from the Greeks to Freud*, Cambridge, MA: Harvard University Press.

Le Goff, Jacques (1986), *The Birth of Purgatory*, trans. Arthur Goldhammer, London: The University of Chicago Press.

— (1988), *The Medieval Imagination*, Chicago and London: The University of Chicago Press.

Levin, Richard (1963), 'The Double Plot of *S.M.T.*', *Studies in English Literature* 3, pp. 219–31.

Linebaugh, Peter (1975), 'The Tyburn Riot Against the Surgeons', in Douglas Hay, Peter Linebaugh, John Rule and E. P Thompson (eds), *Albion's Fatal Tree: Crime and Society in Eighteenth-Century England*, Harmondsworth: Penguin Books, pp. 65–117.

Litten, Julian (1991), *The English Way of Death: The Common Funeral Since 1450*, London: Robert Hale.

Loades, David (1997), 'John Foxe and the Editors', in David Loades (ed.), *John Foxe and the English Reformation*, Aldershot: Scolar Press, pp. 1–11.

Lupton, Julia Reinhard (1996), *Afterlives of the Saints: Hagiography, Typology, and Renaissance Literature*, Stanford, CA: Stanford University Press.

Markham, Gervase and William Sampson (1622), *The true tragedy of Herod and Antipater*, London, STC 17401.

Marshall, Cynthia (2002), *The Shattering of the Self: Violence, Subjectivity, & Early Modern Texts*, Baltimore: The Johns Hopkins University Press.

Marshall, Peter (2002), *Beliefs and the Dead in Reformation England*, Oxford: Oxford University Press.

Massinger, Philip (1976), *The Duke of Milan*, in Philip Edwards and Colin Gibson (eds), *The Plays and Poems of Philip Massinger*, Vol. I, Oxford: Clarendon Press.

Masten, Jeffrey (1997), *Textual Intercourse: Collaboration, Authorship, and Sexualities in Renaissance Drama*, Cambridge: Cambridge University Press.

Maus, Katharine Eisaman (1995), *Inwardness and Theater in the English Renaissance*, Chicago and London: The University of Chicago Press.

Middleton, Thomas (1978), *The Second Maiden's Tragedy*, ed. Anne Lancashire, Manchester: Manchester University Press; Baltimore: Johns Hopkins University Press.

— (1988), *Five Plays: Thomas Middleton*, ed. Bryan Loughrey and Neil Taylor, London: Penguin Books.

— (1997), *The Revenger's Tragedy*, ed. Brian Gibbons, 2nd edn, London: A & C Black; New York: Norton.

— (2002), *The Revenger's Tragedy*, ed. Lars Engle, in David Bevington et al. (eds), *English Renaissance Drama*, New York and London: W. W. Norton.

More, Thomas (1529), *A dyaloge of syr T. More. Wherin be treatyd dyuers maters, as of the veneration [&] and worshyp of ymagys*, London, STC 18084.

— (1532), *The cõfutacyon of Tyndales answere*, London, STC 18079.

— (1533), *The second parte of the cõfutacion of Tyndals answere*, London, STC 18080.

— (1981), *A Dialogue concernynge heresyes & matters of religion*, in Thomas M. C. Lawler, Germain Marc'Hadour and Richard C. Marius (eds), *The Complete Works of St. Thomas More*, Vol. 6, Part I, New Haven and London: Yale University Press.

Mueller, Janel M. (1997), 'Pain, Persecution, and the Construction of Selfhood in Foxe's *Acts and Monuments*', in Claire McEachern and Debora Shuger (eds), *Religion and Culture in Renaissance England*, Cambridge: Cambridge University Press, pp. 161–87.

Neill, Michael (1997), *Issues of Death: Mortality and Identity in English Renaissance Tragedy*, Oxford: Clarendon Press; New York: Oxford University Press.

O'Day, Rosemary (1986), *The Debate on the English Reformation*, New York and London: Methuen.

Orgel, Stephen (1996), *Impersonations: The Performance of Gender in Shake-*

speare's England, Cambridge: Cambridge University Press.

Otten, Charlotte (1986), *The Lycanthropy Reader: Werewolves in Western Culture*, Syracuse, NY: Syracuse University Press.

Owst, G. R. (1926), *Preaching in Medieval England: An Introduction to the Sermon Manuscripts of the Period, c. 1350–1450*, Cambridge: Cambridge University Press.

— (1961), *Literature and Pulpit in Medieval England*, Oxford: Basil Blackwell.

Park, Katherine (1994a), 'The Life of the Corpse: Division and Dissection in Later Medieval Europe', *Journal of the History of Medicine and Allied Sciences* 50:1, pp. 111–32.

— (1994b), 'The Criminal and the Saintly Body: Autopsy and Dissection in Renaissance Italy', *Renaissance Quarterly* 47:1, pp. 1–33.

Parker, Patricia (1966), *Shakespeare from the Margins: Language, Culture, Context*, Chicago and London: The University of Chicago Press.

Parker, Roscoe E. (1933), 'The Reputation of Herod in Early English Literature', *Speculum* 8, pp. 59–67.

Paster, Gail Kern (1993), *The Body Embarrassed: Drama and the Disciplines of Shame in Early Modern England*, Ithaca, NY: Cornell University Press.

Pelikan, Jaroslav (1974, 1978), *The Christian Tradition: A History of the Development of Doctrine*, Vols 2 and 3, Chicago and London: The University of Chicago Press.

Pettegree, Andrew (2002), 'Illustrating the Book: A Protestant Dilemma', in Christopher Highly and John N. King (eds), *John Foxe and his World*, Aldershot: Ashgate, pp. 133–44.

Plato/Republic (1992), trans. G. M. A. Grube, rev. C. D. C. Reeve, Indianapolis: Hackett.

Platt, Colin (1996), *King Death: The Black Death and its aftermath in late-medieval England*, Toronto and Buffalo: University of Toronto Press.

Pollard, Tanya (1999), 'Beauty's Poisonous Properties', *Shakespeare Studies* XXVII, pp. 187–210.

Rainolds, John (1972), *Th' Overthrow of Stage-Playes* (1599), in J. W. Binns (ed.), facsimile reprint, New York: Johnson Reprint Corps.

Richardson, Ruth (2000), *Death, Dissection, and the Destitute*, Chicago: The University of Chicago Press.

Rubin, Miri (1997), *Corpus Christi: The Eucharist in Late Medieval Culture*, Cambridge: Cambridge University Press.

Sawday, Jonathan (1995), *The Body Emblazoned: Dissection and the Human Body in Renaissance Culture*, London and New York: Routledge.

Scarry, Elaine (1985), *The Body in Pain: The Making and Unmaking of the World*, Oxford: Oxford University Press.

Schmitt, Jean-Claude (1998), *Ghosts in the Middle Ages: The Living and the Dead in Medieval Society*, trans. Teresa Lavender Fagan, Chicago and London: The University of Chicago Press.

Scot, Reginald (1584), *The discouerie of witchcraft*, London, STC 21864.

Shakespeare, William (1957), *Macbeth, ed.* Kenneth Muir, the Arden Edition, Cambridge, MA: Harvard University Press.

— (1991), *Hamlet*, ed. Harold Jenkins, the Arden Edition, London: Methuen.

— (2003), *The three-text* Hamlet: *parallel texts of the first and second quartos and first folio*, eds Bernice W. Kliman and Paul Bertram, New York, AMS Press.

Shell, Alison (1999), *Catholicism, Controversy and the English Literary Imagination*, Cambridge: Cambridge University Press.

Shuger, Debora Kuller (1990), *Habits of Thought in the English Renaissance: Religion, Politics, and the Dominant Culture*, Berkeley: University of California Press.

— (1994), *The Renaissance Bible: Scholarship, Sacrifice, and Subjectivity*, Berkeley: University of California Press.

Sinfield, Alan (1983), *Literature and Protestant England 1560–1660*, London and Canberra: Croom Helm.

Siraisi, Nancy G. (1990), *Medieval and Early Renaissance Medicine: An Introduction to Knowledge and Practice*, Chicago and London: The University of Chicago Press.

Spencer, H. Leith (1993), *English Preaching in the Late Middle Ages*, Oxford: Clarendon Press.

Stafford, Barbara Maria (1991), *Body Criticism: Imaging the Unseen in Enlightenment Art and Medicine*, London and Cambridge, MA: MIT Press.

Staines, David (1982), 'To Out-Herod Herod: The Development of a Dramatic Character', in Clifford Davidson et al. (eds), *The Drama of the Middle Ages: Comparative and Critical Essays*, New York: AMS Press, pp. 207–31.

Stallybrass, Peter (1991), 'Reading the Body and the Jacobean Theater of Consumption: *The Revenger's Tragedy* (1606)', in David Scott Kastan and Peter Stallybrass (eds), *Staging the Renaissance: Reinterpretations of Elizabethan and Jacobean Drama*, New York and London: Routledge, pp. 210–20.

— (1992), 'Transvestism and the "body beneath": Speculating on the Boy Actor', in Susan Zimmerman (ed.), *Erotic Politics: Desire on the Renaissance Stage*, London and New York: Routledge.

Steinberg, Leo (1983, 1996), *The Sexuality of Christ in Renaissance Art and in Modern Oblivion*, New York: Pantheon; rev. Chicago and London: The University of Chicago Press.

Steiner, George (1998), 'Introduction', in Walter Benjamin, *The Origins of German Tragic Drama*, trans. John Osborne, London and New York: Verso, pp. 7–24.

Stewart, Susan (1987), *On Longing: Narratives of the Miniature, the Gigantic, the Souvenir, the Collection*, Baltimore and London: Johns Hopkins University Press.

Streete, Adrian (2001), '"*Consummatum Est*": Calvinist Exegesis, Mimesis and *Doctor Faustus*,' *Literature and Theology* 15:2, June, pp. 140–58.

— (2003), 'Reforming Signs: Semiotics, Calvinism and Clothing in Sixteenth-century England', *Literature and History*, 3rd ser., 12:1, Spring, pp. 1–18.

— , 'Ecce homo: *Imitation and the Early Modern Subject*', unpublished essay.

Stubbe, Peter (1590), *A true discourse declaring the damnable life a. death of one Stubbe Peeter, a sorcerer*, London, STC 23375.

Todorov, Tzvetan (1984), *Mikhail Bakhtin: The Dialogical Principle*, trans. Wlad Godzich, Minneapolis: University of Minnesota Press.

Topsell, Edward (1607), *The historie of foure-footid beastes … etc.*, London, STC 24123.

Traub, Valerie (1992), *Desire and Anxiety: Circulations of Sexuality in Shakespearean Drama*, London and New York: Routledge.

— (2002), *The Renaissance of Lesbianism in Early Modern England*, Cambridge: Cambridge University Press.

Turner, Victor (1988), *The Anthropology of Performance*, New York: PAJ Publications.

— (1982), *From Ritual to Theater*, New York: PAJ Publications.

Tyndale, William (1528), *The obediēce of a christen man*, Antwerp, STC 24446.

— (1530), *An answere vnto Sir T. Mores dialoge*, Antwerp (?), STC 24437.

Valency, Maurice J. (1940), *The Tragedies of Herod and Mariamne*, New York: Columbia University Press.

Voragine, Jacobus de (1993), *The Golden Legend: Readings on the Saints*, trans. William Granger Ryan, Princeton, NJ: Princeton University Press.

Webster, John (1974), *The Duchess of Malfi*, ed. John Russell Brown, Revels edn, Manchester and New York: Manchester University Press.

Weimann, Robert (1978), *Shakespeare and the Popular Tradition in the Theater: Studies in the Social Dimension of Dramatic Form and Function*, ed. Robert Schwartz, Baltimore and London: Johns Hopkins University Press.

Weller, Barry and Margaret W. Ferguson (eds), *Elizabeth Cary's The Tragedy of Miriam, the Fair Queen of Jewry* (Berkeley and Los Angeles: University of California Press, 1994).

Wells, Susan (1985), *The Dialectics of Representation*, Baltimore: Johns Hopkins University Press.

White, Helen C. (1963), *Tudor Books of Saints and Martyrs*, Madison: University of Wisconsin Press.

Willbern, D. (1986), 'Phantasmagoric Macbeth', *English Literary Renaissance* 16, pp. 520–49.

Willis, Deborah (1994), 'A New Gorgon: Engendering Horror in *Macbeth* and Contemporary Film'. Unpublished paper, submitted to seminar at the Shakespeare Association of America.

Woolf, Rosemary (1972), *The English Mystery Plays*, Berkeley and Los Angeles: University of California Press.

Young, Karl (1933), 'The Christmas Play from Benediktbeuern', in *The Drama of the Medieval Church*, II, Oxford: Clarendon Press, pp. 189–96.

Index